Born in Sydney, Australia, in 1947, Jeff McMullen was a small boy when he accompanied his father, a member of the RAAF, to live in Penang at the height of the Malay Emergency. He has been attracted to far-flung destinations ever since. Indeed, there is little of the world McMullen has not seen as an ABC foreign correspondent, *Four Corners* reporter, or later as the longest-serving reporter on Australia's *60 Minutes*.

A trilogy of *Four Corners* films from the war zones of Central America won McMullen a United Nations Media Peace Prize in 1984. An hour-long film on the slaughter of the indigenous people of Guatemala was screened before an American congressional committee and influenced its vote to suspend military aid to that regime. In 1988 McMullen won an International Current Affairs Award (Pater) for his story about the effort to save the life of Ian Grey, a young Australian missionary who faced execution in Mozambique after assisting the Renamo guerillas in one of the most violent African conflicts.

While McMullen has been a household name in Australia, his stories also have appeared on CBS's *60 Minutes* and the PBS network in America, as well as the BBC, the CBC, South African networks, and even Russian television.

McMullen has worked on a number of projects to help the disadvantaged. He is a patron of the Merry Makers group that introduces Down's syndrome children to the joy of music and dance; supports Youth Insearch of Australia which arranges weekend camps and counselling for teenagers in trouble; and is a patron of the Melbourne-based Mirabel Foundation which supports children left behind by parents who died of drug addiction. In May 2001, McMullen was asked to help launch the SANE Australia campaign to seek more government assistance for people with depression and other mental illnesses.

McMullen and his wife, Kim Hoggard, live in Sydney and have two children, Claire, aged seven, and Will, aged six.

A Life of Extremes is his first book.

Jeff McMullen

a life of
extremes

Journeys and Encounters

HarperCollins*Publishers*

HarperCollins*Publishers*

First published in Australia in 2001
by HarperCollins*Publishers* Pty Limited
ABN 36 009 913 517
A member of the HarperCollins*Publishers* (Australia) Pty Limited Group
www.harpercollins.com.au

HarperCollins*Publishers*
25 Ryde Road, Pymble, Sydney, NSW 2073, Australia
31 View Road, Glenfield, Auckland 10, New Zealand
77–85 Fulham Palace Road, London, W6 8JB, United Kingdom
Hazelton Lanes, 55 Avenue Road, Suite 2900, Toronto, Ontario M5R 3L2
and 1995 Markham Road, Scarborough, Ontario M1B 5M8, Canada
10 East 53rd Street, New York NY 10022, USA

National Library of Australia Cataloguing-in-Publication data:

McMullen, Jeff. 1947– .
    A life of extremes: journeys and encounters.

    Bibliography.
    Includes index.
    ISBN 0 7322 7053 7.

    1. McMullen, Jeff. 2. Television journalists - Australia -
    Biography. 3. Foreign correspondents - Australia -
    Biography. I. Title

070.92

Cover photo of the author by Phil Donoghue
Cover and internal design by Melanie Calabretta, HarperCollins Design Studio
Typeset by HarperCollins in 11/14.5 Sabon

Printed & Bound by Griffin Press, Netley, Australia on 79gsm Bulky Paperback

5 4 3 2 1
04 03 02 01

For Kim, Claire and Will

Contents

CHAPTER ONE

UNFORGETTABLE STRANGERS

A child, wide-eyed, ran up to the gate of a cottage in the Australian bush. Soldiers in khaki were marching along the dirt road between the gum trees.

'Where's your mum, Snow?' asked the stranger, limping to the gate.

'Inside,' the little boy answered, eyes fixed on the first gun he had ever seen.

While his mother bathed the soldier's badly blistered heel on the front steps of the house, the boy found out that the stranger's name was Bluey. They were not going to war. Just marching. To nowhere in particular.

The boy burbled about a magpie that talked and the wasp nest in the honeysuckle above the gate. For trading these secrets he wanted to know where the soldier had got his gun.

'Some people think guns grow on trees,' Bluey said, eyes twinkling.

'If I put your gun in a hole, will it grow a gun tree?' the boy asked.

'I'd like to bury it, Snow.'

A smile spread slowly across Bluey's red-whiskered face as the boy ran off to find his hoe, the one Dad had given him to start a garden in the bush.

'Thank you, Joyce,' the soldier said, pulling on his leather boot. He waved goodbye as the kid arrived with the hoe, and Bluey disappeared down that road to nowhere.

Why do we remember strangers? Why do their words linger long after they have gone? So much of life's noisy detail fades so quickly, but the unforgettable strangers travel with us for the rest of our lives. It is the poetry of the road, from voices we have never heard before and perhaps will never hear again. Courage, kindness, humour and sometimes wisdom can flow from these chance meetings. The simple joys of life are shared along the way.

I began to write stories about interesting strangers at the age of nine, pasting in photographs and adding sketches to illustrate what I called 'The True Story of Penang'. This island off the coast of what was then called Malaya was our home in the 1950s when my father joined the RAAF squadron based at Butterworth, battling about five thousand guerillas, most of them ethnic Chinese trying to create a communist state.

The Malayan Emergency began in 1948, the year after I was born. Babyboomers like to think we live in peacetime, but there are always wars going on somewhere. I have been to more than three dozen armed conflicts. This one started when the communists killed just three men, white planters who were the backbone of the colonial Malay economy. Ironically, the guerillas were led by a man who was once a British hero. Chin Peng had even been awarded an OBE for his struggle against the Japanese invaders during World War II. His aim was to topple the government of Malaya by attacking the plantation owners, the rubber tappers and the tin miners. The terror campaign also targeted any villager who did not support the guerillas. Children were butchered in front of their parents. District officers were beheaded. It was a grim introduction to the real world for a young Australian boy.

My father, Jack, was eager to do his bit for the country. His father, a fine horseman from the Hunter Valley of New South Wales, was in the 30th Battalion of the Australian Imperial Force which fought in France during World War I. Grandfather's postcards from his training camp in Egypt joked about endless marches and sand in his boots. He never said a thing in later dispatches about being wounded, evacuated, patched up and sent back in to fight again. After rotting in the trenches and suffering from the blistering effects of mustard gas, he was shot a second time in France and spent six months in hospital battling to walk again. Perhaps in gratitude, years later he led the fundraising drive to build Maitland Hospital, the first real medical care for the coalminers and cattlemen of the Hunter Valley. I have letters from the townspeople of Branxton saying that he was always a generous man but the war made him more so. As a young boy I remember him hobbling about cheerfully, always glad to be alive. Like most veterans of war, Grandfather did not talk much about it, but it was obvious that his son was very proud of him. As soon as he could, Jack turned his back on cattle and the bush and set out to see the world. The air force was his wings and mine.

What made the Malayan campaign highly successful, with a very different outcome to the war in Vietnam soon afterwards, was the effectiveness in cutting support for the guerillas in the countryside. The Australians won the hearts and minds of the civilian population of Malaya. To destroy Chin Peng's camps the RAAF used Lincoln bombers and Sabre jets, and an Australian army battalion and British troops fought their way through the jungles. Into the early 1960s our men in khaki drabs and wide-brimmed hats kept searching for the communists up near the border with Thailand, but by that stage the enemy was on the run and hardly a threat.

'I hope we don't find them,' Jack said, when one of his three sons asked why the terrorists were still hiding, 'because a lot of them now are just poor hungry people.'

You could never call Jack a warmonger. He had considerable knowledge of Malaya's problems, a sensitivity about the tensions between the Malays and ethnic Chinese, and a strong conviction that massive change was coming to much of Asia faster than most of the world imagined. Yet, unlike many of his generation, he was not gripped by lingering fear of Japan or any other fast-growing Asian nation. He ridiculed the Domino Theory and even in the early years of the Vietnam War told anyone who would listen that MacArthur was right and we shouldn't be there.

Malaya, for the children of the Australian servicemen, never seemed like a war zone. It was a place of delight and discovery. In Penang's rubber plantations we found something irresistible in the white latex dripping from the 'V's carved into the trees by the Malay tappers. It was hard to believe they were going to make tennis balls and even Mum's brassieres out of that sticky stuff. And who knows how many condoms were never made because of those snowy-haired larrikins who emptied the tappers' cups or filled them with stones. Sometimes the Malay workers would chase us with machetes, screaming like madmen, until we made it to a coconut tree which formed a bridge across a deep monsoon drain. On the other side we would hide in the tall grass and laugh until our sides ached, before slowly wandering back to our house on the edge of the warm Penang sea.

It was an enchanted island through the eyes of boys so young. We swam under mountain waterfalls and built cubbies with bamboo thicker than a man's arm. Little black monkeys came down from the jungle. Occasionally an enormous python slithered across a track. Each day in Penang was an adventure.

A favourite place of mine was the Pure Cloud temple, for there, for the first time, we saw 'magic', a show that had us both intrigued and sceptical. Venomous snakes coiled around candelabra on the altars as devotees sat dangerously close, lighting sticks of incense which Jack said kept the snakes doped. It was an early lesson in organised religion and our agnostic father was enjoying our education. Each exotic sight prompted so many questions and our mother Joyce, a devoted Catholic, was having difficulty trying to explain why Christians believed the snake represented the devil, but in the Pure Cloud temple the vicious viper was like a god.

In the port of George Town, there were so many different shrines, mosques and temples that we soon worked out there had to be a lot of gods, no matter what Mother or the Pope said.

At the end of narrow laneways, behind high walls and dragon-covered gates lived very strange gods indeed and none of them looked like Jesus. The Chinese temples had huge golden Buddhas, fat and leering. At Sri Mariamman, where the Hindus worshipped, there was Krishna in a wonderful chariot drawn by white horses.

In the churches back home, there was always a life-sized sculpture of the dying Jesus nailed to a wooden cross, blood trickling from the crown of thorns and the spear wound in his side. In Penang, we saw living men, wild-eyed Indians in linen loincloths, parading with spears sticking through their arms and into their chests. Dangling on fish-hooks through their cheeks were floral tributes to their god, not a Christian god but one they obviously took seriously. No one died. There should have been pain but no one seemed to be hurting. Religion was full of myth and mystery, but it also was just another spectacular sideshow.

St Mary's Cathedral in Sydney once had seemed like the biggest building in the universe, with the only stairway to heaven. After wandering through the maze of the Kek Lok Si temple, staring at its pagoda of 10 000 buddhas, and joining the sea of Muslims barefoot on the prayer rugs of the Kapitan Kling mosque, we knew that there was far more to the story than we had been taught by the nuns in Australia.

School was a half-day affair in Penang, because of the heat. We had classes at the old Governor's residence and played on the lush lawns a running–wrestling game called 'British Bulldog'. In the afternoon we swam with the Malay and Chinese children who lived in houses on stilts by the sea or in *kampongs*, small villages surrounded by giant thickets of bamboo.

I used to cut out pictures from Penang's newspapers and take my own photographs on a box camera. I also began a journal, writing stories and poems that captured fresh experiences in an immediate way. This became a lifelong habit. I found to my great delight that once I had collected my thoughts in this way the impressions were indelible.

It was a great age to begin exploring the Orient. Penang was the oldest British settlement in Malaya but the tea parties at the big

houses along Millionaires' Row were not as interesting to us kids
as the sights, sounds and smells of George Town.

Jack led us through streets crowded with bicycles, handcarts,
trucks and trishaws. We bought paper cones filled with crushed
ice in lurid reds and blues that made us remember the bright
feathers of the crimson rosellas in the bush we had grown up in.
But how different were these bamboo street stalls to Sydney's
shops, behind glass, protected from the Australian weather by
jutting metal awnings! On our little island they just rolled down
cane blinds or old canvas when it rained. The local children loved
to walk barefoot in the street until their thick dark hair was
slicked down and their singlets and shorts were soaked.

After the monsoon the air was filled with the sweet smell of
tropical fruit, blended with spices wafting from steaming woks.
Malays, Chinese and Indians peddled their foods in a chorus of
different languages. There were ducks hanging on hooks, baskets
of fish of every size, dried stingrays, piles of sea snails, even some
large, dried, flattened rats.

'There's dinner,' said Jack, pointing to the rats as, laughing, we
headed into a noodle house.

We watched big families squatting with chopsticks in the open
doorways of their houses. But not everyone had a bowl of rice.
In Penang we saw poverty for the first time, images that would
stay with us for life.

Children our own age scavenged for scraps of food on the
street. People slept on pieces of cardboard in the drains. Old men
with ribs poking through shrivelled skin came up to us as we
travelled through town in a trishaw. Women with babies often
begged for coins at the front gate of our house. Joyce believed
it helped to give them something. Jack said the beggars and
their children would keep coming back. They were both correct.
My father smiled as he watched my mother handing over money,
food and clothes, because she said she loved all children and it
was the right thing to do.

We discovered that barefoot Malay boys and girls liked the
same kind of fun we did. We would take a kite, rub glue along the
string below the tail and then roll the string in broken glass to

give it a jagged cutting edge. When the kites were high over the *kampongs*, we would saw away at one another's painted paper monsters, colours streaming, kids screaming, as old rivals tangled once again. If you cut through someone's string with your kite, a whole world of children seemed to empty into the streets, running, pushing, laughing, all in the game together. Whoever caught the runaway kite kept it. But the real fun was in the chase.

CHAPTER TWO

THE BOY SOLDIER

Bring down the barbed wire that runs through the mind,
dividing brothers ...

(JOURNAL 1973)

The kid wore a cap, raked back like a baseball player's, but it wasn't a bat he was holding. Javier Blancher was eleven years old and the rifle he was cleaning with a piece of string and cloth looked older than he was. The Sandinistas, the revolutionaries who overthrew Nicaragua's dictator, Anastasio Somoza, in 1979, were using everything they had, including boys like Javier, to defend their hold on this small Central American country against a counter-revolution.

Up in the mountains near Jinotega, the Sandinistas were trying to protect their coffee crop and trucks from attack by the counter-revolutionaries known as the *contra*. Young Javier was in the Sandinistas' village militia. He sat with his back to the wall of his commander's bunker, sheltering from the sun high over the deserted square. If he had not been at war, this kid would have been kicking a soccer ball around in the dust, or marking out a diamond to play baseball, the game of the Yankees whom he would come to hate. Instead, Javier and the other boy soldiers would file out of the village at dusk to patrol the hills.

In Nicaragua guns did not grow on trees. Javier's gun was an AK-47 and everyone knew Cuba's President Fidel Castro was supplying the Sandinistas with these Soviet weapons.

The Nicaraguans were slipping guns to leftist guerillas trying to overthrow the military government of neighbouring El Salvador. The United States feared that Marxist revolution would spread throughout Central America and into Mexico. The boy soldier did not understand the politics of the war but he was experiencing the terror. The kid had begun to fight so young he had a rough time at first even carrying that heavy rifle.

Sometimes the militia would set a trap for the *contra*, who were fewer in number than the Sandinistas but better armed with grenade-launchers and automatic weapons. One night the *contra* turned the tables and caught Javier's patrol in an ambush. The kid lay in the dark, shooting back at the flashes until his rifle jammed. The *contra* fire got heavier. Javier kept his face pressed into the dirt with his hands over his head, until the patrol leader told them to crawl out of there. Leaving his rifle behind in the panic, the boy ran smack into a tree in the darkness. His head was spinning but he kept on running and falling, then running again, until he was back with his mother at home.

The next day, to prove a boy soldier could be as brave as a man, Javier crept back alone to search for his rifle at the site of the ambush. He found the gun. He also came across the headless body of his cousin who had been shot in the fighting and then mutilated with a machete. Javier had kept his eyes on the rifle, just as they were now as we sat together. Staring into the shimmer of heat, I thought of that young Australian kid who years before had wanted a rifle, before he really understood what it could do.

We were running along a rutted mountain road with mortars exploding ahead of and behind us. Tom Sigale, an American cameraman, and I were with a unit of the Sandinista regular army, close to the border with Honduras.

It was hard trying to run and shoot. Shoot film, that is. We never carried guns. The Sandinista captain offered me one but I said I was just a storyteller.

I spent most of my first two decades in journalism as a foreign correspondent for the Australian Broadcasting Corporation. In Nicaragua in 1982 we were filming an hour-long documentary for the *Four Corners* program, one of three I did from the Central American war zones. The sound-recordist in our team had been left far behind, sick with fever, resting safely in a little church. A camera assistant also had fallen back after being unnerved by the sight of a Sandinista soldier executing a badly wounded *contra* at point-blank range. I was trying to be reporter, producer and sound-recordist, but Tom and I had too much film gear in our packs and after several weeks in the hills we were close to exhaustion. We had driven in jeeps into the mountains, through passes known to be ambush alleys, past the blackened wreckage of trucks destroyed by the *contra*. Then we walked from village to village as the Sandinistas hunted down the marauding enemy. Up and down those steep, almost conical peaks we trekked, sweating during the day and freezing at night. The Sandinistas were not interested in sharing our load, as they were dragging a heavy mortar with them. But they were in no position to use it now.

As Tom and I rounded a bend in the road, running hard, one of the Sandinistas, a *politico* assigned to keep an eye on us, started spraying his machine-gun wildly into the trees. We slid under a barbed-wire fence and into a ditch. I was so out of breath it felt as if my heart would tear right through my chest. We rolled camera and sound just as a rifle-fired grenade from the *contra* tore a few posts from the fence. My mouth was dry. I could feel the pulse in my forehead. This tom-tom beat of the brain brought a strange slow motion to the battle. Bullets from the Sandinistas arched up in white tracers towards some *contra* a few hundred metres ahead of us. The field of dry grass started to smoke and burn. Flames were licking at a tree where a *contra* was dug in with the grenade-launcher. In a creek bed to our left I heard groans from another *contra* who was wounded. There was more shooting and his moaning stopped. Then, just as suddenly as the battle had started, most of the *contra* stopped firing. We could see at least five dead and the others began to withdraw, covered by their man with the grenades.

A Sandinista captain, just twenty-four-years old, waved at us to follow him as his men rushed towards the hilltop. Tom and I were running again, legs made of jelly, up the slope, panting, down a dip, up again, everything burning now, the smoke choking us, the heat and our own fear almost smothering the reason we were there.

In battle, unarmed, the mind operates like the shutter of the camera, frame by frame, recording the no man's land we had entered, the space between life and death. The sheer absurdity of the situation, of our vulnerability and the fragility of every life around us, was an unforgettable feeling. While I have seen valour and cowardice, victory and defeat, my strongest sense of battle is that it makes no sense at all. This total breakdown of reason can almost overwhelm you. We were watching men from the same country killing one another. Yes, I know it can happen in any town, under any roof. But seeing it again and again and remembering that split fraction of time between the shot and the scream, I decided that war must be an insane impulse on our evolutionary journey, an impulse that we must master to become civilised.

(JOURNAL 1983)

Look back. Look ahead. Keep your eyes open in the smoke.

At the top of the hill, under the tree, the *contra* with the grenade launcher lay dead. A Sandinista prodded him with his rifle. Film was still rolling through our camera. Was this the reason we were here? Was this the face of war? This dead man had no face left. His body was covered in blood. His arms were muscled. His chest was pumped up. His skin was the same rich brown colour of the Sandinista standing over him. They were both Nicaraguans. They once spoke the same language. I felt then so deeply the lesson that history had been trying to teach us for so long. Civil wars end in a terrible silence, when we confront the enemy for the last time and have to admit that we are not much different after all.

We filmed the war in Nicaragua from both sides. Tom Sigale's footage in the *contra* camps was the first convincing proof that the United States was supplying the counter-revolutionaries in a covert operation. In 1983 it was still being called the 'secret war in Nicaragua', but Americans would see this film and hear *contra* commanders boasting that they were 'freedom fighters', the term President Ronald Reagan later used to justify the fight against the Marxist Sandinistas. Washington congressmen would watch the film as crate after crate of American guns and ammunition was unpacked by the *contra*. The Central Intelligence Agency had created a well-armed fighting force. Even their uniforms and boots came from north of the border. *Gracias*, Uncle Sam!

That night with a golden moon over the mountains, the Sandinista soldiers shared with us a bottle of their white rum. They were all young men and women eager to hear about the other guerilla wars we had filmed in El Salvador and Guatemala.

'How can the United States provide weapons to so many armies which terrorise peasants?' they asked.

We talked about the ninety-odd times in history that American troops had come south of the border. Imperialism was the simple explanation favoured by revolutionaries. In plain terms it was the greed of multinational companies and the eagerness of the United States to protect its economic investments. The Sandinistas took their name from their hero, Augusto Cesar Sandino, who half a century before the current struggle had fought in the same northern hills against American troops sent to preserve the old order. Now it was the American fear of communism, the resulting contest with the Soviet Union in every conceivable arena and the threat of instability this produced so close to home that convinced the Reagan Administration to involve the United States once more. It is one of the curiosities of the American brand of democracy that within such a great and powerful society so many fear communism. The rugged individualists sensed another wrestle to the death was coming. Instinctively, the eagle had to show its talons.

I told the Sandinistas that once they had dressed their socialist revolution in military uniform it was almost guaranteed that Reagan would see them as the enemy. And besides, before Reagan came to power, Jimmy Carter had tried to give careful support to the fledgling Sandinista government. Washington's ambassador to Nicaragua, Walter Pazzulo, had told me that the Sandinista leadership had been mistrustful to the point of paranoia about any American assistance. A very wise diplomat, Pazzulo was convinced right from the start of Reagan's secret war that military solutions would not work in Central America.

'Our role there is mindless. I don't see the problems in Central America being resolved by rifles, no matter what the Marxists say about power coming out of the end of a gun. There are too many forces at play and real change will not come about that way in Nicaragua, Guatemala or El Salvador. If we are on the side of pushing for military solutions we are on the wrong side of history in the whole area. You've got to demilitarise this region and try to eliminate the animosities and fear. A rational approach would be to build up the institutions and help the people of the whole region develop. If, as I see it, the Sandinistas, because of their failure to govern well, are starting to lose the respect and support of the Nicaraguan people, isn't it better to allow that change to come naturally?'

I could not tell the Sandinistas that in just over a month's time I was due to marry a very bright and beautiful woman who worked in Reagan's White House. That certainly could have endangered the lives of my crew. Afterwards I did tell my wife-to-be that it was a very strange feeling to be shot at with bullets paid for by her Administration. When I challenged one White House official, pointing out the disastrous consequences of American support for the *contra*, who were largely the remnants of Somoza's hated National Guard, I realised that many of Reagan's most senior staff were not fully aware of the agenda being pursued by Lieutenant Colonel Oliver North of the National Security Council. A Congressional investigation much later revealed that North and others secretly were selling weapons to Iran for its war against Iraq, and then diverting

millions of dollars of the profits to pay for the arms going down
to the *contra* in Nicaragua.

The Sandinistas I was drinking with agreed that you could never
trust *gringos*. They joked that if I were shot dead by the *contra*,
Ronald Reagan would say I was a blue-eyed Russian there to help
the Marxist revolution. With our rum bottle draining towards
empty we traded songs, as soldiers do in war.

After several weeks of fighting in the most dangerous mountains
up north near Jinotega, I got to know the men and women of this
patrol. We walked together, ate together and slept together,
huddled for warmth without tents or blankets. These young
Nicaraguans revealed a horrible truth. Fighting was all they
seemed to know.

I asked them whether the Sandinistas also mutilated the *contra*
when our camera was not around. Of course they did. I once
saw a Nicaraguan churchman with his ears cut off by a bayonet
and his throat slashed. At least 45 000 had been killed in the
revolution to overthrow Somoza and thousands more would die
during the counter-revolution. With a population of just over two
million there were 25 000 in the Sandinista army and a militia of
50 000. An entire generation was being indoctrinated into the cult
of violence.

It is one of the greatest horrors of our modern world to see
children at play in this game called war. Although it is against
international law for anyone younger than fifteen to go into
battle, UNICEF says there are hundreds of thousands of children
fighting in wars started by adults. In the West African nation of
Sierra Leone, I met ten-year-olds who had killed many times in
their savage civil war. They smoked marijuana mixed with
gunpowder and then went on a rampage, doing whatever their
commanders asked of them. I was astonished to hear some of
these very young children admit that they had mimicked their
older brothers and joined in the rape of elderly villagers.

The same ten-year-olds had hacked off limbs as part of the terror campaign intended to make people vote for their side in the dirty war.

In Central America I came to understand how this happens, how children like Javier Blancher are militarised. When he found his cousin's head severed from his body, Javier was deeply traumatised. Doctors have learned that the physical development of the brain of a child like this often is retarded and the mechanism for dealing with conflict or even emotional challenge is severely damaged. Javier had come to see fighting as his only choice. His life was war.

By the time our thirty-strong patrol had made it back to the village of Cua, nine Sandinistas had been killed. These exceptionally high losses had an extraordinary impact on everyone. The bodies that were brought in were laid out on wooden benches in a crude chapel. Outside, two carpenters banged away making rough-sawn coffins. Women and children wept over their loved ones. Fathers too.

I sat with Javier Blancher as an old man clutching a bottle came weaving across the square towards us. He was very drunk, and sobbing. Earlier I had watched this man as the body of his nineteen-year-old son was lifted from the back of a truck. He had stood with a crowd gathering and proudly eulogised his son in a strong voice. The young man had died for the homeland, and by God he would give the lives of his three sons still in the army to defend the revolution.

As the day faded, so did the old man's resoluteness. The pain of his loss and the fear of what very likely would happen to his sons, Victor, Manuel and Juan, had found its way to his heart.

No one could comfort the old man. The Sandinistas would not look him in the eye. And so he stopped in front of young Javier and me.

I could not look away. I just held out a hand. I thought of my own father and how he would feel if he lost any one of his sons. I thought of all the mothers of all the soldier sons. The old man dropped his bottle and flung his wiry arms around my neck, crying uncontrollably in a deep, convulsive agony.

This Nicaraguan father's grief is one of my enduring memories of the real pain of war. It is stored in my head and my heart, a dark negative, flicked up occasionally onto a vivid screen. I often see the face of Javier too, his faint smile, only a trace of childhood left, his innocence lost because of war.

The children of the world
are taught to hate,
to tear their hands
on our barbed wire,
and yet they look beyond
the walls of the playground
we have built.

(JOURNAL 1983)

CHAPTER THREE

GOING TO EXTREMES

*High up in the Himalayan mountains surrounded by
spectacular peaks I said goodbye to the rest of our team
and flew off to the highest war on earth. The extremes of
madness can be as irresistible as extremes of beauty and
this journey involved both. I was headed for a
battleground near K2, a mountain so glorious it is worthy
of the worship it is given. Up here at the top of the world,
India and Pakistan were waging war.*

(JOURNAL 1990)

We were squeezed into a very small Pakistani army chopper, climbing slowly between the awesome mountains. Just below us was the magnificent Siachen Glacier, claimed by both India and Pakistan. These mortal enemies had been disputing the border for decades, losing thousands of lives in periodic artillery duels, infantry clashes and helicopter battles.

Apart from the pilot, my only companion was *60 Minutes* cameraman Phil Donoghue. Even dressed for winter warfare in white battle fatigues we could feel the severe cold. The pilot had oxygen but we did not and the unpressurised chopper, aptly called a 'Llama', was throbbing hard to reach the war zone 6300 metres above sea level. Along the way we spotted the wreckage of several big cargo helicopters whose engines had been unable to handle the high altitude. It seemed mindless that two nations that could barely feed themselves were wasting millions of dollars this way.

We crossed breathtaking alpine valleys and several smaller glaciers. It was easy to see why adventurers had been tantalised by these peaks. They were some of the world's most challenging mountains, but climbers had been driven away by the war. India and Pakistan each had about six thousand soldiers dug into this blindingly white battlefield. Our pilot told us that many men had slipped to their death in the deep crevasses or been buried under avalanches.

The chopper came down on the biggest glacier I had ever seen, a massive, mind-boggling beast of ice devouring giant boulders and everything else in its path. I stared at this awesome force of nature and then at the snow-covered ridges that were pocked with dark scars from incoming artillery shells. This was how man left his mark on these heavenly heights. I said to Donoghue, 'Isn't this the most absurd place to fight a war?'

The only human life we could see appeared to be moving in slow motion. Against the grandeur of the Himalaya the Pakistani troops looked like toy soldiers, tiny and insignificant. These men had to spend from six months to a year fighting at over 6000 metres above the rest of humankind. An army medical officer admitted that after just thirty days at this difficult altitude, the mind and body begin to crack.

The Himalayan air was so thin soldiers were struggling to drag a mortar thirty paces, all the while gasping for breath. I could feel a light-headedness and a slight dizziness caused by the lack of oxygen, but Donoghue, with his shock of silver curls and a few days growth on his chin, was lugging his Arriflex camera and film magazines and puffing on a cigarette.

Although the Siachen Glacier is often swept by blizzards, on this day the sky was bright blue and the snowy peaks dazzled us with their perfection. The master cameraman was breathing hard now, trying to contrast this beauty with the ugliness of war.

It was so cold that touching the metal film magazines stung our fingertips. For the soldiers, trying to load an artillery shell could strip the skin from bare hands, and for every one killed by a bullet, nine more died of altitude sickness, from blood clots on the brain or lungs crippled by the freezing air. Hundreds of troops on both sides had suffered severe frostbite. Yet neither India nor Pakistan would surrender their claim to the glacier, and just to the south both nations were struggling over who should own Kashmir. To most of the soldiers this war of attrition was futile. To us it seemed almost surreal.

One man was sitting miserably on his own. He no longer cared about the invisible line drawn across the Himalaya because he was so sick he feared he would never see his wife and children again. His name was Hosef and he asked whether I would take a photograph of him and mail it with a letter to his family in Rawalpindi in Pakistan. I did as he asked. Hosef then pulled from his pocket some rocks he had found in the mountains. At times he had been so bored with this crazy war and the weeks of waiting for the next attack that he had used the army's dynamite to blast boulders like a mad prospector. He pressed into my hand an uncut gemstone. A large red ruby it turned out to be, but to this day I have kept the stone just as that soldier handed it to me, as a reminder of the man and the mountains.

On the roof of the world it seemed that we had come to the heights of man's insanity. Donoghue and I took a long look at this place, so glorious it belonged not to men but to angels, and then at the same moment we both began to laugh, until there were tears in my eyes.

Together Phil Donoghue and I have filmed some of the worst chapters of the grimmest century of human history. We have walked through the minefields and over the bones left by the Khmer Rouge in Cambodia. We have shared the horror of the child soldiers at war in Africa. Twice we have journeyed to the edge of the human abyss to document the genocide in Rwanda. In this observer's role, looking at life through a lens, there is a danger that it will all become surreal, like a movie that might be over soon, letting everyone go home. A heart, a mind, a nervous system can only stand so much and then some people shut down, closing themselves to the horror of war, the agony of famine, the sheer folly of mankind's gravest mistakes. Donoghue always keeps his eyes open and what he films has a clarity, a balance of light and darkness.

Our journeys also have taken us to places of the most exotic beauty. We went to those glorious extremes because nature gave us perspective, and maintained our sense of wonderment and enthusiasm to celebrate the exhilarating side of the human race. We have travelled to many forbidden places, the most remote corners on earth and have witnessed human endeavour on the most spectacular scale. One story about ten thousand men tearing ships apart by hand on the beaches of Gujarat in India won Australia's Golden Tripod, the highest cinematic award for excellence. But the prize we always cherished most was the experience itself. The life of the travelling storyteller is one of living and learning. All the dangers and the fatigue are worth enduring for that chance to share so many true wonders of the world.

I have worked with some of the finest cameramen around the world and their artistry has brought much of the power to my storytelling. The best of them, like Phil Donoghue, understand the natural choreography of action. They are magicians with light, both portrait artists and painters of landscape. Like thieves, they are hungry for the stolen moment. The unforgettable strangers so often provide them with the unforgettable images. Above everything else, however, these great visual storytellers prize authenticity and originality. To achieve that they go to dangerous extremes.

*Rebels from the Chilean armed forces moved towards
Allende's palace. Leonardo stepped out of a doorway
with his camera rolling. A captain waved a gun as other
soldiers jumped from a truck. Leonardo was filming.
They were shooting. Shooting at him. He was hit. You
bastards. Screaming, 'La Prensa, La Prensa'. The
soundwoman, terrified, dropped the tape-recorder. More
shooting. Leonardo's camera had it all. I wonder about
his last thoughts. 'I am bleeding ... I am dying. Now, I
am my camera.'*

(JOURNAL 1973)

As I arrived in Santiago to cover the first attempted coup against President Salvador Allende in June 1973, the cameraman I had hired was at the airport in a coffin. I drove slowly towards the city, excitement replaced by apprehension, trying to imagine the last seconds of his life. When I met President Allende inside the palace shortly afterwards he was aware of the death of Leonardo Henrichsen, the brave and talented freelance cameraman many of us foreign correspondents used in South America. While filming this aborted coup not long before Allende finally was overthrown by the Chilean military, Leonardo had captured the horror of his own death. Allende was told that the troops mistakenly believed Leonardo had been holding a rocket-launcher, not a camera. The President promised us he would help the widow and her family, but he seemed subdued by an even greater sadness, a sense of impending doom. Only a few months later the palace was in flames and Salvador Allende, the world's first democratically elected Marxist leader, was dead.

> *I lay on the ground outside the university as the army*
> *poured a murderous fire into the classrooms defended by*
> *Allende's last youthful supporters. Later in the soccer*
> *stadium a few of us foreign correspondents were herded*
> *onto the centre of the pitch to see at least seven thousand*
> *Chileans held prisoner there. Many of them, like the*
> *singer Victor Jara, were tortured and secretly executed.*
> *A German reporter with me was beaten savagely with a*
> *rifle butt. There was fear everywhere on the streets, even*
> *behind closed doors. Chile's greatest poet, Pablo Neruda,*
> *died suddenly after General Pinochet's troops sacked the*
> *libraries, burning piles of books.*
>
> (JOURNAL 1973)

Democracy was in flames in Chile and so was the film of my memorable final meeting with President Allende. My new freelance

cameraman had used a cracked film-magazine. This simple error let
flashes of light onto the film, destroying one of the last historic
images of President Allende with his back to the wall. You will thus
understand why I have the deepest admiration for men and women
who, under the greatest pressure, are able to capture life or death
through a lens.

The first legendary combat cameraman I saw in action was Neil
Davis. We met during the Vietnam War years in Bangkok. I was
a green kid, the youngest foreign correspondent ever sent away
by the ABC. At eighteen I had been posted to Papua New
Guinea where I explored the country with a Chimbu mate,
hitched a ride on a DC-3 to the Trobriands, the 'Islands of
Love', and reported on some of the tribal battles between
Highland warriors. Looking back on my eighteen and a half
years with the ABC and a commercial television career spanning
sixteen years as a reporter on Australia's 60 Minutes, I think my
main interest was always in going the extra mile to find original
stories. But when I plunged again into the Southeast Asia that
I had discovered as a boy, I still had much to learn from the
old master.

Neil Davis enjoyed the kind of intense experiences that made
me appreciate journalism as far more than a job and rather a
way of life. Davis was in touch. He knew so many people,
from the street to the palaces, from the bar district to brigade
headquarters, that it gave him an awareness that eluded many
pundits, politicians and diplomats of the Vietnam War era. As a
staff cameraman for the news agency Visnews, Davis knew
Southeast Asia.

He was very Australian, a big, blond larrikin from Tasmania,
but he also was a gentle, keen-eyed traveller who learned most
of what he understood about life in Vietnam and Cambodia,
particularly on the battlefields. While it was not uncommon to
hear some of his colleagues refer to 'gooks' and 'noggies', Davis

respected both friend and foe. His film from the frontlines was proof that there was bravery as well as brutality on both sides, and seasons of war where triumphs hid approaching defeats.

Instead of competing with the pack of photographers that usually flew with the Americans, Davis's specialty was filming with the Vietnamese, South Koreans and Cambodians. His contacts even allowed him to slip away with the Viet Cong forces that killed dozens of other correspondents.

It was Davis's ideological view of the war that I was most interested in when I peppered him with questions about the morality of Australia's 'All the Way with LBJ' policy. I wanted to know what Davis thought of America's Gulf of Tonkin Resolution, that official excuse for entering the war; what he made of Australian motives for joining the battle; and whether he saw any justification for so many civilian deaths, the special mark of the wars of our century. If Davis was amused or scornful, he showed no more than a gentle smile and the knowing look of a man who knew a bit about combat.

I explained that being younger than Davis and his peers I would soon face the possibility of being drafted to Vietnam, not as a reporter there by choice, but as a conscript, called up by a lottery as mindless as Russian roulette. I knew some other young reporters back home who were planning elaborate manoeuvres to avoid conscription, not because of any moral opposition to the war or even an understandable fear of being shot, but simply because they disliked the idea of giving up a couple of years of their career.

I did not burn my draft papers and registered for possible military service for the same mixture of reasons my grandfather accepted his orders to fight in World War I and my father served in Malaya. I was not much interested in what was acceptable to my peers but concerned with my own conscience. I obeyed the law on military service because at that time I saw no clear, overriding moral reason to oppose it. While going to university, however, I was impressed when I read for the first time the argument of the American political philosopher Henry Thoreau that one should not contribute in any way to an unjust war.

I began to examine more closely the government's justification for sending troops to Vietnam.

Suddenly the Vietnam Moratoriums began and I was out in the streets as a young reporter covering the biggest mass demonstrations our country had seen. It was an odd situation. I knew some of the student leaders marching in the front ranks, yet I had to try to maintain objectivity in my coverage of these events. I admired the ideal of non-violent civil disobedience but could not see the point of demonstrators spitting in the faces of the police and provoking violence. The Moratoriums taught me to be suspicious of the extremes of propaganda from both sides of any argument. But the more I learned about Vietnam and its history the more it seemed we were heading towards a tragedy. I listened carefully to my father's warnings about the dangers of trying to find winners and losers in this war. Neil Davis happened to agree with Jack.

I was quite surprised when Davis told me that he had arrived in Southeast Asia as green as I was, that he had pushed extremely hard to get to Vietnam because he simply wanted to film any war and that he found it hugely exciting. Well that is honest, I thought, but a bit disappointing. Just as Damien Parer's courageous filmwork during World War II had made him a legend, Davis and many of his generation were in Vietnam to test their mettle professionally. But he said some were a lot better at it than others. He had gone through military training during Australia's earlier period of National Service and believed that this helped prepare him for covering combat. Many of his friends were killed, like the photographer Sean Flynn who that same year had disappeared while riding his motorbike in Cambodia. Davis admitted he still liked the challenge of filming war, even as he came to understand it.

Patiently, the veteran explained that the Vietnam War was much more complicated than the simplistic and erroneous media portrayal of ugly Americans and Australian 'grunts' mindlessly destroying the innocent Vietnamese. Davis saw neither side as morally superior. He said most Vietnamese wanted peace, just like most people in most wars. So why were the Vietnamese still at war? Davis believed that the great powers, the United States and the Soviet Union, had invested their war technology, their economies and human capital in the struggle between communism and democracy. Now everyone was trapped.

> *Like many who have spent time with armies on both sides*
> *of a conflict, Neil Davis has a hard time finding any*
> *morality in this war and tells me it is tragically misguided.*
> *He says the North and the South both want*
> *independence. Neither has 'God on its side'. When*
> *judging our political leaders and their grand policies, as*
> *well as the conduct of the men on the battlefield, he uses a*
> *fairly simple test. What is fair and what is foul? Davis sees*
> *soldiers first as people, recognising that they all have*
> *personal stories before they become part of this killing*
> *business. He tells me that he believes the Vietnamese most*
> *certainly could work out a unified government without*
> *this scale of death and destruction as the superpowers*
> *goad both sides.*
>
> (JOURNAL 1970)

Our greatest combat cameraman did not seem bothered by the prospect of a communist government in Vietnam, even when I reminded him of Mao's execution of perhaps fifty million people during the Cultural Revolution in China and Stalin's purges in the Soviet Union. This seemed to be his blind spot. When Davis later had to leave his favourite city, the Cambodian capital of Phnom Penh, as the fanatical Khmer Rouge drove over a million innocents to their slaughter, the old Asia hand rightly was horrified. Here was a clear case of genocide but the western powers were unwilling or unable to stop it. History's most difficult choices surely include bold international intervention at such times to prevent a perceived greater evil. There are just wars and occasions when united world action is not only warranted but morally essential. Nonetheless, there is a strong consensus, even among many of the military men who were engaged in it, that the Vietnam War involved a series of grave political miscalculations that led to disaster. I found Davis's advice incredibly useful and quite prophetic.

My marble was not drawn out of the lottery barrel and so I watched the end of the war from the command centre in Washington. There I reported on the biggest peace marches in American history. On the same Washington Mall today you can run your hand over the smooth stone of the Vietnam Veterans Memorial feeling the names of just some of the dead, sensing the cost of this debacle. The French certainly created the colonial mess in Vietnam. The United States made a mistake by not embracing Ho Chi Minh's very early overtures and later lost any chance of political support at home or abroad by indiscriminate bombing that killed far too many civilians. Australia blindly accepted the Domino Theory and forgot most of the lessons learned in the successful military campaign in Malaya. A wiser western diplomacy in Vietnam may have steered the North and South towards a political solution, as Neil Davis argued. In the most terrible war of my lifetime, one of the world's great nations lost perhaps a century of progress, not to mention more than two million lives.

It was no surprise when in 1975, as the first North Vietnamese tank crashed through the gates of the Presidential Palace in Saigon, Davis was there filming. With typical confidence he calculated correctly that there would be no bloodbath. When a North Vietnamese soldier stuck a rifle into his ribs Davis defused a dangerous moment by saying in Vietnamese, 'Welcome to Saigon, comrade. I've been waiting for you.' Davis captured the image of North Vietnamese victory just as surely as his film of the last helicopter lifting off from the roof of the American embassy in Saigon was the haunting image of defeat. He *was* his camera at such moments. It was a talisman that protected him, gave him a charmed life, but sometimes that magic or luck runs out.

Like a shooting star falling across the sky
I see my life, its glory and its end,
opening in the clouds over a desert night,
with animal breath held deep
in a canyon of silence.

(JOURNAL 1979)

In East Timor in 1975 five Australian-based newsmen were trapped in the most dangerous of wartime situations. They had positioned themselves with a much weaker force up against a powerful, advancing enemy. They had gone to the town of Balibo, occupied by FRETILIN troops, just inside Portuguese Timor, hoping to get the first film of an Indonesian invasion of this small neighbour. One of the journalists, Greg Shackleton, filed a memorable final report, clearly aware that an attack was imminent. Shackleton and his colleagues may have remembered Neil Davis filming the North Vietnamese march into Saigon.

The Balibo Five appeared to trust that painting an Australian flag on the walls of the house where they took shelter and the fact that they held passports and press credentials would establish their neutrality. They almost certainly were moved to take such a great risk knowing that the world had not seen proof of Indonesia's covert operations or preparations for the full-scale attack on Dili in which another Australian journalist would die. While some reporters pulled back from Balibo, the five who stayed were killed when Indonesian commandos and some Apodeti (Timorese allied with Jakarta) troops launched a dawn attack on Balibo. There has been controversy ever since over exactly how these cameramen and reporters died.

Soon after the Indonesian invasion Jakarta's spokesmen claimed that the Australians had been fighting alongside FRETILIN troops, 'controlling and directing the fire', according to one outrageous official statement. Although I admit I would pick up a gun and try to shoot my way out of trouble if the alternative were certain death, there is not the slightest evidence to support

Indonesia's excuse for what was clearly cold-blooded murder. Jakarta simply was trying to exploit a dubious report from a high-level Timorese at the scene of the battle. This account was disputed immediately by all those who knew the Australian newsmen, especially Greg's widow, the eloquent Shirley Shackleton. She kept demanding from the Australian government a full investigation and was not prepared to see the Balibo Five buried under a dirty lie.

In 1976, after a high-level intelligence lead, I broke the story that most of the Australian newsmen had not been killed accidentally in the heat of battle but had been executed. At offices of the United Nations in New York I interviewed Timorese politician Jose Martins, who had written the original false report which became the basis of Indonesia's official explanation of the deaths.

As the President of the Kota Party in East Timor, Martins originally had supported the Indonesian invasion, claiming it would bring about a provisional government representing all political factions. He admitted he had been an apologist for the invaders and during the fighting provided liaison between the pro-Indonesian forces and Jakarta. Now he said he wanted to withdraw the Kota Party from the provisional government. He claimed it was the atrocities committed by the Indonesian army that persuaded him to switch allegiances.

Jose Martins told me that he arrived at the scene of the battle in Balibo, just two hours after the fighting on 15 October 1975. He said that he interviewed an Apodeti commander and some of the Indonesians. He was given conflicting accounts, but offering his diary notes as some degree of proof he said there was a consensus that all of the Australians were shot or stabbed by troops under the Indonesian command. Three of the dead Australians then were dressed in FRETILIN uniforms by the Indonesians, propped up behind a gun and photographed. No photograph has ever surfaced, but other Timorese have come forward over the years to confirm and also deny Jose Martins's story.

As the world knows, the Indonesian army massacred countless unarmed East Timorese civilians after that initial invasion. This had a much greater impact on the Australian public than on our politicians who compromised our national integrity by accepting the 'geopolitical reality' of Indonesia's 'right' to Timor. The killing of the Balibo Five is a reminder that the current generation of Indonesian militarists includes some murderous liars. Australian diplomats, intelligence analysts and military commanders were briefed by the Indonesians about the covert invasion, but no one thought they should warn the Australian newsmen in Balibo that the invaders wanted no witnesses.

This was a hard way for all Australian journalists to learn a universal lesson. Reporters and cameramen sometimes have to trust their lives to governments and armies. We must try to anticipate their strategies. To survive all kinds of warfare, we have to accurately assess the intelligence and character of the officer in charge, the strength of his force and the threat posed by his, but not necessarily our own, enemy. It is hard to avoid becoming a pawn in somebody else's war game. Yet sometimes the greatest danger is when reporters and cameramen go it alone in war.

It was a fellow ABC correspondent, Mike Carlton, who nicknamed Derek McKendry 'Sundance'. The two of them were a bit like the Redford–Newman pair in that movie, swaggering into some trouble spot or out of a honky-tonk with a girl on either arm. Mike Carlton had a wild afro and did a wonderful Mick Jagger impersonation with his Indonesian rock band. In Vietnam he also was fond of impersonating American war correspondents, parodying the propaganda that was being handed out at the 'Five O'Clock Follies' in Saigon, the official briefings when newsmen were handed the latest useless body counts. Mike Carlton and Derek McKendry were a formidable team in the field because they understood the futility of reporting the war the way the military machine wanted it. Whenever they could they hitched a ride somewhere else to find a real story.

After surviving the Vietnam War (and all those nights together) McKendry and Carlton must have felt that they had charmed lives. But it was not with Carlton that 'Sundance' shot his last battle. In 1979, the New Zealand-born McKendry was sent into Zambia with another talented ABC reporter, Tony Joyce. They went to film skirmishes on the border with Rhodesia (now Zimbabwe) and were driving a dangerous road when armed men suddenly surrounded their car and blocked their way. Joyce, a man of considerable wit and word-power, protested strongly. In a flash of madness, an African gunman leaned in through the window and shot Joyce in the head at point-blank range. McKendry, sitting next to him, lived to tell us the horrific details, but it was many years before he could pick up a camera again. The kind of images he had seen are too terrifying to put on television and it is no wonder McKendry swore off ever again filming bloodshed.

Tony Joyce is remembered for his great sense of humour. I can replay the last dinner I had with him and his wife, Monica, when they were posted to New Delhi. There was always so much laughter wherever this man went, but Joyce also was a very serious reporter, always hungry for an original story. It made me angry later when I heard some journalists mumbling, like they did after the deaths of the Balibo Five, that Joyce had made a terrible miscalculation, losing his life for a story that was of little consequence. Here were an excellent journalist and first-rate cameraman taking that extra risk to get original film that would make their coverage exceptional. This was a commitment to truth and a great public service.

As Reinhold Messner, a mountain climber who had survived many assaults on all of the world's highest peaks, once told me, 'You have to know when to go on and when to turn back.' But no matter how much experience you have, there is always that unpredictable random act of insanity, the sudden, savage death that awaits many a camera team, even the best of them.

Just six years after Tony Joyce was killed, Neil Davis, perhaps the luckiest man throughout the Vietnam War, picked up his camera for the very last time. By September 1985, Neil had filmed in so many combat zones that another military coup in Thailand must have seemed like a routine assignment. He crouched in the Bangkok streets with his soundman, Bill Latch, covering the battle between rebel soldiers holed up in a radio station and loyalist Thai troops manning machine-guns and tanks outside.

One of Neil's mates, another Australian cameraman Gary Burns, and his Thai soundman, Daeng Kariah, also were trapped in the battle. They were behind a low telephone junction box as tank shells and machine-gun bullets exploded around them. Bill Latch was hit in the stomach and legs. Neil Davis was almost torn in half by shrapnel. His last words, the veteran's inglorious epitaph: 'Oh shit!'

Gary Burns, who was lying between Neil Davis and Bill Latch, escaped without a scratch. Ever so bravely, he dragged Neil's bleeding body away from the tanks. All of us who liked and respected Davis, who had hoped his luck would hold forever, watched his last story with horror. He had been wounded many times before, but that competitiveness, that skill at positioning himself to get such extraordinary pictures while allowing a reasonable chance of survival had pushed him to extremes of danger. Neil Davis had gone on because he liked covering war. The last image he filmed was of his own head sagging in front of the lens. *Now, I am my camera.*

CHAPTER FOUR

LAST OF THE TRIBE

For longer than we have been here
The cypress pines and cottonwoods
Have watched the stream
Of life and death,
But after all of the wars
And warriors on these plains,
is it only the trees that really do
'remember the Alamo'?

(JOURNAL 1978)

Canyon de Chelly, Arizona, has a serenity that will stay with you for life. One of the world's greatest ever architects, Frank Lloyd Wright, described the canyon as 'America's masterpiece'. The last Ice Age began the work of art and then time painted the walls in red, black and sun-bleached white. Water flowing down the 300-metre cliffs added long blue-black streaks to the painting. The eyes wander, feasting on the beauty of the canyon, its clear waters and green cottonwood trees, until you see the ruins of human settlement.

The vast caves, the adobe cliff dwellings and the stone ruins on the floor of Canyon de Chelly are a haunting monument to the ancient Indians, the Anazasi, who settled here around 350 AD. Hundreds of rock paintings and petroglyphs tell part of the story of their mysterious exodus. Spanish conquistadors on horseback invaded the area in the sixteenth century. By the time that white American settlers pushed westward, the Anazasi had disintegrated as a nation and the Navajo had settled in Canyon de Chelly. Kit Carson and his gunmen brought them into submission, destroying their homes, their livestock and even the canyon peach trees. The Navajos were forced to march 483 kilometres to the Bosque Redondo reservation in New Mexico, the Long Walk that is remembered so bitterly by the surviving southwestern tribes, who eventually were allowed to return to Canyon de Chelly.

It was here that I got closest to America's soul. The great silence that envelops the adobe ruins, the stirring beauty of Canyon de Chelly and its sheer perfection of scale explain the attachment of humans to this land. Here you discover a sense of place.

I first passed through these so-called 'Indian lands' in the mid-1970s on my way to one of the last militant displays by the surviving Native Americans. When some young radicals of the American Indian Movement, led by Russell Means and Dennis Banks, took over the trading post at Wounded Knee in South Dakota, I crawled past FBI sentries to report from the inside during this tense political showdown. There was a long siege, a gun battle and a federal agent was killed.

Russell Means, a handsome Oglala Sioux dressed in buckskin with hair in braids, was in a solemn mood as he defended his violent tactics at Wounded Knee. No one cared how fast his people were dying. This was a desperate last stand for cultural survival.

Sitting on the back of a pick-up truck surveying the misery of the Pine Ridge Reservation, Means sadly described how the Sioux, once the dominant plains nation, had been herded into today's state of despair, crowded into these derelict houses and stripped of their pride.

There was fierce resistance against white settlement in the decade after the Civil War, so the young cavalry leader General George Custer was given a new command over the US 7th Cavalry to wage war against the Sioux and the Cheyenne. The plains tribes had their own great leaders idolised by Russell

Means, warriors like Crazy Horse, Red Cloud and Chief Sitting Bull. Their fate and that of their people was a mixture of tragedy and treachery.

Peace treaties with the whites were supposed to guarantee the Sioux the Black Hills of South Dakota. But in 1874 Custer reported the discovery of gold and the treaties were ignored in a stampede by the panhandlers, the gold miners who came from all directions to stake their claim on the Sioux lands. Most of the Native Americans began to withdraw to the government reservations. A proud Chief Sitting Bull rode off to Canada, determined to stay a free man, but when he slipped back into South Dakota in December 1890 he was killed by those he once considered brothers, renegades in police uniform sent to arrest him. Some of Sitting Bull's men joined the last warrior fighting, Chief Big Foot, who led a wandering band of about 350 Sioux. It was these final resisters on America's western frontier who were surrounded in the snow at Wounded Knee and gunned down by the 7th Cavalry.

While historians still argue over the facts, Russell Means described the Battle of Wounded Knee as a 'murderous slaughter'. He said there was plenty of evidence that the band of Sioux had agreed to be escorted peacefully to the government headquarters on the Pine Ridge reservation. They camped for the night along Wounded Knee Creek but many of the cavalry began to question the Sioux about the infamous battle of Little Bighorn in Montana in which Custer and 265 of his men were killed in 1876. There is a compelling oral history passed down by the Sioux that says the reconstituted 7th Cavalry was bent on revenge.

On the cold morning of 29 December 1890 the Sioux suddenly were surrounded by the cavalry, ordered to surrender their weapons and then mowed down by rifle and cannon fire. Unarmed women and children huddling in a ravine not far from where we were sitting were among those butchered. Russell Means believed that the cavalry had been primed for officially sanctioned genocide in order to destroy the Native American resistance. The slaughter certainly ended the American Indian Wars.

As Russell Means showed me some of the earliest war photographs, including a disturbing picture of Chief Bigfoot frozen in the snow where he fell, eyes fixed in a terrible death mask, I could only wonder how today's Native Americans would survive. Poverty, poor health and alcoholism were threatening to finish off what the 7th Cavalry had started. They were corralled by white indifference and unable to escape the vast sadness of the reservations. They were denied an apology or any recognition that Wounded Knee was indeed a massacre. US military history still clung to its version of events, describing the bloodshed as a 'misunderstanding' and pointing out that twenty-five soldiers also died when the canyons erupted with gunfire at close range.

Russell Means told me that his people had no other choice but to fight through the courts to establish the truth. After the longest legal case in US history, involving over half a century of litigation, the Supreme Court ruled in 1980 that the government had broken the treaties and stolen the Black Hills from the Sioux.

A full century after the massacre at Wounded Knee the US Congress conducted its own investigation and in 1990 passed a resolution expressing 'deep regret' for the deaths of the 350 Sioux. The Wounded Knee Survivors' Association, descendants of the few who lived to challenge the army whitewash of the massacre, rejected this belated and limited expression of sorrow, insisting that only a formal apology, an explicit 'sorry' from Washington, would acknowledge that this was unconscionable mass murder.

This will seem eerily familiar to many Australians disappointed by Prime Minister John Howard's refusal to say sorry in a formal way for the official policies that decimated the Aborigines. From frontier massacres and deliberate poisoning to the forced removal of the 'stolen generation' of children there is a disturbing pattern to the conquest of indigenous people and the theft of their lands. I have made many films around the world about their struggle for survival and have found that most of the ruling powers, despite the evidence, are reluctant to admit that these slaughters were officially sanctioned. The American army, in fact, decorated many soldiers involved in the massacre at Wounded Knee, presenting them with Medals of Honour.

My own long march to find out the truth of what has been inflicted on indigenous societies has taught me that much of great value is lost each time the so-called advance of civilisation devours the last small tribes on earth.

Wading ashore through giant lily pads on a tributary of the mighty Amazon I found a solitary house on stilts in the jungle. A scrawny Indian woman was sitting at a pedal-driven sewing machine, making clothes for half a dozen small children. She was on her own, far from civilisation. I learned that the woman's husband and relatives had been shot by soldiers flying overhead in the same helicopters that were being used to spray Indian villages with highly toxic defoliants. Some of the children gathered around, tugging on my arms. On a swampy mound nearby they showed me the tiny white gravestones of other children who had died as the family struggled for survival. I felt the eyes of the living and the dead as I drifted back down the Amazon. Who will tell the world what is happening to the Indians? Does anyone really care?

(JOURNAL 1977)

While filming the destruction of the Amazon rainforests in the 1970s, I witnessed the campaign by Brazilian commandos to wipe out troublesome Indians who stood in the way of the timber and mining barons. I learned to my horror that most Brazilians, with their eyes fixed on economic prosperity and greatness as a nation, saw the Indians as subhuman, a kind of vermin that had to be swept from the frontier by any means. They shot them, poisoned them and gave them diseases that killed the Indians at an astonishing rate.

When Brazil was discovered by the Portuguese around 1500 it is estimated there were between three and five million indigenous people. Contact with the white man has decimated their number to around 200 000. This slaughter has not been confined to Brazil, however, as there is evidence of similar carnage in many parts of South and Central America. As this area was not well travelled by Australians twenty years ago (and Americans knew little more about the wars going on south of their border) I made many documentary films there to try to bring out the truth.

The genocidal campaign against the last indigenous majority in the Americas, the Indians of Guatemala, was barely reported in the 1980s because it was so physically challenging and dangerous to get there.

After two decades of military rule in this lush and beautiful Central American country, a guerilla war was widening and I set out to get the story. Even after hearing from some of the guerilla leaders hiding in Mexico, I was not fully prepared for the horror I discovered. The military dictator, General Rios Montt, a born-again Christian zealot, had ordered nothing less than a scorched earth policy against the Indians he saw as pagan savages.

I secretly entered Guatemala with cameraman David Brill
and the help of American sound-recordist Pamela Yates
who knew how we could hike in through southern
Mexico and illegally cross the Guatemalan border.
We rendezvoused with the guerillas, a rag-tag band of
lightly armed and poorly fed Indians, and then tried to
keep out of sight of anyone who could alert Rios Montt's
soldiers to our presence. Our mission was to carefully
interview massacre survivors in different parts of the
country and then to crosscheck their stories. For a war
out of reach and out of sight for most human rights
observers this was the first step to try to establish the
conduct of the army and the death toll. We also contacted

medical organisations and some of the religious groups
whose liberation theology led them to protect the
indigenous population. The Indian leaders were convinced
that they were being targeted for genocide.

(JOURNAL 1982)

The Guatemalan army had more than thirty thousand soldiers in the field and over thirty helicopters supplied by the United States. Our first interviews indicated that at least five thousand Indians had been butchered in just one of many sweeps by the army as it destroyed any village even suspected of feeding the guerillas. It was a macabre crusade with a particular kind of savagery, blessed by the so-called 'Christian' leader, Rios Montt. Indian children and the mothers who bore them were hunted like animals. Soldiers crushed the skulls of Indian babies on river rocks. There were heads impaled on stakes and more than three hundred people were burned to death in a church as soldiers raked the windows with gunfire. An old woman was made to watch as troops raped her granddaughter and then forced the young girl to look as they slashed the old woman with machetes. The sermon preached by God's own general was that only terror would stop the Indians in the countryside from joining the guerilla war and overrunning the government. This was most certainly a genocidal campaign, the kind that the United Nations had sworn to prevent.

As we started another long walk, this time out of Guatemala carrying the film evidence that we hoped might alert the world and stop the killing, a dark storm burst over us. The track soon was deep in mud. It was exhausting as we slogged on kilometre after kilometre. David Brill and I slept on the ground, Pamela Yates in a hammock slung between trees. We were low on food and water, cold and hungry and very tired. When the Guatemalan helicopters came over searching for us, we rushed for the trees and hid. Only when the sound of the chopper had faded would we emerge and go on walking. We understood that if we were trapped in open ground we would be shot on sight by the Guatemalan troops, but we did not expect the trouble we encountered from the Mexican army once we had dragged ourselves back across the border.

Although the Mexican government tolerated the presence of many leftist political leaders on its territory, the border patrols like the one that swooped on us were a law unto themselves. The three of us were led into a bush hut at gunpoint and ordered to show the visas that had allowed us to enter Guatemala. We had none, of course, not even a filming permit for Mexico, because declaring our intentions would have made the journey impossible. It was an extremely tense situation because we had been warned by the guerillas about a degree of co-operation between the Guatemalan army and some of the Mexican border patrols. We were trying to stay calm and think fast as the Mexicans talked on their radio and among themselves for some time. When we heard another Guatemalan chopper in the distance we knew that the worst possible outcome would be to be handed back to Rios Montt's butchers.

The Mexican officer told us that the Guatemalan military knew where we were and where we had been. Unshaven and covered in mud, I told him that we were so sick and tired we would not be needing visas for another trip to Guatemala. 'Wouldn't it be easier to just let us go?' The Mexican officer glared at me with contempt. Then he asked me what we had been filming in Guatemala. I said simply, 'The civil war and it is dirty.'

As he looked us over, two filthy Aussies and a pretty tousled Yankee, with no cash in our pockets and not much else worth stealing, the Mexican must have decided that we had to be crazy to have made this journey. At any rate, finally he let us go. Deeply relieved but not daring to smile, we walked off into the rain towards the safer mountain villages in the Mexican state of Chiapas.

David Brill was cussing because he had insisted on lugging his heavy tripod, his 'lucky legs', on this gruelling trek. Like Neil Davis, David was a Tasmanian who had risen from boy-photographer to top-flight cameraman. 'I beg your pardon,' he would sniff, feigning great insult, 'I am a cinematographer, not a cameraman.' When he arrived in New York in the 1970s this delightful but highly eccentric example of the species was not wearing the *de rigueur* multi-pocketed cameraman's jacket. 'Sir David' preferred a well-cut blue blazer and cravat, with a red silk handkerchief. He had been desperate to cover the war in Vietnam and emulate the feats of Neil Davis, but by the time he left Southeast Asia the young Brill knew that he had filmed too much conflict. It gave him an intensity he could never shake. David was so keen to become the ABC's first full-time cameraman in the United States that he paid his own fare to New York and bought his own camera gear including that tripod.

I had Pamela Yates's bulky tape-recorder over one shoulder and the camera in my other hand. Our backpacks were heavy with the several dozen precious cans of film. As I led the way down a steep, muddy slope, my feet suddenly shot out from underneath me. To prevent the lens smashing, I took a wicked knock on the elbow and let out a stream of expletives, probably loud enough to be heard back on the border, certainly capable of startling a friendly *campesino* wandering home through the hills. The little Mexican farmer came out from the bushes and climbed down to help lift me out of the mud. As Brill and Yates caught up with us, we all burst into laughter, including the Mexican.

The stranger lived not far away and offered us a place to sleep for the night. In minutes he had tied all of our camera gear, including Brill's 'lucky legs', onto the back of the smallest donkey I had ever seen. None of us objected. The man's family, Mexican Indians sympathetic to the indigenous Guatemalans, welcomed us not like strangers but distant kin. They fed us well and with warm blankets we slept soundly for the first time in days.

After an American Congressional Committee in Washington listened to my testimony and viewed our *Four Corners* documentary on Guatemala, it voted to suspend military aid, including those dreaded helicopters, until Rios Montt stopped the slaughter of the Indians. It was hardly a victory. A whole decade of horror for the Guatemalan Indians left about one hundred thousand dead and another forty thousand officially listed as 'disappeared', a common euphemism in the wake of these military dictatorships. At least four hundred Indian communities were wiped off the earth. So much for the 'Christian Crusade'.

> On the Equator
> in the Amazon rainforest
> a jungle cat sleeps
> with one eye open
> on the brown men
> wearing sticks through their lips,
> and the other eye
> on the white men
> with crucifixes round their necks,
> 'praising the Lord' and
> falling down in a swoon,
> and I wonder, which tribe
> is stranger?

(JOURNAL 1990)

When I walked into the midst of the naked Indians, deep in Brazil's Amazon jungle, I certainly looked as strange to them as they did to me. This 'lost tribe' had never seen a blue-eyed, fair-haired white man. I had never seen people wearing what looked like a length of broomstick through their lower lip.

Some of the women had painted their entire bodies red. They wore nothing but a headdress of white feathers. The men had a small strip of bark tied around their penis to signal (I learned later) that they had a relationship with one of the women. As the throng of excited people gathered around me, prodding and poking and exploring the stranger, a small boy casually unzipped the fly of my green dungarees. I suppose he wanted to know whether I wore a bit of bark too.

As days and then weeks passed with this small Amazon tribe I learned that the *potoro* worn through the lip was the totem that identified these Indians as a unique people. On the map they were located up north towards Suriname, living along the Cuminapanema River, but it was true to say that we had found them somewhere in the Stone Age. They were the most remote and primitive people I had ever encountered and the privileged time I shared with them was the most extraordinary experience in all of my travels.

The first contact with the tribe had taken place only a couple of years before my arrival in 1990, when fundamentalist Brazilian Christians belonging to the Florida-based New Tribes Mission cheered the discovery of another lost tribe for their crusade. The missionaries had orders to learn the language of these poor souls so that the Bible could be translated into that tongue and then the New Tribes Mission would move on until all of God's work had been done.

These were noble motives to the three missionaries who knew that in other parts of the Amazon some of their ilk had been killed by headhunters and cannibals. The New Tribes Mission tried to dodge the arrows and poison darts from blow-guns by first flying over a region and dropping trinkets. When first contact was made on the ground, metal axes were handed over and almost at that instant the Indians of the Cuminapanema area and their stone implements became museum exhibits of the future.

The New Tribes Mission had not been given permission to contact these Amazon people, according to Sidney Possuelo, a ranger with FUNAI, Brazil's under-resourced National Indian Foundation. Sidney led my freelance film crew into the Amazon to gather proof that the missionaries were trespassing. Most Brazilians took little interest in what was happening to their native people. To our disgust we found that this tribe had been lured away from their three separate settlements by the promise of modern axes and a little food if they settled around the jungle outpost the missionaries had named 'Esperance' (Hope).

The missionaries picked up weapons when they first saw us coming. They never used them against us but plainly regarded us as the enemy because our camera was a very powerful threat to their unauthorised presence there. Possuelo told me that FUNAI had known of the existence of these mysterious Indians, having spotted them from the air. A decision had been made to leave them in the relative safety of their isolation as it appeared they had avoided contact with neighbouring tribes for as long as anyone could remember.

Although the missionaries were well ahead of us in understanding the language, which they believed was similar to that of a larger Amazon group, the Tupi Indians, most of their time was spent in Bible study and they could answer few of our questions. To Possuelo, the tribe looked remarkably different to any other he had encountered previously.

Before the missionaries had arrived the Indians had been farmers, using a few small clearings in the jungle to grow cassava, whose starchy, tuberous roots were made into flour. The area was thick with enormous Brazil nut trees which supplied both food and the wood and husks needed to make many of the Indians' artefacts. They had a few clay pots as well and used woven sieves to prepare the cassava flour that was part of every meal.

After the first week of living in the jungle I found a new friend, Toru, one of the Indians' spiritual leaders. We shared some of the most intriguing conversations I have ever had, purely through sign language and a series of basic words we established. I would sit by the fire, for instance, and learn the word for 'fire', then discover the associated words for the sun and light. Toru pointed at me and said 'kirahi' (meaning, maybe, 'white man' or 'stranger') and speaking of himself and others in the tribe he used the word 'zoe'. This may have meant 'us' or perhaps it was the name the tribe called itself, as Cuminapanema, the name used by the missionaries, was, of course, the name of their river. It was a slow but delightful process to listen and learn.

One day Toru led me to the potoro tree and explained that when his children, boys and girls, were about so high, perhaps seven or eight, a very thin stick would be inserted in their lower lip. Later they would get a larger potoro like Toru's. As we walked through the rainforest Toru pointed out the tall tree that he took his name from and told me that the little girl who followed us, Tacee, had the name of an ant.

Toru took me fishing Amazon Indian style. With rocks he made a small temporary dam in a nearby stream and then used a weed called *timbo* to turn the water a milky white. A short while later, with his bare hands, he lifted from the stream several large fish he called *traira*. They were stunned but still alive. He dismantled the dam and the stream ran on, just as it always had for Toru's people.

By scratching marks in the dirt to indicate days spent wandering in the jungle, Toru told me that his tribe also liked to fish and hunt from their old villages. This was necessary to find the best game, like wild boar, which they would drop with their bows and arrows.

I gave Toru no gifts, just my undivided attention whenever he wanted to show me something in his rainforest, like the poisons he rubbed on the tips of his arrows. Like most Amazon Indians, Toru believed that his potions gave him power to move safely through a world where animals and bad spirits intermingled. When I showed Toru the few photographs I had from home, his eyes opened wide at the sight of the first dog he had ever seen, my large German shepherd, Ned Kelly. Half the tribe had to have a look at those big jaws and sharp teeth, nuzzled so close to the dog's master. I was introduced to Toru's family pets: small green parrots, a black monkey, and a big furry rodent called a *paca*, all tethered with short lengths of twine. It was a surprise one night when the rodent and the monkey were barbecued for us.

Often I sat with the Indians late into the evening listening to the sounds of the jungle. There were strange bird cries I had never heard before. Was that a tapir crashing about? Someone went to check. The women settled back with the babies in hammocks slung under the thatched roofs of huts the Indians had built near the mission. The men sat quietly in small groups and occasionally one voice would be raised to communicate with a man in another group some distance away. I touched Toru's elbow and nodded towards the canopy of stars. He pointed a finger and traced a path across the sky. I thought of the ancient mariners crossing the oceans by their knowledge of the heavens. As I lay back in my hammock before going to sleep, listening to the murmurs from the Indians and the cacophony from the jungle, I wondered where this tribe had come from and where they were headed.

An anthropologist at the University of São Paulo, Dominique Gallois, who studied the tribe in 1991, told me that the 'Zoe', as she called them, were so different to other Amazon tribes they may have migrated from the Brazilian coast thousands of years ago. Perhaps they had wandered here, one of the most inaccessible areas up near the border with Suriname, to find a place of their own away from the dangers on the coast. But with the arrival of the missionaries, all the menace of our world had come to them.

Sidney Possuelo soon discovered that many of the tribe had malaria. The missionaries already had counted almost fifty deaths among the Indians. Our film team, on the insistence of the Indian ranger, had gone through very thorough medical checks to make sure no one arrived with even a common cold. Possuelo angrily declared that the missionaries had not been so careful. He blamed them for the diarrhoea, respiratory infections and, in particular, the malaria that had felled so many of the Indians. With no natural immunity to new diseases and no magical protection from the men with crosses around their necks, the tribe was in grave danger. Possuelo said that when the Indians had been living in their three separate villages, there had been several hundred members in the tribe.

The missionaries agreed that was true. I walked around two empty villages, abandoned long huts and cassava fields already half overgrown by the jungle. It was a very eerie experience. I kept wondering whether this was the end of another small race. Back at the missionary settlement, I went from hut to hut and counted a total of just 135 Indians. The tribe looked like it was dying before our eyes.

Toru led me to some small mounds in the jungle where newborn infants had been buried. The custom among many Amazon tribes devastated by illness is to do away with the babies when mothers are too weak to feed them at the breast. Male or female, it does not matter. Many of the women carried small monkeys on their backs and I think I understood Toru to say that these were child substitutes for a tribe that was losing too many children. The men began to cut their hair in a different, shaggy style that symbolised the decline of these people and their passage through bad times.

For these animists, vitality and even survival depended on being able to control the numerous supernatural forces they saw in nature. As a shaman, Toru was responsible for trying to ward off the demons that were threatening the tribe. He seemed wary of the missionaries but unthreatening and quite passive about their presence. This community was the most peaceful I had ever seen. During our weeks with them I did not see a single incident of violence or aggression and this was something that no one could adequately explain.

One morning Toru and some of the women led me down to the stream where they bathed. Everyone was naked and it appeared to be some kind of cleansing ritual. I was asked to drink from the clean water, while the women lathered up in a ceremonial way downstream. It was their way of inviting me to share in an evening that I would never forget.

For days the Indians had been preparing a special brew for this night. I had witnessed the fermentation of manioc in other parts of the Amazon and the use of hallucinogens blown into the nostrils, but this tribe had brewed a different kind of jungle juice using large dark berries. I had absolutely no idea what it was but that night I was determined to try it.

At sundown, I sat with Toru as several men began the chant that signalled the start of the ceremonies. People slowly gathered, quietly taking their places on the ground and together we watched the great ball of fire fade into a glorious jungle sunset. We ate a tapir slow-roasted on glowing coals in an open pit. Then we drank the magic brew. The night, from that point, was like a dream of gleaming naked bodies, white feathers plucked from the birds of the rainforest, deep guttural chanting, red-painted breasts and buttocks, hands passing food, soft touching, low voices, a sky full of other worlds embracing us, travelling through time, dark primal fears, joyful bursts of light, sharing the stars with the people of the *potoro*.

> *Every time a tribe like this disappears with their language,*
> *their culture, their traditions, a whole universe of*
> *knowledge disappears with them. The original custodians*
> *of a land have the greatest experience of how we can live*
> *in harmony with nature. Without this balance our*
> *development will be unfulfilling and possibly short-lived.*
> *The importance of Toru's people cannot be measured only*
> *in their numbers. I understand evolution but do not*
> *accept that human civilisation should be built any longer*
> *on the destruction of entire communities of human beings.*
> *Unfortunately too many Brazilians for too long have been*
> *prepared to accept the sacrifice of the Amazon tribes.*
>
> (JOURNAL 1990)

Sidney Possuelo told me that this small tribe was among the last two thousand Amazon Indians living in complete isolation. Why had the Brazilian government failed to protect them? Why did so few Brazilians care? The ranger could only shake his head sadly, ashamed that his sophisticated society could behave with such arrogance and ignorance. But he was most angry with the missionaries who had no right to go there at all, especially without adequate health checks or enough of the vital medicines to safeguard these vulnerable people. It was no good saying that contact would have been made anyway. It was these men of God who had made the contact that was destroying the tribe. The missionaries said that they had no idea whether the Indians wanted them or not. In the beginning the Indians had been sullen and restless. I found these truthful admissions quite staggering.

I asked one of the missionaries to come and look at several of the most seriously ill Indians lying helplessly in their hammocks. He agreed that it was malaria and admitted some of the missionaries had been suffering the illness. Of course they had not contacted the Brazilian government or any health team because they had no official permission to be there.

Sometime afterwards, when I flew to Sanford, Florida, to question the head of the New Tribes Mission, Mel Wyma, at first he insisted that none of his three thousand missionaries had made contact with this tribe along the Cuminapanema River. When I presented Wyma with the photographic evidence and the allegation by the Brazilian Indian ranger that the missionaries had spread illness to the tribe, Wyma calmly admitted that this sometimes happened no matter how careful the missionaries were about their own health. God had commanded them to make contact with the superstitious Indians who, after all, were living in spiritual darkness. The New Tribes Mission had no blood on its hands. These Stone Age people would have disappeared even if not contacted by the missionaries. No matter what anyone thought, this was God's work and when there were no more lost tribes God's work would be done. It then would be time for the Apocalypse.

Before leaving the Amazon, I walked with Sidney Possuelo and some of the Indians to a spectacular waterfall where we swam together, trying to preserve in our minds the extraordinary beauty of this place and the uniqueness of its people. We knew that they desperately needed to be returned to their own villages and social organisation, that they needed medical help, legal rights and true protection. But most of all Toru and his people needed some recognition from us of their human value.

After a quarter of a century of listening to many of the Amazon tribes, Possuelo understood that we had given them very little reason to admire us westerners, despite our technological superiority. He said that the Amazon Indians still believed they lived at the centre of the natural universe. They believed they were more important than the missionaries who dropped gifts from the sky. They knew that they had far more knowledge than us about the extraordinary wilderness that belonged to them. Worst of all, they seemed to know that contact with our civilisation was killing them.

I said goodbye to Toru's wife and children with a gentle embrace and then placed an open hand on Toru's heart. I knew I would never see him again. It had been a journey to the past, an exhilarating, unique, mind-jolting experience. I left the Amazon thinking that sometimes the truth has a power and beauty that can inspire others to action. The story of the people of the Cuminapanema was shown in scores of countries around the world. I also sent the film to the Brazilian government, some anthropologists, the New Tribes Mission and the United Nations.

As it happened, our timing was perfect. There was a political upheaval in Brazil shortly after that and to my great delight Sidney Possuelo was promoted to become head of the Indian Foundation. He met with Brazil's president, Fernando Collor, and showed him our story. The result of this meeting was the expulsion of the New Tribes Mission from the Cuminapanema River and an investigation of similar missionary work all over Brazil. Aware, no doubt, that the eyes of the world were on this 'lost tribe', FUNAI sent in a health team and started taking care of the sick. After the malaria and influenza were stabilised, the tribe's health slowly began to recover.

The anthropologist Dominique Gallois recently told me that Toru's people, the 'Zoe' tribe, today number 152. Meeting the strangers from outside the Amazon, according to Gallois, had aroused curiosity about the white man's cities and for the first time the tribe had shown an interest in meeting other Indians in the region. If this contact with our world were allowed to happen according to the pace and terms of the people of the Cuminapanema, it would be a wonderful end to this story. But even well-intentioned protectionist policies breed reliance on the white man and the true independence needed to guarantee the survival of culture too often is lost. In 1997, the Brazilian government began the long legal process of recognising that this part of the Amazon belongs to Toru's tribe. The right of the Indians to their native lands is guaranteed in Brazil's Constitution, but unfortunately while gold and diamond miners, oil explorers, timber cutters and other land-grabbers are free to challenge the Indian holdings and stake out their own patch of the Amazon, the real future of Toru's people is as uncertain as the day he met his first white man.

CHAPTER FIVE

MIRACLES AND MADNESS IN MOZAMBIQUE

Espionage usually meant death by firing squad in Mozambique and in November 1987 it looked as though a young Australian missionary, Ian Grey, was headed for execution. Tall and handsome, with a face not unlike those traditional Christian paintings of Jesus, he had been recruited by a secretive Christian group to help Africa's most bloodthirsty guerilla army wage a terror campaign against the Marxist government of Mozambique. Over one hundred thousand people had been butchered by the guerillas calling themselves Renamo, or the Mozambique National Resistance, and there was no sympathy at all for Grey when he was caught red-handed.

Ian Grey's diary logged his secret missions carrying supplies and relaying intelligence between Renamo and their clandestine foreign supporters. An entry headed 'PR for Renamo' led to one of the most serious criminal charges, that he had been actively inciting rebellion and support for the guerillas who had been attacking hospitals, blowing up railway lines, destroying food supplies and pushing over four million Mozambiquans into starvation.

Mozambique had a population almost the size of Australia's but it was fair to say that most people in Toowoomba, Queensland, where Grey came from, had no idea where the capital Maputo was or how the son of a local plumber had ended up in jail there. At the Trinity Revival Centre, a Pentecostal church in Toowoomba, Grey's father Alan, mother Val and two sisters joined the congregation in hymns and prayer for Ian's safety. They had that gleam in the eye, the look of fervour that suggested that whatever happened they would accept it as God's will. The pastor and the family then 'laid hands' on me, and with loud exaltations asked God to give me the strength of the Holy Spirit on my mission to Mozambique.

At *60 Minutes* we had decided to try to save the life of the misguided Australian missionary and establish the truth of the grave charges against him. My colleague Tim Kupsch telephoned the celebrated human rights lawyer Geoffrey Robertson in London and asked him whether he would fly to Mozambique and try to make a case against sentencing Ian Grey to death. Through excellent contacts in southern Africa, Robertson soon established that the young Australian was an innocent abroad, duped by a right-wing American group that believed bringing down a Marxist government was the work of God. As the eloquent counsel set out from London for Maputo, hoping to plead Grey's case before a military court, we arranged for a father who had seldom travelled out of his hometown to fly with us to Africa.

Alan Grey was a hardworking man who believed he had given his children the wisdom of the Ten Commandments and the faith that could save them from hell. He could not believe that his son was a soldier of fortune or a 'soldier for Jesus', as Ian described himself during his first five months in prison. When Alan telephoned a few of Ian's contacts in small American churches he was given an apocalyptic description of the war in Mozambique and told that the Marxists very likely would put the young missionary to death. Alan was so distraught and out of his depth he walked like a man in a trance. His only plan was to beg for Ian's life. I was hoping that the father might persuade his son to see the light and make a confession that might give Robertson a chance of obtaining clemency.

As we flew to Mozambique, Alan explained how his son had

been like any other young Australian until a motorbike accident and a brush with death converted him into the deepest of believers. Ian wandered the world looking for a way to thank God and in Jerusalem he found it. The Holy City is not only the seat of many traditional religions, it is riddled with doomsday cults and other extremist groups. Through 'mystical prayer sessions' and elaborate brainwashing by means of films and slide shows, Ian was transformed into a man on a mission, one prepared to spend all of his money on a high wheelbase, four-wheel-drive vehicle equipped with long-range fuel tanks for God's crusade into darkest Africa.

The Shekinah (Glory of God) Ministries that shone the light of conversion into Ian's innocent eyes was an American Pentecostal group fanatically opposed to communism. Its literature carried the slogan 'Burn Mozambique!' and through a network of similar groups like the End Time Handmaidens these fundamentalists trawled the Bible Belts of the world to find money to pour into the Renamo-controlled areas of 'the Marxist devil's land'. Shekinah's director, the Reverend Michael T. Howard, recruited Ian Grey by promising tent meetings that would deliver thousands of Bibles and a crusade so powerful that the Marxist government would be swept from Mozambique within two years. Other shadowy figures were making very sinister plans for the young Australian.

Renamo was the frontline terror force for a secret campaign by the old apartheid regime of South Africa to destroy Mozambique's Marxist government. The guerillas got direction for their attacks through a military cipher machine linked to the South Africans. There was a covert pipeline of military support for Renamo, but one vital weapon they did not have was Stinger ground-to-air missiles to battle Mozambique's helicopters. Ian Grey says these weapons were promised by a network of right-wing American conservative groups more interested in 'commie' bashing than Bible bashing. Groups like Free the Eagle were anxious to fight communists everywhere and became skilled at raising money for this cause. Ian Grey's vital role was to relay intelligence messages between the Renamo commanders and the lobbyists organising the funding for the terror campaign.

As we drove into Maputo past several blackened buildings we could see that the guerilla war had come within a few kilometres of the capital. Alan Grey was shocked by the wanton destruction caused by Renamo's machine-guns, mortars, rockets and grenades. In the days ahead I would take him to a hospital to see some of the youngest victims. One of Renamo's most appalling tactics was to wait until the wounded had been brought into thinly staffed field hospitals and then to launch deadly raids on the helpless and bedridden victims. Alan had never seen as much as a person with a bullet hole before and was stunned to see children who had been shot, stabbed, mutilated and burned by Renamo. How could Christian soldiers shoot innocent, unarmed children? An aid worker described an attack on the northern town of Hermoine where more than four hundred people were hacked to pieces and infants were bayoneted in their cribs. Most of the country was a dangerous battlefield and the tally of foreign aid workers killed by Renamo had passed thirty. It would have been hard, almost impossible, for any Australian father to believe that his son was mixed up in such an ugly war.

I showed Alan a neutral assessment of the Mozambique conflict by Chester Crocker, a black American diplomat responsible for the US State Department's refusal to aid Renamo. In the 1980s Washington was sending secret aid to Nicaraguan 'freedom fighters' battling the Marxist Sandinistas, and some right-wingers like Senator Jesse Helms were screaming that Renamo deserved American military aid too. But the State Department said it was a myth that Mozambique remained 'a dangerous, compliant client of the Soviet Union', and in truth Renamo's monstrous crimes made the rebels totally undeserving of American aid. Alan Grey slowly was forming his own idea about the truth.

The 'truth', in the eyes of some Christian fundamentalists, often appears to mean twisting the words of Jesus Christ or digging up arcane passages from the Bible to justify extremely violent crusades. The truth in Mozambique was patently clear. The Renamo rebels were nothing but baby-killers and the so-called 'Christian' groups aiding them were rebels of another kind who had veered away from the mainstream churches to actively support this fanatical guerilla war. The Shekinah Ministries' propaganda machine was milking money from people who really believed that the battle against communism and a global race war would precede the Apocalypse.

After a few days in Mozambique Alan Grey told me that he was beginning to think his son had joined the 'baddies, not the goodies'. He was having dreams about the women and children in the hospital, the amputees sitting sad and silent on the verandahs. Alan also had guidance from others trying to save his son's life, including the then-Australian Prime Minister, Bob Hawke, the Foreign Minister, Bill Hayden, and special envoy Laurie Alexander who negotiated very skilfully with the government of Mozambique. I could see that leading Alan Grey around Maputo through a daily round of official meetings was draining him, but he was determined to do everything he could to save his son's life. A proud and honest man, he assessed all of the information step by step as if he were laying out a tough plumbing job back in Toowoomba. I still felt that the father was the key to his son's fate.

Geoffrey Robertson has flown to Maputo without any payment to try to save Ian Grey from the firing squad. Robertson told me that he was in two minds at first, because despite Ian's innocence Robertson worried that his so-called 'missionary work' had involved actively supporting the senior Renamo commander with communications and logistics. Meeting young Grey in jail and his father here at our old hotel has convinced Robertson that Ian was just a messenger boy, not a spy. No spy in the history of espionage had ever been arrested with such an open and detailed diary in his possession. What will the military tribunal think though when the court martial begins, because many of these senior officers know men killed by Renamo? Personally, I think Ian Grey and the others involved in this missionary madness

have contributed to Mozambique's tragedy but I cannot
support the death penalty. His astonishing naivety
suggests he deserves mercy not execution.

(JOURNAL 1988)

Geoffrey Robertson arrived in Mozambique without having
official permission to represent Ian Grey before the Revolutionary
Military Tribunal. There was a savage war going on and in this
part of the world there were no trials in the western sense.
The government of Mozambique usually gave its enemies a local
lawyer to explain what was happening and then proceeded to
swift and forceful punishment. Robertson had an old friend in
Mozambique who gave him good advice on how to negotiate
access to the Revolutionary Military Tribunal as a special counsel.

A heroic white South African lawyer, Albie Sachs, had taken
sanctuary in Mozambique after attacks on his life by the agents
of apartheid. But even in Maputo they had tracked him down,
planting a car bomb that almost killed him. It mangled one of his
arms and he had a long battle just to walk again, but Sachs went on
campaigning against violence and injustice in southern Africa.
When I talked with this courageous man about Ian Grey's
chances of living, I fully expected a tirade about Renamo. But
understanding the ways of Africa, Albie Sachs pointed us towards
the People's Assembly of Mozambique which recently had passed
a law offering amnesty to guerillas who gave themselves up. This
amnesty stated that it was 'founded on a deep belief in the capacity
of man to change'. It sounded like the godless government so
despised by Shekinah was capable of Christian mercy.

Our first real opportunity came when we organised a meeting
with Mozambique's Foreign Minister who listened patiently to
claims by Robertson and myself that most Australians knew very
little about the wars in Africa and that this ignorance made
someone like Ian Grey vulnerable to a life-changing conversion.
This meeting created the breakthrough. Geoffrey Robertson
was invited to make a special address to the three high-ranking

commanders of the Revolutionary Military Tribunal. The biggest obstacle was that the defendant seemed hellbent on destroying himself, as he still was refusing to make a confession.

When I met Ian Grey for his first media interview since his capture he had the shell-shocked look of a man not used to rough imprisonment. He described, somewhat uneasily, the interrogation techniques favoured in Mozambique. He spoke of the almost unbearable heat of his prison cell and then being forced to stand in a 'confession box', about two metres tall and not much wider than his body. This near-suffocating space was just big enough for an average-sized man to squeeze into, but the lanky Grey could barely move. He was also slapped about the face during the interrogation sessions. This treatment made Ian start thinking of agreeing with the enemy to save his life, but he stubbornly refused. He clung to the idea that he was a soldier of Jesus Christ. It could not be wrong to preach the Gospel, and if they went ahead and shot him, that must be God's will too. You may call it faith or fantasy, but when a young missionary has that zealous look in his eyes, that beatific expression, it takes a small miracle to break the spell. Ian Grey's eyes opened to the truth only when his father was allowed fifteen minutes with him and told him bluntly that he had been deceived.

Ian said that he was like a cobra up ready to strike and then his father, a gentle, humble man, suddenly confronted him with sharp and surprising words. The truth was like a hammer blow. Alan cried and told his son how much he loved him but he wanted him to understand that he had been misled about the Renamo guerillas. He also had been misled about the real message of the Gospel. Alan said that Jesus never believed in insurrection against the Roman government. He said give to Caesar what is Caesar's. This was the kind of Christian logic that struck Ian right in the heart and he cried in his father's arms.

Alan Grey told me that he was not angry with his son but with the American zealots who had led Ian into the wilderness and then abandoned him. Shekinah's other foot soldiers and the money traders who had done the deals had fled the temple. Perhaps they wanted a martyr? The imprisonment of the Australian missionary had made front-page news in the *New York Times*. An execution by firing squad would bring an outcry from church groups and condemnation of Mozambique's government as it struggled to get foreign aid to feed its starving people.

When Alan Grey discovered that there was starvation just outside the city of Maputo, he was almost overcome by remorse. He was dumbstruck that his son had contributed to the Renamo terror campaign. He met local Christians in their church practising their religion quite freely under the Marxist government and their accounts of Renamo's violence had a strong impact. This was enough for the father. He asked God for forgiveness and prayed for a miracle.

Ian Grey came before the Revolutionary Military Tribunal and to the surprise of his captors he not only made a tearful confession but he begged them for mercy. He explained that Shekinah Ministries had lied to him about the destruction of whole villages including Christian churches, blaming the Marxist government, not Renamo. He spoke candidly of the bargain he had made to collaborate with the guerillas in exchange for permission to preach the Gospel. He admitted carrying intelligence for Renamo and gave up the names of the Americans who had been helping bring in weapons and communication equipment, as well as wheeling and dealing to get Renamo the Stinger missiles it so desired. Describing himself as a naive messenger boy, ignorant of Mozambique's long struggle for independence, he sobbed and asked the country to forgive him.

'Today was not a *Hypothetical* my friend,' I said to Grey's counsel that night.

'You're telling me.'

'Geoffrey Robertson before a Revolutionary Military Tribunal with his client facing the death sentence.'

'It's not the Old Bailey,' Robertson smiled.

Robertson knew that the Revolutionary Military Tribunal had sentenced many people to death for giving similar assistance to Renamo. This brilliant barrister, principled, passionate and logical as always, played his best card last. He went into the courtroom, as he put it, with one hand on the Bible and the other on the

Geneva Convention, and asked the three senior military commanders to consider how their mortal enemies would exploit a death sentence for an Australian missionary who clearly had been duped.

'I asked the commanders to use their own military cunning, to see that by executing him by firing squad they would be doing more for the enemies of their country than anything else because they would make him a martyr. They would make his death a propaganda victory for their enemies. I told the Revolutionary Military Tribunal that Renamo and others would be quite happy to see Ian Grey condemned to death and so they should think coldly and clearly about some other possible conclusion.'

*Ian Grey was acquitted of the most serious charge,
espionage, which carried the death penalty. He was
convicted of four other charges including inciting
rebellion. Geoffrey Robertson says they could have locked
Ian up for thirty years on that charge alone. He has been
sentenced to ten and a half years in prison, a very lucky
escape in the circumstances. Ian was enormously relieved,
emotional and tearful as he warned other young
Christians coming out of Bible colleges to beware of
dangerous propaganda and not follow in his footsteps.
Alan Grey is in a state of shock, believing that he got
his miracle.*

(JOURNAL 1988)

Twenty-two months after his arrest in Mozambique, Ian Grey walked back into the church in Toowoomba where he had begun the journey that transformed him from an ordinary Australian into a dangerously misguided soldier of Jesus. His family and the rest of the congregation were overjoyed to have the prodigal son home again. Tears streamed down many faces as they sang the very hymn we had heard at the start of our mission, 'Nothing is Impossible for Thee'.

'The fact that I am alive is miraculous,' Ian told them and I know he believed it.

Under an amnesty announced by the government of Mozambique, Ian did not even serve the decade in prison that he no doubt deserved. But he fully understood the scale of the devastation and suffering caused by Renamo and it weighed heavily on his conscience. By naively carrying messages about heavy armaments he had played a very serious role in a vicious war.

Alan Grey still was having dreams about the bullet holes, the amputees, the tiny children who were the victims of this madness. He had come to understand that there was a great difference between missionaries who tended wounds and others who caused them.

'The moment you bring politics into Christianity or Christianity into politics you are in real trouble,' he told me in Toowoomba.

'God help us Alan,' I said, 'look at the world.'

'Without his help, without our prayers, maybe you wouldn't have gone over there,' Alan said.

'I know you are going to tell me now that the Lord works in mysterious ways,' I replied, smiling.

'Yes, well he does, doesn't he?'

CHAPTER SIX

A MAN FROZEN IN TIME

On an autumn day, a long, long time ago, a man pulled on his backpack, grabbed his bow and arrows, a knife and an axe, and walked high into the Tyrolean Alps. It is a great mystery what happened next but at an altitude of about 3200 metres the man lay down in a rocky hollow and died. Possibly he was caught in a very strong storm that the Austrians call a *foehn*, with violent winds of more than 100 kilometres an hour. After a few weeks the body dried out, birds pecked here and there, but then snow came, burying the stranger. Soon the huge Similaun Glacier moved down the mountain grinding everything in its path, everything except the man's body with his clothing, backpack, food and weapons, all remarkably preserved in a three-metre-deep basin of ice. Life went on down in the valleys and over the ages people forgot about the stranger until the summer of 1991 when the glacier thawed a little. After fifty-three centuries frozen in time, the ancient wanderer came back to our world.

I set out to meet the Iceman thinking that anyone who lived that long ago had to be some sort of primitive, a caveman in skins, certainly uncivilised by our standards. After all, this man had walked the earth over three thousand years before the time of Jesus Christ. On my way to the Alps I made a stop at Oxford

University where the carbon-dating lab had used small samples of skin and bone to figure out the Iceman's age. These same Oxford dons had shattered the myth of the Turin Shroud, announcing that the impression of Jesus Christ was a medieval fake. But I encountered great excitement about the Iceman. Separate scientific tests at several European institutions had come to the same conclusion. This man had lived in the late Stone Age, about 5300 years ago.

In Innsbruck, Austria, I met John Romer, the great British archeologist famous for unravelling the mysteries of Egyptian tombs and the lands of the Old Testament. Romer has one of the best investigative minds I have encountered. If you have seen him on television clambering about the pyramids with his captivating Yorkshire accent and distinctive straw hat, you will remember that he also is a brilliant communicator, a barrel of a man full of wit and wisdom. On this adventure he travelled with his partner, the author Elizabeth Romer, whose insights on European food — she wrote *The Tuscan Year: Life and Food in an Italian Valley* — were an unexpected bonus as we tried to establish some facts about the Iceman.

A backpack with a U-shaped frame, a grass net and a small animal-skin pouch found alongside the Iceman had spilled some tantalising clues. He had been carrying sloe berries which Beth expertly described as a wild blue-black fruit related to the plum. It would have been a rather bitter snack, Beth suggested, more suited to making jam or bathtub gin. The real value to us of this tiny wild berry was the fact that it is found on trees in late summer or autumn. We had at least a rough idea of when the Iceman had gone wandering.

As our helicopter carried us higher towards the Similaun Glacier, John Romer was full of admiration for this ancient man who had climbed these awesome mountains where most of us would not last a night. The Iceman stood about 1.6 metres and weighed around fifty kilograms, and he must have been incredibly fit. We stepped out into the cold of the glacier, dressed in our modern winter gear and marvelled at the ingenuity of the Iceman's clothing. He wore a fur cap and garment made from patches of deer, chamois and ibex skin skilfully stitched with sinew. His shoes were made of leather and stuffed with grass for insulation and over his shoulders hung a woven grass cape, similar to those used by shepherds in these Alps even a century ago.

The locals believed that the Iceman probably was a shepherd as stock had been grazed on the high meadows for thousands of years. But what on earth led him to the top of the Alps? Romer said my simple question was far more useful than all the speculation. To say he was a shepherd did not tell us much. The first shepherds lived off the blood of sheep, mixed with milk and their own urine. They were hard, tribal men. Their very survival depended on how they responded to their natural environment. To establish the truth about the Iceman we had to stop guessing and look at the evidence.

Our guide led us to the spot where the Iceman was discovered by hikers. We could see the rocky ledges that had protected the tomb of ice as the huge glacier passed over the top of him for more than five thousand years. In this icy grave temperatures were between 0°C and −8°C but even this did not explain his extraordinary state of preservation. It looked as though the Iceman had been air-dried and then snap-frozen, until fifty-three centuries later he popped out of the glacier.

An unforgivably clumsy excavation by a team using a jackhammer, a pick and a ski pole had largely destroyed the archeological value of the site. The Iceman had been taken down the mountain, examined carefully and, thankfully, safely stored in a freezer at the University of Innsbruck. The professors pronounced that he was the most intact ancient human ever found. The Egyptians, of course, had removed the brain and vital organs from their mummies in the tombs. The Iceman was complete, with the bizarre exception of his penis and most of his scrotum. The scientific team believed that this bit of his equipment was stolen, along with other souvenirs, over the weekend of his discovery on the mountain. So much for civilised modern man!

From an age with no written history, a time of considerable mystery to us, an almost complete man and the articles of his everyday life had been transported to the present. It was possible that so much about our past could be revealed by this one ancient man. As I visited the University of Innsbruck with John Romer, I wondered whether the Iceman's style of dress, his weapons and the contents of his pack could tell us more about him, his people and what he was doing so high in the Alps. So much was uncertain, with even estimates of the man's age ranging from thirty to fifty.

The Iceman wore one item of decoration, a small white circular stone, polished and threaded on a tassel of string. To Romer, it was no different to someone today wearing, say, an Egyptian hieroglyph around his neck. He had no idea what it really meant.

A couple of 5300-year-old mushrooms strung on a knotted leather cord were of far greater interest to the scientists because traditionally fungus had been used to fight infection. The 'lost tribe' of Indians I met in the Amazon still used the same kind of medicine. The University of Innsbruck team speculated that we were looking at the world's oldest first-aid kit, but John Romer just chuckled.

To the archeologist, one of the fascinating things about history is that it tells us more about the person writing the explanation than about the subject itself. The Iceman had lived at a time when to survive each day he had to be a lot better informed about nature than we are, yet he still died mysteriously on the mountain. Instead of trying to imagine what had happened, John Romer began by recognising that we knew practically nothing about this period of history in this particular area. Over the centuries mountain soil had been washed down over the sites of small settlements on both the Austrian and Italian sides of the Alps. What was most exciting to Romer was that the Iceman came from the very time when modern European life was beginning. He was really our first modern man. We could look him in the eye as a real human being, see how he was dressed, what he had been eating and, most wonderfully of all, we could hold his beautifully balanced copper axe, his flint knife and a magnificent half-finished bow.

The Iceman's dogwood arrows tipped with flint were not only the first ever found from the Neolithic period, the sophistication of the feathers glued to the shaft with resin suggested a knowledge of ballistics way beyond what scientists had imagined. A dozen of the arrows were unfinished, as was the massive bow not yet notched for a sinewy bowstring. These were important clues. Yew was the best wood in Europe, but hard to find in the Tyrolean Alps. The Austrian scientific team speculated that the Iceman set out from the south in what is now Italy, crossing the high barren ground and walking down to the treeline towards what is now Austria to search for yew wood to complete the bow and make more arrows. A sudden storm left him trapped at the crest of the Alps where he died. That is pure guesswork. But, adopting John Romer's approach, it seems reasonable to suppose that at some point the Iceman searched far and wide to find the rare yew wood for his longbow, just like the one supposedly used by Robin Hood. The Iceman was the type of person who wanted the very best weapon.

The bow was a classic killing instrument, its arrows strong enough to sink deep into very big animals. Another fascinating clue that caught Romer's eye was the Iceman's fondness for tattoos: there were blue lines and crosses behind his knees, on one ankle and his spine. The ancient Egyptians drew the same symbols to represent the hunter and his animal prey. This was a historical pattern. The tattoos may have had something to do with a belief in strength and power. In John Romer's view, the Iceman was a powerful, thinking man, not stupid and certainly not a savage. My prejudice about this ancient human being was dissolving fast.

In a heavily secured room at the University of Innsbruck we looked at the new 'time machine' that at a cost of US$10 000 a month was trying to replicate the temperature and the humidity of the glacier, the near-perfect preservation technique that brought the time traveller to us. Professor Werner Platzer told us that if the university team could safeguard the Iceman until DNA technology improved, perhaps a future generation would learn far more than we could about this ancient man.

'Perhaps in 200 years we will get him to talk,' chuckled Romer as we walked from the freezer.

'We might keep him going for 200 years,' I said, 'but I wonder whether he will last another 5000?'

We did not disturb the Iceman's peace. He had been poked and prodded and sampled enough. The photographs and film we studied had been taken with haste before hot lights thawed the last preserving shroud of cold that kept him safe in the twentieth century. If you looked past the damage caused by the weight of the ice and the brutal excavation it was, as Professor Platzer said, a 'nice face, perhaps handsome'. His dark hair had been trimmed short. He was tanned and clean-shaven. But it was his hands that interested John Romer.

'When I am on a dig,' he told me that night over dinner, 'I see workmen with split nails and hands a great deal rougher than this. The Iceman's nails are manicured. This tells me that he did not do heavy manual work in his clan but had a skilful role, probably using that longbow and Stone Age axe.'

'Could he have been a warrior for his tribe?' I asked. 'Is there evidence of war in his time?'

'I think one of the big things we have done with history in general is to create a myth that there were always huge nations fighting enormous battles,' Romer said. 'Most people never went to war. Go back just two hundred years and you see how ordinary people thought it was the nobles who fought battles. Britain's Victorian historians have reported everything as if it were World War I. I don't believe it was like that. It was a few guys thumping one another. The Iceman may have used his axe to chop wood or to kill his friends. We just don't know.'

All we could be sure of is that the copper axe was well made and sharp. It would not blunt like the earlier flint tools. All the Iceman's tools were so expertly fashioned that he clearly depended on them. He probably used them for just about everything. The longer I spent with John Romer the more I enjoyed this approach to history, ancient or otherwise. He could see the Everyman and tried to understand him. He looked at the Iceman and wondered what he said about us in our modern world.

The twenty-first century promises the most extraordinary advances in human knowledge and technology. In medicine and science we are poised for breakthroughs that could extend human life expectancy, cure much suffering and give so many people a chance of health and happiness. So why does modern life seem so confusing and unsatisfying to millions of people, as demonstrated by the global epidemic of sadness and loneliness? The World Health Organisation says that depression soon could be our leading disability, costing more people the chance for productive lives than almost any other illness. There is plainly something troubling in the way we look at our world. We have become desensitised to so many things around us, the condition of other people and other nations, the wellbeing of our society, of our local community, even of our families. Many people are no longer attuned to the health of their own bodies despite all of the knowledge we possess. For all of our sophistication something is out of kilter in modern civilisation.

The Iceman, in Romer's view, was more in tune with the world than we are. He was much more aware than we are of the earth and the sky, and how the seasons changed. He probably was more sensitive to things inside his own body and could live in a fashion that most of us are not capable of anymore. Yet men of his day had nowhere near the life-expectancy we enjoy. Clearly something dark and terrible happened on the mountain, which cut short the Iceman's life.

The mystery of how the Iceman died was only resolved recently, a full decade after the discovery of his frozen corpse. A research team at the South Tyrol Museum of Archaeology (which now houses the Iceman) in Bolzano, Italy, found a flint arrowhead embedded in his left shoulder. He had been shot from a low angle, the arrow just missing a lung, with signs of heavy internal bleeding signalling a painful death. Now the strength of John Romer's historical method seems even more impressive. All the speculation, that the Iceman was exhausted, broke his ribs, had a fall or just fell asleep and froze to death, was all wrong. The Iceman had died a most violent death. Now we are left wondering whether it was his enemies across the Alps or one of his own tribe. I have learned from Romer that there is so much we don't know that it is best to stay with the established facts about any event in the past.

The archeologist gave me a whole new way of looking at human progress and time through the ages. The western world has agreed to begin its calendar from the birth of Jesus Christ, a mere two thousand years ago. The Chinese and Islamic people preserve the traditions of their own sense of time, but it is still a slight variation on a modern theme. Mostly we think of the calendar in terms of our own lifetime. It is what is happening to us that we are most preoccupied with, but the archeologist challenges such thinking. He uncovers the bricks and bones of ancient history to remind us that the true story is much older, the journey longer and more intriguing.

In the Iceman's day, his calendar was based on the seasons: good and bad, wonderful for living or threatening his survival. Until that last day on the mountain he was the master of his universe. This ancient traveller gave me a greater appreciation of the talents of every human being and the place of the individual in our concept of civilisation. His death is a reminder of the tragedy and violence along the road of human history, each of us facing that possibility of a cruel fight and a savage, senseless death. Or will we climb to new heights and resolve conflict intelligently? The Iceman invites us to understand the different ways the human mind can work — not primitive or intellectual, not savage or civilised, just different. He helps us to understand that people may look, behave and think differently but the values found in this diversity are what make humans such a wonderful species. The Iceman certainly melted some of my unfounded ideas and ignorance about the past and I began to experience his world and mine afresh.

In the still pools
I look at the reflection
of the traveller's face,
a man lined by the road,
hitched to a larger wheel,
drawn on to beauty
and the light.

(JOURNAL 1985)

Meeting John Romer inspired me even more than the Iceman. As much as I would have loved to share an ancient brew with the Iceman, I could talk to Romer over wine for hours every night. It was a measure of his intellect that he loved a challenging idea, even if it was pure heresy to his colleagues.

'The Aborigines may be the oldest continuous civilisation on earth, so maybe your beloved Egypt was not the *only* cradle of civilisation,' I challenged him.

'Yes, but you will have to be the man to prove it,' Romer replied laughing.

'How can anyone be sure? We've really only just begun to dig in our own backyard.'

'Dig on, brother. You're bound to make some surprising discoveries and the press will write, as they always do, that it's the biggest discovery since Tutankhamen's Tomb.'

In the 1970s Romer had led the first excavations in the Valley of the Kings since the discovery of Tutankhamen's Tomb in 1922. While often highly critical of archeological blundering and plundering, Romer has explored the tombs and temples of Egypt for almost three decades with great passion and sensitivity. His scholarly volumes and epic television series have illuminated the wonders of the ancient world through his staggering knowledge of art, literature and history. But he was most interested in discovering the truth wherever it could be found.

I am walking in the footsteps of Jesus Christ with the most wonderful guide I could ever hope to join me. Who has not wondered about the intersection of history and faith that occurs here in Jerusalem? Is it possible to discover the truth? Can John Romer, after a lifetime studying the biblical lands, tell me who is this man who has influenced the world so powerfully and profoundly for two thousand years?

(JOURNAL 1992)

There is another man frozen in time, a man worshipped as God by at least one billion people, a man who has had a greater impact on history than any other individual, and yet the historical Jesus is a mystery. As we sat on the recently excavated ancient stone steps of the Temple of Jerusalem, Romer explained the conundrum with a true story of an archeologist friend of his, a Christian, who made an intriguing find in a cemetery on the Mount of Olives. He dug up a skeleton of a man who possibly had been crucified. The coffin was inscribed in Aramaic: 'Jesus, son of Joseph', but the archeologist never published the discovery. Romer was amazed and said it could have been *the* Jesus. The archeologist said no, *the* Jesus rose from the dead and went to heaven.

Who was this man Jesus? Son of God, a carpenter's son from Nazareth, an inspired prophet of love and understanding, or a seer of the Apocalypse? A sage like Gandhi who cared about the downtrodden or a revolutionary who questioned the ruling order and conventional wisdom? A holy man with no plan for a Church or a genius who absorbed the prophecies of the Old Testament and acted them out to become the world's first great humanist, promising civilisation a clear moral destiny?

'If you have to ask you will never know' is a common response from devout Christians, but such an answer is not good enough. As we work out our relationship to the cosmos, contemplating the very essence of our existence, surely a central question must be where does Jesus stand? Was it chance or divine providence that put this man on earth? Was it the sheer force of his personality or the power of his mind, the spell of ancient prophecy, the events of his day or those that came later that shaped modern civilisation and gave so many some sense of purpose and fulfilment?

'His name as a man was Jesus,' said Romer to really begin at the beginning. 'Jesus Christ is a Christian term for a god. We have no historical proof that the man ever lived. Jesus is a character in a book.'

Now the archeologist was on his treasured ground, examining the few facts we have about the 'greatest story ever told'. The Bible, in Romer's view, is the heritage of modern western civilisation, expressing a unique sense of order and human destiny. It is the story of how some of civilisation's oldest ideas, such as salvation through morality, passed from the east to the west. It is a literary construct that allows each of us to think about our place in the universe. The story of Jesus, which is really a series of incidents and a series of sayings, is by far the world's most effective tale.

As an archeologist, Romer has the same problem dealing with Jesus as he does with Hamlet, Prince of Denmark. In Shakespeare's great play, Hamlet lived in the castle of Elsinore. In the last few years archeologists have gone to Elsinore and dug it up. But that does not prove the existence of Hamlet, nor does it prove that he stood there and said, 'To be or not to be'.

As a historian and a world authority on ancient literature, Romer was prepared to say that the men who wrote the book about Jesus really knew what they were talking about. The character called Jesus, the time and place all seemed to fit together. Even a historian has to take some things on trust. None of us has met Alexander the Great but the biographical writing about him convinces us that he lived. Jesus had such an immediate and immensely powerful effect that historians believe that he existed. Unlike Alexander, Jesus was a humble man and so we have no coins of the day with the face of Jesus on them, no truly contemporary inscriptions telling us of his passing. But if you read the Gospels as you visit certain places, as John Romer and I did in Palestine, it is easy to assume that you are walking in the footsteps of Jesus.

We drive north from Jerusalem along the West Bank, through military checkpoints, past kilometres of barbed wire and the wreckage of modern fighting. Then the ruins of Jericho, where the walls came tumbling down, start erasing the present and we slip back to the past. Near Tiberias on the Sea of Galilee a group of Christians is baptised. I remember Martin Scorsese telling me a few years ago about the John the Baptist sequence in his film The Last Temptation of Christ *and how he imagined the throng of the crowd, the music and fervour of ancient*

*times. Not much has changed here. There is still religion
in the air. Scorsese, ever the old altar boy and ex-
seminarian, liked the idea of a human Jesus struggling to
come to terms with his responsibility and destiny. How
will we know this other than through the sayings of the
man himself? In the afternoon light of a glorious summer
day John Romer and I walked towards the ruins of
Capernaum where it is believed the public and political
life of Jesus began.*

(JOURNAL 1992)

The flowers, the trees and the Sea of Galilee itself are exactly
like the world of the New Testament. Capernaum is where
Jesus lived in the Gospels, where at the age of twenty-nine he
recruited his apostles while he stayed in the house of a local
fisherman named Simon, known to us now as St Peter, the first
Pope. To the archeologist the most compelling reason to believe
that Jesus had been here is the fact that within a hundred years
of his death a large church was erected over the house said to
be St Peter's. Romer and I were standing in the ruins excavated
by Franciscan archeologists, a meeting point perhaps of faith
and science.

It was here on the shores of Galilee that Jesus, we are told,
worked astonishing miracles. We strolled over to another house
said to belong to the Roman centurion who asked Jesus to heal
a paralytic servant. *Pick up thy bed and walk.* The miracles, to
Romer, were simply part of a world order we no longer have.
It did not help to try to explain them like a trick: Jesus did not
really turn water into wine, he did not really raise people from the
dead but hypnotised them and wore inflatable boots to walk
across the water, and so on. All of this ranting and raving had
flooded the world with crazy books about Jesus. There had been a
whole industry merchandising the life of Jesus for two thousand
years but it did not tell us much about Jesus. It told us about the
people writing the books and the people making money from

religion. Romer believed that it was helpful to see the miracles as a way of trying to understand an ancient world where everyone believed that being ill was a condition of sin or evil, like the last of our animist tribal people today, and for the ancient ones miracles happened every day. A modern, psychological explanation of how Jesus might have swayed the masses or cured the ill with hypnosis missed the important truth that the people of his time all believed in miracles. It was natural for the Gospels to be full of them even if the stories were written many years later.

At Qumran, about an hour's drive south of Jerusalem,
I climbed the cliffs alongside the ruins of an ancient
settlement and then crawled on all fours out of the sunlight
and away from the fierce desert heat into the cool shade of
a cave. It was here that a Bedouin shepherd boy found the
Dead Sea Scrolls in 1947, the year I was born. For all my
life people have been fighting to control these treasured
documents, arguing over their interpretation and meaning.
The discovery of the Dead Sea Scrolls has long promised
to reveal the truth, at least about the world of Jesus.
(JOURNAL 1992)

Although various ancient books have been found scattered throughout the Middle Eastern desert over the centuries, the 800 Dead Sea Scrolls include major biblical texts more than a thousand years older than any others in existence. The meaning of the scrolls has been one of the great religious controversies of our time, partly because of rivalry between Jewish and Christian scholars. There has been so much secrecy, jealousy and intrigue that until quite recently the real importance of the sacred scrolls was in danger of being lost. After enjoying the rare privilege of inspecting some of the original bits and very tiny pieces of this literary jigsaw puzzle, I am going to leave out the wild speculation

about what the scrolls tell us about Jesus Christ and share the far
more fascinating facts.

Carbon dating of the documents and other analysis indicates
that the Dead Sea Scrolls were written over a long period of time,
from two centuries before Christ through to the destruction of the
Temple of Jerusalem in 70 AD. Of the 800 scrolls only four are
virtually complete. Most of them are written in ink on leather,
parchment and papyrus. But one scroll is unique. It is inscribed
on copper, a scroll that would be expected to last a very long
time. Dubbed the 'Copper Scroll', it was written around the time
that the Romans were destroying Jerusalem.

Romer says the Copper Scroll indicates that the entire collection
of Dead Sea Scrolls is an extraordinary library of sacred and
esoteric texts removed from the Temple just before it was sacked.
The Copper Scroll has been ignored by some scholars because it
includes a strange list of directions to where other important
scrolls had been hidden, along with a huge quantity of treasure.
There were two important discoveries of ancient scrolls hidden in
pottery jars many centuries before the Dead Sea Scrolls were
found. The fact that only the Copper Scroll was written in the
colloquial Hebrew of the day and in the dry style of an accountant
suggests that it was an inventory of an extraordinary literary
treasure, and possibly of a decent hoard of gold as well. While
others scoff at the Copper Scroll's indication of undiscovered
treasure, Romer calculates that the accumulated wealth of the
Temple of Jerusalem certainly would amount to a fortune and that
it may still be lost in the Judean desert. Dig on, brother!

When we visited the locked vaults of the Jerusalem Museum to
inspect some of the jealously guarded secrets of the Dead Sea
Scrolls we left all certainty behind. We entered a peculiar,
obsessive world of Jewish, Christian and secular scholarship
competing to find coherent meaning in thousands of tiny
fragments of something that was never one book but a library of
texts written and collected over a considerable span of time.

Romer believes that the Dead Sea Scrolls are of huge importance
because they offer proof that around the time of Jesus Christ the
Bible was nothing more than a collection of sacred texts. The

evolution of ancient morality and wisdom was scattered through many different stories that in the future would be gathered between two hard covers and presented to the world as the greatest story ever told. It was only after the cataclysmic destruction of the Temple of Jerusalem that the religious leaders, desperate to preserve the culture and sacred laws forever, decided to edit, refine and distil this belief system as the Bible's Old Testament.

The Dead Sea Scrolls include prophecies that created the expectancy of a Messiah in an Apocalyptic End Time. As these texts are so much older than others in existence they support the view that from very ancient times some Jews began to consider the idea of a Messiah who would die to lead them to salvation. This has always been one of the central tenets of Christianity, which Christians would say began with Jesus. This underscores Romer's belief that regardless of religious faith, the Bible conveys the development of human thought as people struggled to work out a moral code and establish their place in the cosmos.

After meeting some of the scholars who have been studying the Dead Sea Scrolls for many years I came to see that rather than looking at the scrolls as one religious message it is better to see them as a collection of writings on morality and other issues. They range from the spiritual to the esoteric and purely fantastic, with bizarre and contradictory messages, just as you would find contradictions and outlandish theories in any modern library.

The Australian author, Barbara Thiering, claims to have found a secret code that locates Jesus in the Dead Sea Scrolls. At the Jerusalem Museum all of the scholars I met vigorously disputed this. Thiering studied, among many texts, the Damascus Scroll that refers to a 'teacher of righteousness', but carbon dating indicates this scroll was written 150 years before the year in which it is widely accepted that Jesus was born, so he cannot be the person mentioned. There were many other high priests and prophets competing for an audience. The scrolls certainly reveal much about what people were thinking in the time of Jesus; they provide a whole world of information about the traditions and religious beliefs of a clearly dangerous age. The destruction of Jerusalem by the Romans surely gives great validity to some of this fearful writing. It is a fact, however, that no one has reported any specific mention of 'Jesus' in the Dead Sea Scrolls.

As so much of the story of Jesus is set in Jerusalem I was eager to find the places where one could say that this was the very ground where Jesus had stood. Unfortunately the Romans destroyed most of the ancient city except for some walls and towers where their troops were garrisoned. They may have left behind the Roman Forum but they quarried most of the heart of Judaism. The long-hidden original steps of the Temple are one of the few remaining places where you can walk on the same smooth stones where Jesus preached. This was where anybody who was anybody came to preach — the Sadducees, the Pharisees, the Essenes — and according to the Gospels, this was where Jesus upset the ruling order and became a man marked for death.

In Romer's view, Jesus was a threat because he said you could talk straight to God, without the Temple, without organised religion. The religion of the day demanded that you pay your money — make an offering in the Temple — to obtain remission from sin. Jesus cut out the middleman. All of the ancient kings had raised revenue, a hidden tax if you like, by getting the population to make an offering to the gods. In the age of Jesus, temple offerings still were central to the fiscal power of the state and so his preaching was a threat to the influence and very livelihood of the priests.

I was curious to know what had made Jesus, an ordinary man born the son of a carpenter, as the story goes, become a preacher of such breathtaking power that so many people hailed him as the Messiah. His sayings recorded in the Gospels often have great beauty in their simplicity and rich layers of meaning: Ask and you shall receive; seek and you shall find; knock and it shall be opened to you ... No man can serve two masters ... Every kingdom

divided against itself is laid waste ... When a person strikes you
on the right cheek, turn and offer him the other ... Which of you
by worrying can add a moment to his life span? ... Let tomorrow
take care of itself. Today has troubles enough of its own.

Romer explained that from the Gospels we have at best an
enigmatic character. The people expected great things from
heaven and so projected onto Jesus their traditional hopes and
imbued his words with great importance. He is the human being
many people still see as embodying most human virtues. It is
marvellous to think that such wisdom came from a nomad
child. Romer said that when we read in the Gospels that Jesus
was born of a virgin in a stable in Bethlehem with a star in the
sky and so on, the story echoed the ancient prophecies of how
the Messiah would be born. The Gospel writers clung to that
story because if Jesus was the Messiah it had to have happened
that way.

We were approaching subjects highly sensitive to many
Christians but Romer's knowledge of the ancient literature
made sense of some traditional Christian beliefs that had
seemed mysterious to me. He said when people talked about
the Virgin Mary we had to remember that in the time of Jesus a
'virgin' was any young, inexperienced woman, not someone
who miraculously had a baby without sexual intercourse.
In pagan mythology, however, there was considerable mystique
invested in the very old idea of a virgin whose powers
transcended the limitations of the human body. The importance
later attached to the virgin birth of Jesus (or the Immaculate
Conception as Catholics refer to it) may have been a response
by Christians to give the birth of Jesus eternal significance. This
appears to have succeeded.

If Jesus was a typical man of his day, Romer argued as we
walked around Jerusalem, it was extremely likely that he was
married. This was interesting because only fairly recently
Christian and Jewish scholars had got together to discuss Jesus
and most agreed that he lived and died a Jew. If you were a Jew
aged thirty, like Jesus, and you were not married, this would have
been so extremely rare that it certainly would have been

mentioned in the Gospels, Romer believed. It would have been a major biographical feature in the stories of Jesus. It was as important to see what had been left out as what had been put in to the New Testament, and in the absence of evidence to the contrary, Romer concluded that Jesus was married like most Jewish men of his day.

We followed an ancient road down the side of the city walls, through the colour and noise and commerce of the modern bazaar, and back into the past. Romer told me that this was the path that Jesus would have walked from Herod's fortress to the rocky knoll that was the Roman execution ground near the gates of the city. Calvary was an awesome symbol of Roman imperialism. They chose this spot just outside the city gates to make the crucifixions a very public punishment, an advertisement to all the poor wretches of the Empire that if they defied the order of Rome they would be tortured in the most terrifying way. The talk of a Messiah who would lead an uprising of the poor against the Romans would be suppressed by the public killing of anyone who was considered a serious threat. The prisoner would be tied to a crossbeam and then nailed up in any horrible fashion that pleased the executioners. Sometimes a victim's legs would be broken so that his whole body would sag and he would suffocate.

As we approached the Church of the Holy Sepulchre which now enshrines the alleged site of the crucifixion, I asked Romer about the strength of the archeological evidence, wondering whether it supported the faith of the millions of people who have made pilgrimages here through the ages. He said that this was the most authentic Christian site in Israel, because the public space outside the city gates was the ideal crucifixion site as well as a traditional burial place. In the third century, just a couple of hundred years after the crucifixion of Jesus, the socket said to have held his cross was carved into a cube of rock and then a golden cross was erected here on the spot where it is believed he died.

From the ground level of the modern church we walked in silence down to the once-secret chambers under Calvary. They were sealed off for centuries because the faithful praying above believed that this path led to purgatory, a place full of suffering, the halfway house for those trying to reach heaven. In the gloomy light as we descended staircases built by Crusaders, I could see the names of ancient pilgrims, holy graffiti, the scribblings of people trying to make their mark on a spiritual world. There are small chapels between the ancient water cisterns and the limestone quarries that reach down into bedrock.

Here science bowed to faith in John Romer's view. He could not prove it as an archeologist, but if Jesus was crucified, then this was where it happened. It was also where he was taken down from the cross, washed and annointed, and then buried in a tomb. We stood together watching a sea of different faces, different faiths, all drawn to a belief in the importance of Jesus Christ, even now.

It is a bitter irony, as cruel as crucifixion, that much of the tomb of Jesus has been smashed to pieces by fanatics threatened by his message of peace and love. This magnifies the sadness that hangs in the air at the place where he died. It made me think how some of the most terrible wars in history have been waged by leaders invoking his name. I have been to quite a few battles myself where the cross of Christianity was worn like a talisman by those who brought only terror. And what would the Jesus who sadly prophesied the destruction of the mighty Temple of Jerusalem think of the vast power and wealth accumulated by his churches today? If you don't need a temple to speak to heaven, if you don't need middlemen, why are vast institutions and whole kingdoms of wealth and real estate an integral part of most religions? Organised religion is big business, just like it was when Jesus lived. Do the millions of people who give this Lord some allegiance, lip-service or lifetime loyalty really live his message? Have the humble words of Jesus brought Christians and the rest of the world harmony?

A journey to look for Jesus the man, through so many places suffused with history, leaves everyone wiser: scientist, sceptic and true believer. If you believe Jesus was the Son of God, this is an eternal truth for which you will thank God. In historical terms

Romer saw the beauty and value of the story of Jesus in a very different way. When Jesus came along, the world controlled by the Roman Empire was a cruel, hard and lonely place. People were longing for faith. When Christianity spread through the Empire it brought down very old class barriers. Even if you were a slave or a woman locked away from society, you could be part of the faith. The early Christians were the poor unfortunates of society and one of Christianity's strongest points was that it helped these people in adversity. The Christians who were ripped to pieces by lions in the arena had something for the first time in their lives that was worth dying for, because of the strength of companionship they experienced believing in the idea of love. Our so-called 'civilised' world is still a dangerous, aggressive place. Jesus still gives some people comfort and for that reason is important.

On a hill above Jerusalem, the pages of the book dissolve in the fading light and the character of a cosmic drama is there to be experienced. The life and death of Jesus are there for contemplation in the beautiful city still divided by religion, politics and a lot of history. My trusty guide was right. The story of Jesus will tell you a great deal about the people who wrote it and even those who still believe in the words, but Jesus the man may be hard to find. In the age in which his story began it is easy to see why he wanted to answer the question we all must face on the journey towards true civilisation. Peace and love make more sense than violence. Ah, but we live in a world far more violent than in the time of Jesus. We have just ended a century in which at least 180 million people died in wars, the most violent age in human history. In the third millennium since the death of Jesus, the man and his message are still frozen in time.

A DIVINE COMEDY

God was the Creator,
the Alchemist, the Geometer,
until someone said NO

God was the Architect,
the Grand Designer, the Watchmaker
of this clockwise universe.
And then came the Master,
the Mastermind and the Masterpiece,
so soon after the Mystery, the Riddle,
the Beginning and the End.
Now, blessing themselves,
some swear God is a Computer.
Oh really? A user-friendly God?
Software or hardware?
Why not God the Gambler?
God of the Dice or God
the Cosmic Crossword Puzzle?
Haven't we changed our minds
enough times to know
God is Zero, Zero?
that's it,
God is merely good.

(JOURNAL 1992)

CHAPTER SEVEN

FALSE PROPHETS AND GODMEN

Charles Manson looked like Jesus Christ in the eyes of his followers. With his dark beard and long, straggly locks, the hippie garb and barefoot pretence to poverty, he had a Messianic appeal to the angry and alienated. When they wandered the desert in California and gathered around fires at night listening to his LSD-inspired visions, the 'Family' heard prophecies every bit as terrifying as the Apocalyptic passages of the Bible. Charlie had a plan to kill the 'rich white pigs' who hung out with the film director Roman Polanski at his house in the Hollywood hills. Everyone would blame 'the niggers', start a 'race war'. Helter Skelter!

One of Charlie's Angels of Death was Susan Atkins, now jailed for life for murdering the pregnant actress Sharon Tate in a crime worse than any horror movie ever made in Hollywood. When Atkins held out her hand to me in a maximum-security prison in California, I noticed that she had painted tiny koalas on her long, witch-like fingernails. It was a personal and bizarre first touch for a reporter from Down Under who knew where those hands had been.

Atkins was wrapped in a tight dress that was meant to show her lean, taut frame and as we walked together past other women lifers her body language said that she was top bitch in the prison yard.

The other prisoners seemed afraid of her, as though she still held the steel blade dripping with the blood of the eight-and-a-half-month pregnant actress.

Sharon Tate's mother, Doris, had warned me that Susan Atkins was quite an actress herself. Perhaps she was capable of a performance that would persuade me that she was innocent and so trigger the kind of chain reaction in the media and the justice system that might lead to her parole. Curiously, Doris Tate had been working to help other prisoners, perhaps to preserve her sanity and belief in humanity after the viciousness of Sharon's death. Understandably, Doris was bitterly opposed to the legal manoeuvring aimed at giving Atkins freedom.

As we walked into the quiet of the prison chapel, Atkins told me that she talked to God a lot. This did not surprise me as she had done too much talking to her Devil and Master, Charlie Manson. In another jail, Manson, too, was serving a life sentence for ordering Atkins and other members of the Family to carry out a series of brutal murders in August 1969. These nights of terror in the Hollywood hills were shocking evidence that the Messianic complex was alive and full of menace in our modern world.

Manson's madness was not apparent to the drug-addled minds of the group of young women and men who obeyed his orders. They did not see him as a deeply frustrated man who wanted to be a star like the rock musicians he knew in California. They certainly did not recognise his behaviour as psychotic even when he rambled about the coming race war that he was going to ignite, even when he promised to lead them down a hole in the ground in Death Valley to escape the final battle of Armageddon.

Looking at Atkins I wondered what had made her so vulnerable to the lunatic ravings and dangerous brainwashing. What had happened to the young girl who once sang in a church choir? Why had she been mesmerised by a man who thought he was Jesus Christ and hailed Adolf Hitler as his hero? She told me she had lost her mother to cancer when she was very young and had a rotten relationship with her father. She had become a topless dancer, lost all respect for herself and had ended up in the desert with a young baby of her own, under the spell of the most amazing man she had ever known. The psychiatrists said Atkins was afflicted with a kind of *folie à famille*, a shared madness that springs up in groups intoxicated by the same crazy ideas. There was a deep-seated hostility in each of his disciples that Manson exploited. He sent his vicious sidekick, Charles 'Tex' Watson, to lead the Angels on the killing spree. A musician, Gary Hinman, was the first killed. Tate and four of her friends were next, and the following night a wealthy couple, Leon and Rosemary LaBianca, were stabbed to death. Atkins had told another prisoner that the Family had killed as many as thirty-five people, but the other bodies would never be found. Even the prosecutors admitted we may never know just how many murders Manson ordered.

Sitting close enough to lean forward and touch my knee from time to time with those long fingernails, Atkins began to flirt with me right there in prison. I was told by the guards that she would exercise half-naked, proposition other prisoners and seemed to enjoy the role of vamp. Her mood changed abruptly when I asked how she could have been so far under Manson's spell that she did his dirty work for him. Her story had changed many times through the investigation and trial process but at various times she had claimed to have stabbed more than one of the victims. She had admitted stabbing Tate again and again, even as she begged to be allowed to live for her baby's sake. Atkins told the actress that she would get no mercy, that she did not care about her unborn baby. She had boasted to another prisoner of liking the taste of Tate's blood. She said she had thought about cutting the baby from the womb.

I reminded Atkins that she, too, was the mother of a child. How could any woman do such a thing, commit a crime that should be unthinkable? With remarkable composure Atkins embarked on a new tack, most likely discussed with her lawyers. For the first time, she blamed her god, Manson, for turning her into an evil angel. Surprise, surprise, Charlie was no longer innocent. Atkins also used the LSD sessions as an excuse, adding that it was only under the influence of this drug that she had allowed Manson to dangle her own baby over a campfire on one of many crazed nights under the stars with the Family. Charlie had intoxicated them all with his mind-bending messages, convincing them that if they slaughtered enough wealthy whites in Hollywood, the blacks would be blamed. This is why she had used Tate's blood to smear the word 'pig' on the door of her house. This was the language of the black radicals. America would be destroyed by the race war and only the Family would survive after hiding in Charlie's secret cave in Death Valley.

As she protested total innocence, Atkins was staring intensely into my eyes, pausing for effect, closely studying my reaction. Doris Tate was right. I watched Atkins throughout a long afternoon in that prison and she gave a performance far better than many on the Hollywood screen. She could smile and smoulder, pout when challenged and when she needed tears she could turn them on like a pro, her whole body quivering as she sobbed out an entirely new story. Now she claimed that the real killer was the only man in the pack that night. It was Tex Watson. He was the murderer. And Charlie Manson had ordered the girls to lie.

Why did I think that Susan Atkins was lying? How could I be sure that this mother–angel–killer had first tortured and then slashed and stabbed another woman full with child? I read the evidence very carefully, whole volumes of evidence. I consulted the prosecutor and discussed weaknesses, errors and 'missing scenes' from the horror movie. I was solidly satisfied with the important facts and, more importantly, so were the jurors entrusted with that responsibility over one of the longest trials in American history. 'But look at her tears now,' her defence attorney said, 'she could not be a killer.' I doubt he believed that and nor did I.

As Truman Capote said, you can see it in their eyes. To murder, you have to suspend your own humanity, even for a deathly second and then for eternity your eyes will look away to the place where you have sent your victim.

Whenever I meet the new Messiahs like Charles Manson, and their dangerous disciples, I find myself looking into their eyes. They are often mirrors of the mind. The honest man or woman may have clear eyes that shine brightly, eyes full of sadness or a look of weariness with life. But the false prophets, the 'Godmen' as they call them in India, have an arrogant glare, a delusion of superiority, that often betrays their madness, their menace and manipulation of their followers.

There are more Godmen and 'miracles' per square inch in Pune, India, than anywhere on earth. At the most famous Sufi temple they have been taking money from followers for the last eight hundred years by chanting the name of a saint to make a seventy-kilogram boulder rise into the air on the fingertips of eleven Sufi priests and their assistants. My new friend Premanand stepped up smiling and said, 'Watch, I'll show you the trick.' It only took four of us with a finger pressed to the rock to hurl it into the air as if it were as light as a basketball. The Sufis chuckled then shuffled away with embarrassment. For Premanand, that was his 1501st 'miracle'.

(Journal 1997)

With his long hair and flowing white beard B. Premanand looks more like a Godman himself than the leader of India's Rationalist Movement who has spent more than fifty years exposing and challenging the miracle merchants. To this thoughtful man, belief in God is a matter of personal choice. As the publisher of a magazine called *The Indian Sceptic*, Premanand's concern is not religion per se but the phenomenal resurgence in our times of self-appointed Messiahs who hold sway over millions of people in the east and the west. Those who feel lost and are searching for meaning, those who are gravely ill, grieving or full of despair, are easily exploited. Premanand and his merry band of followers decided to become guru-busters.

In a dirt-poor village outside Pune in southern India, I watched a Godwoman, Tai Maoli, expertly work a crowd of about twelve thousand people. Every Thursday they came in huge numbers because she told them that she was a living god who could heal the sick and purge demons. As I pressed through the crowd towards the stage where she held court, some women were whirling and shaking as if they were possessed. Half-naked men rolled in the dust and kissed the 'sacred' dirt with the tip of extended tongues. A band, crashing brass cymbals and chanting, had the crowd in a frenzy of expectation. As I swept back the curtain screening the Godwoman from her worshippers I came face to face with a thirtysomething wily peasant type with a satisfied grin on her face. She had a strange all-male entourage led by a cross-eyed *aide-de-camp*.

'How often do you perform miracles?' I asked Miss Maoli.

'Only on Thursdays,' she replied via my translator.

Premanand, who was in hiding to avoid being stoned to death by a mob that hated his irreverence towards the Godwoman, had explained how her first 'miracle' had established power over the villagers. About a year before we arrived, Tai Maoli had claimed that a pair of golden slippers had risen magically from the desert sands. This was an ancient trick performed by planting the golden slippers above a heavily seeded patch of soil. After judicious watering, the 'proof' that she was a living god capable of miracles popped up from the ground and the career of another holy roller was launched. She used another old trick, mastered long ago by Premanand, in which magic smoke and ash appeared mysteriously from a 'sacred hole' in the ground. I stood behind a couple of her white-suited followers and smiled as they fanned the smoke into a twenty-five-metre tunnel that emerged right under the sacred site.

I did not see anyone cured of illness, but the believers enjoyed the show so much that they stuffed about forty thousand rupees into her donation box. They were given small vials of 'miraculous holy water' and Maoli's blessing in return. Every Thursday, this seductress in a shimmering gold sari raked in a fortune, more than any of her followers could make in a year. The Godwoman told me that for 10 000 rupees I could have my name inscribed on her temple, the one they were going to build soon.

From around the world highly educated people searching for something missing in their lives come to Pune. They meditate and meet masters who explain the paths of eastern transcendentalism. Many at least temporarily abandon the western addiction to materialism, change their diet, their clothes and their way of living. For some, these pilgrimages to the east are profoundly moving, deeply spiritual and inspiring. As Premanand and others have explained to me, India offers some of the most powerful philosophies in the world.

'To each his own,' Premanand told me over tea, 'but the exploitation of philosophy has created a big business called religion. The Godmen and women, the swamis, sadhus and all the other reverend gentlemen who do business in the east and west must be honest with people.'

India's most famous living rationalist (the great Sri Jawaharlal Nehru deserves that eternal honour) has exposed some stunning frauds who exploited the misery and poverty of other people. One Godman who claimed to be 800 years old was 'busted' when Premanand discovered a very modern photograph taken when the Godman was a youth. He shut down a Godwoman because she was giving people dangerous treatments without a licence to practise medicine. Wherever Premanand found shysters claiming that their mental powers could light candles or bend spoons, he would gather a crowd and perform these 'miracles' himself. His repertoire includes piercing the body, standing on swords, drinking snake venom and producing gold from thin air. Sometimes the believers become angry and try to attack the guru-buster, but on other occasions they laugh. A Sri Lankan Godman, Jappanam Siddhan, used to claim that God helped him break coconuts with his bare skull. Premanand exchanged one of his bags of tenderised coconuts with a sackful of hard ones. The embarrassed Godman tried to save face by telling his followers that he had seen a naked woman bathing that morning and it had upset his supernatural powers.

If Premanand himself has a mantra it is Nehru's call to search for the truth and not to accept anything without testing and trial. The Rationalists have visited about seven thousand Indian villages and Premanand is encouraged when they open the eyes of the young to frauds and tricksters. But Premanand and the Rationalists met their match when they took on India's greatest Godman, Sathya Sai Baba.

Omniscience and omnipotence are merely two of Sathya Sai Baba's humble claims, along with the suggestion that he is a reincarnation of all gods including Jesus Christ. After growing up in a small village in southern India he announced his divine status at the age of fourteen and has since built a worldwide following of millions with centres in most western countries. I have met devotees around the world eager to praise his mystical messages and wholeheartedly endorse claims that he has brought people back from the dead, healed the sick and made objects materialise. His followers within India include many of the rich and powerful, a High Court judge, senior politicians and several past prime ministers. As T. N. Seshan, a Harvard-educated former civil service boss, said to me in New Delhi, faith has no reason. Seshan had *seen* Sai Baba make a gold ring materialise out of thin air. He had *seen* Sai Baba present some of India's leading politicians with similar miraculous gifts. He also had seen Sathya Sai Baba grow extremely rich.

Premanand and other rationalists conducted exhaustive investigations of most of the supernatural acts attributed to Sai Baba and found no evidence to support the claims of miracles. Secret videotapes showed, naturally, that the rings and necklaces materialising out of thin air were fairly sloppy sleight-of-hand tricks performed a lot better by more entertaining magicians. The stunt that had most international visitors swooning with admiration — the 'miraculous' appearance of *vibhuti* or holy ash as Sai Baba walked among his followers — was a simple trick using talcum powder. Try it yourself. Mix the talcum powder with water and bake it for a couple of hours until it turns into a solid cake. You can hide the lot inside a 'magical urn' or keep a piece in your hand. Abracadabra! With a touch of your hand you too are a miracle worker, although perhaps not devilishly clever enough to be a Godman.

The Rationalists amused the whole of India by challenging Sai Baba in the High Court on the grounds that he was making gold necklaces materialise and yet did not have a government licence to manufacture gold. The judge took the view that the Godman was using spiritual power to make the gold. There was no violation of the Gold Control Act because the gold came from God. Although the Rationalists left the court laughing, they recognised that it would take a miracle to dethrone India's biggest Godman.

Despite the setback, Premanand carries on the art of questioning, previously practised by the greatest minds that ever lived. Copernicus and Galileo were persecuted for giving truthful answers, but who is laughing now as the earth goes round the sun? St Augustine's youthful brilliance retreated into a traditional adult conservatism when he suggested that curiosity was but a childhood disease and that it was futile to try to discover the secrets of nature and to dream of the stars. Although the new Messiahs always have told us to stop asking questions, men like Bacon, da Vinci, Descartes, Newton, Darwin and Huxley kept looking for answers. Premanand has taken scientific thought out of the hallowed halls of academia and made it his life's work to demonstrate the art of questioning to the one billion Indians who often seem too busy surviving to think. Before I said goodbye to this remarkable old Indian, Premanand told me that he only had one question for the new Messiahs whether they were in the east or the west: 'Can you prove it?'

The Indian guru-buster is cheered on by an international group of scientific thinkers now battling the same explosion of superstition in America, Europe and Australia. Some of the greatest minds of our age, from the late Jacob Bronowski to Carl Sagan, have lamented this retreat from knowledge and the widespread acceptance of uncritical thinking, demonstrated by the rush to worship men and women claiming supernatural powers.

In the American state of Georgia I saw thousands flock to a woman who simply calls herself Nancy, claiming to deliver messages from the Blessed Virgin. The sceptics said that the proceeds had established Nancy on a very nice farm. Australia's own seer, calling himself 'Little Pebble', gave me his predictions for the coming Apocalypse when he would be the last Pope to lead God's children to heaven. Some of his former followers wondered why he was so interested in making pretty teenage girls the queens of his earthly kingdom. I have stood in an Arkansas stadium and watched the Reverend Benny Hinn, the tele-evangelist, summon gravely ill people onto his stage, desperate mothers pushing wheelchair-bound children and terminally ill cancer patients shuffling forward. Benny would lay hands on them to 'heal them with the power of God', and then ask his television audience of millions to keep sending in donations. In many cases the self-styled Messiahs, like the Reverend Jim Jones or David Koresh, led their followers to a hellish end right here on earth. That does not stop them coming.

The new Messiahs have been appearing all the way through recorded history, and yet despite their scaremongering about the Apocalypse they have not led humankind to heaven or even earthly harmony. When the gurus ask people not to use the most powerful organ we have developed over several million years of evolution, to turn off the brain and surrender to faith, they divert our collective energies, distract our communal concentration and slow down the progress we need to make to ensure survival of our species.

If it takes 100 000 years or so for a new, higher order of species to evolve from the old, why waste our precious time? Science is not an alternative religion as the New Messiahs claim. The questions that children ask us about the earth and fire, lightning and rain, life and death, have answers that we all are biologically capable of understanding. Human intelligence is the key to our evolutionary destiny. With the knowledge now in the most extraordinary libraries that have ever existed, the opportunity for self-discovery and enlightenment can be shared by billions of people. Imagination, creativity and critical thinking have an extraordinary beauty. Only the truth brings fulfilment, and unlike the hocus pocus of the Godmen, the truth can stand testing.

In Kathmandu a horn blows at dawn and people file through the Himalayan mist and the stone ruins towards the temples. Petals are sprinkled and prayers are offered. It is a serene hour and people are smiling peacefully. Within sight of the crumbling piles of yesterday's cremations, a young man with impeccable English leads me to his sadhu, a 'living god' who looks to me like a wild-eyed man with dreadlocks who has smoked a lot of ganja. The sadhu offers to 'materialise' one million dollars on my doorstep in Sydney ... if I give him $US250. Or, he says smiling, he could dangle eight to ten bricks from his penis. Why? Why not, I guess, if you are a Godman.

(JOURNAL 1997)

CHAPTER EIGHT

THE FORBIDDEN CITIES

In Samarkand, that fabled city of turquoise mosques and golden domes, Uzbeks, Kirghiz and Afghans wind their way through the alleyways to the holy places where so many before them have come for a thousand years. In the silence of the Shah-i-Zindeh tombs or the great mosque of Shir-Dor-Madrasah stand some of the USSR's 43 million Muslims who don't appear to believe that God is dead under Marxism.

(JOURNAL 1984)

Legend has it that the ancient market of Samarkand in Uzbekistan first brought the west the paper I am now writing on. This oasis at the crossroads of the oldest caravan routes between east and west has had a powerful allure for me ever since reading as a child Coleridge's enchanted poem, 'Kubla Khan'.

Samarkand was closed to western journalists for many years but in 1984, the Orwellian year, I found that the soul-destroying darkness of totalitarianism was beginning to lift in the Soviet Union. Did Lenin and Marx really expect conformity from 280 million people in fifteen republics speaking more than a hundred languages? How could the Kremlin possibly brainwash so many ethnically diverse people in eleven different time zones spread across one-sixth of the world's surface? When I slipped through the Iron Curtain to some of the long-forbidden lands of the mighty Russian Empire I discovered a world as exotic as when Marco Polo travelled here seven hundred years ago.

In Samarkand I joined pilgrims walking through the desert heat to the shimmering beauty of a magnificent mosque, the dome clad in minute turquoise tiles and lined with gold. The prophet Mohammed probably would have been amazed that after his death his system of belief spread around the world. Islam also inspired an explosion of talents, a great flowering of intellectual, artistic and scientific accomplishments in the mysterious east, little known to most westerners.

I followed an old Uzbek man hobbling on crutches into the hilltop observatory of Ulug Bek, a medieval astronomer and enlightened thinker. It was a very strange place because as I descended into the gloom I noticed it housed no telescope. How could this Uzbek have plotted the planets and over one thousand stars so accurately without the western world's great discovery? The answer lay before me. With a perfect marble arc, originally over sixty metres long, and an ancient measuring device called an astrolabe, Ulug Bek had built a gigantic sextant. Unfortunately, this wise man's quest for knowledge and questioning of Muslim orthodoxy so unsettled his countrymen that he was assassinated by his own son in 1449.

I began to think about how the ancient world plays tricks with the eyes and the mind as I walked down to the marketplace in Samarkand. The scene before me had not changed much since Marco Polo's time. It was bedlam. Here was a dancing bear cruelly tethered for the amusement of wanderers from every corner of the east. The sound of haggling blended with the wailing of eastern music and the laughter of children darting through the crowd. Dark-skinned women wore bright silk robes over ankle-length pants. A shaman sold cures, travelling musicians played strings and wooden flutes, and wild-eyed, barefooted wanderers spread grubby blankets to hawk the age-old trading goods of the silk routes. Spices, meat, fruit and vegetables, hand-woven rugs, gold and silver lamé and uncut gemstones had been sold like this for centuries. The teahouses, offering shade from the fierce heat, politely welcomed all travellers as they have in Samarkand for the last 2500 years. Only when I got to the central plaza where children were playing in a fountain in front of the inevitable, giant-sized portrait of Lenin did the modern reality intrude that I was still inside the ugly walls of concrete communism.

While it seems extraordinary now that the Red Army could have managed to hold onto all these exotic pieces of the mighty Soviet Union for more than seventy years, there once was a power more feared than communism and it ruled an even bigger empire. In 1220 Genghis Khan and his Mongol horsemen devastated Samarkand when it was truly one of the great cities of the world. You can see the ruins of the ancient gate where the terrifying hordes burst in, slaughtering the last defenders and half of the civilian population. Flaming arrows set fire to the oldest mosque and burning oil was catapulted onto the golden city. The destruction of Samarkand, Bukhara, Herat, Urgench, Baghdad and other magnificent cities set back their progress for many centuries.

Follow the silk route further east and you come to the land of the Great Khan, a sweep of green steppe, mountains and the Gobi Desert. In the Mongolian capital, Ulaanbaatar, the statues of Lenin and Marx have been torn down, replaced by the fierce image of Genghis Khan who was restored to hero status when communism fell in 1990. Even during the years of Russian domination the Mongols clung to this cultural heritage, the inspiration, the sheer strength of their legendary sovereign. Their real flag was never the hammer and sickle, but a banner made of horsehair as in the days of the Khan.

When I flew over the vastness of Central Asia it staggered me to think that a single Mongol warrior had been capable of such guile and terror that he had united his own tribal land of little more than one million people and then led an army of not much more than 110 000 men to conquer half the known world.

I stared at the map. In the twelfth and thirteenth centuries, the
Mongols had subjugated millions of people all the way from the
coast of China to the river Danube, from the Yellow Sea to the
Mediterranean. This was a man I would have liked to meet ... to
ask him, 'Why?'

Where did his lust for conquest come from? Did the boy, born
Temujin, merely set out to avenge the poisoning of his father by
rival tribesmen but find he could not rest until he wiped out the
tribe? Did he acquire a taste for blood when he killed a half-
brother who stole his cache of fish? Was he addicted to
psychopathic violence? Or was it the exhilaration of military
victory as he conquered other tribes that shaped this remarkable
man who at the age of forty realised his destiny as Genghis Khan,
ruler of the world?

Asking the Mongols about the Great Khan was like asking the
British about Churchill or the Americans about Washington. Now
that they were free to forget about Marx and Lenin everyone saw
their future greatness in the past. In Ulaanbaatar the long-banned
film *Genghis Khan* was screening daily. At the Mongol circus
where daredevil riders balanced on galloping horses, camels and
even yak, the star of the show always was the superhero, Genghis
Khan. The young man we hired as our translator while filming in
Mongolia proudly told us that Genghis Khan was a genius who
united his people for the first time and then outwitted and
outfought all of his enemies.

Every Mongol kid could tell us how Genghis Khan was the
greatest horseman who ever rode the plains and how the short
but strong-legged Mongol ponies were more agile and had far
more stamina than Europe's finest cavalry mounts. The boys and
girls could list all of the Great Khan's weapons, beginning with
his powerful bow and three quivers of armour-piercing arrows,
the lance with its deadly barb, the sabre sharp enough to
decapitate, and the dagger strapped to his arm that carried a
small leather shield. Frankly, no one much enjoyed my suggestion
that there was a great deal of historical evidence indicating that
Genghis Khan also was a master of vicious psychological warfare,
a butcher who ordered the massacre of whole armies and

countless millions of civilians when he needed to teach the rest of the world a terrifying lesson.

When his generals circled the Caspian Sea they left a trail of slaughter through Turkey, Georgia and Russia. Genghis Khan, his sons and grandsons waged war in an astonishing way that certainly no longer occurs, forcefully recruiting the armies they conquered to serve the Mongol cause. Civilians were made to transport the baggage of war. Mongol women followed the marauding horsemen, finishing off the wounded and collecting the deadly arrows that time and again would cut down great armies superior in number to the khan's hordes. There is no doubt that Genghis Khan was a military genius, patenting the false retreat and the vicious counter-attack. The legacy of this is that neither the Russians nor the Chinese trust the Mongolians today even though there are a mere two million of them in the north, and about three million in the Chinese territory of Inner Mongolia.

*In 1209 Genghis Khan and his men set out on horseback
from a valley near Karakorum, the ancient capital of
Mongolia. I reached the old city by Russian helicopter,
a bulky, trembling beast called a Mi-8. The khan is said to
have ordered his men not to piss in the rivers of Karakorum
and to keep their stock out of the water too. The traditional
explanation is that the khan had decreed the world's first
environmental laws out of respect for the land and
understanding of what man and beast needed to survive.*
                                                    (JOURNAL 1992)

Karakorum in the thirteenth century was the headquarters of the most awesome fighting force of the Middle Ages, a mobile band of killers more feared than the Crusaders who had marched across the Holy Land. In that sense Karakorum was briefly the most powerful city in the world, but perhaps because of its dedication to conquest it never became a great centre of civilisation. I walked among the forlorn ruins, broken walls and shards of pottery, all that is left after the Chinese armies eventually beat the khans at their own game, destroying the last symbol of Mongol supremacy in 1388. My young guide insisted that the khans were never really beaten by foreigners but by their own disputes that weakened the great Mongol Empire and guaranteed its decline.

Curiously, although there have been many treasure seekers looking for Genghis Khan's bounty, no one has found his grave. After he died in pain, possibly suffering from typhus, his body was carried to Mongolia for burial with forty fine horses and forty virgins to give him pleasure in the next world. Some of the gold and jewels plundered during about sixty savage years on earth also were buried with him. According to several accounts, his followers rode horses over the burial site to scatter the dirt and hide all traces of the grave and its treasure. I would be more interested to find some satisfying record of this terrifying warrior's summation of his life.

The khan's very last campaign was against the mysterious kingdom of Xi Xia in what is now eastern China. Its crime was refusing to send horsemen to support Genghis Khan's destruction of so many great cities to the west. We are told one of his final orders from his deathbed was to send his troops to annihilate everyone in Xi Xia, erasing a culture that had its own written language and advanced art. Genghis Khan was a butcher to the very end.

Genghis Khan worshipped a god called Tengri, ruler of the heavens. Although he had conscripted many soldiers of Islam, Christianity and Buddhism, he seemed to have absorbed little of the real wisdom of these philosophies. Conquest had brought his largely illiterate people a little knowledge, such as a more advanced script. He had enlisted foreigners to show him how to build a government. But he certainly destroyed more of civilisation than he built. Most chronicles from his day suggest that the great Genghis Khan was addicted to conquest itself, a warrior who loved nothing more than making war.

In Karakorum I have been thinking about the legacy of
the Mongol khans and how it relates to the evolution
of humankind. Of the last 5000 years only a couple of
hundred have been free of a major war. Even though my
friend John Romer was right and most men did not
participate in these wars, our history and indeed
archeology bears all the scars of so much destruction
caused by a few. The khans seem to have drawn and
quartered half of Asia. They had the Chinese and the
Russians suppressed for over a century. But what came
out of this conquest apart from a temporary unity forged
by violence and not mutual self-interest? When Kublai
Khan's ships got down to Java they were defeated by our
northern neighbours and the Burmese on their elephants
scared them off too. Terror has its limits. The only age
more terrible than Genghis Khan's is our own. But there
is no evidence that the great technological wars of the
twentieth century have advanced human civilisation
despite the death of 180 million people, mainly civilians.
Genghis Khan and his ilk have led us nowhere.

(JOURNAL 1992)

The human phallus as a symbol of conquest is at least as old as
the war cry. You find displays of penis power in most primitive art
forms and in the warrior tribes that still exist today, from New
Guinea highlanders wearing enormous penis gourds to World
Championship wrestlers and modern Olympians bulging in their
Lycra tights. It is understandable that some might spend a little
time thinking about this part of the male anatomy, but in
Karakorum I was surprised to see that the penis had been elevated
to the plane of worship.

As you enter Karakorum's only surviving Buddhist monastery,
built in the sixteenth century, it is hard to miss the well-endowed
penis stone as usually there is a line of young women waiting to
touch it. The girls coyly approach, glance around to see the smiles

of their watching friends and then gingerly touch the stone, hoping that soon they will be pregnant. There was a very good chance of that happening around here in the old days, as a lot of the Buddhist lamas behaved more like typical men, flouting their vows of celibacy, spreading venereal disease and, for a time, ruling Mongolia with a greedy, power-hungry theocracy. In the twentieth century, the communists put an end to that by executing an estimated fifteen thousand lamas and senselessly destroying hundreds of magnificent Buddhist temples. They are still digging up skeletons from these brutal purges of the 1930s. Now that communism has fallen, the temples are slowly being patched up. The girls will go on patting the penis stone, because in Mongolia the oldest traditions do not die.

With a fanfare of martial music, Mongolians on horseback carrying horsehair flags cantered into the stadium outside Ulaanbaatar, for the beginning of Naadam, the annual games held in July when the Mongols celebrate their warrior culture. There are wrestlers in leather boots, skimpy blue briefs and tight-fitting red jackets open across the chest. There are archers — men and extremely beautiful women — wearing brilliantly coloured tunics tied with a golden sash. There is also a lot of choral singing, connecting the crowd and contestants to the most ancient traditions. These tournaments once were held after the victories of Genghis Khan. There is still plenty of aggression displayed in the wrestling which brings the victor tremendous national fame and a grand title: Falcon, Elephant, Lion and then, if you keep knocking them down, Giant. There is a man here who has won ten years in a row. His modest title? 'The Eye-pleasing, Nationally Famous, Mighty, Invincible Giant'!

(JOURNAL 1992)

One of the most stirring human spectacles I have ever seen was the descendants of Genghis Khan racing their horses, not on a track, but over thirty kilometres of dusty steppe at full gallop with the greatest glory to the leading bunch. These races for boys and girls between the ages of six and twelve were the highlight of the Naadam festival when thousands of nomadic herders gathered outside Ulaanbaatar.

After spending more time in that ugly, squat city polluted by oil stacks, its horizon scarred by a messy tangle of powerlines between depressing apartment blocks, it was exhilarating to be out on the treeless plains to see this richly coloured painting, the great sea of *ghers*, circular tents made of felt and canvas, as the nomads camped like the armies of Genghis Khan. Long-maned horses grazed nearby or were being lovingly groomed by their owners. Every Mongol wore the traditional *del,* the knee-length jacket tied with a sash, boys carrying saddles and leading their ponies, girls tending the sheep and goats. Despite the vastness of the camp there was an unusual and very enjoyable peacefulness among these wandering people who liked the silence and the isolation of life on the steppe.

They do not like fences in Mongolia. These nomads are free to drive their herds of sheep, camels, goats and cattle hundreds of kilometres to fresh pastures. It is a hard life but a fairly self-sufficient one. They literally live off the sheep's back and sometimes a camel's. A fine camel can produce six kilograms of hair a year and in the communist era the nomads relied on the yield to double the miserable wages paid to state workers. Some now own motorbikes, television sets and radios. The *ghers*, however, are still very simply furnished with a marital bed, soft bedrolls for the children and pillows for reclining spread around the woven rugs. A small Buddhist altar is usually the only decoration. The nomads' 'colourful' handmade clothes are folded in battered trunks. Food and dishes are stacked in painted wooden cabinets. There is nothing elaborate, everything can be dismantled and packed in a yak-drawn wagon with only a few hours work.

In the bitterly cold winters temperatures get down to –45°C on the steppe, but the nomads survive by doubling the *gher*'s outside layers of felt, piling up more animal skins and rugs on the floor, and fuelling their small stoves with dried animal dung. The smoke escapes through an opening in the sloping roof that lets in the only light. It is cosy inside the *gher,* with a feeling of intimacy among the family members who share their food from a single plate on a low wooden table. Their most exotic dish is *boodog,* which is a goat carcass filled with hot stones and roasted slowly from the inside.

The nomadic custom is to warmly welcome perfect strangers. I was offered a bowl of *airaq,* a drink of fermented mare's milk that may not be refused without great insult to the host. As this was a friendly family with a fine horse-breeding tradition and a very good chance of winning one or two races, I accepted a second and third bowl of *airaq,* something I would later regret. I was then fed chunks of cheese, made from the same mare's milk, and a bit of bread, topped off with a brand of vodka named 'Genghis Khan'.

When it was time for the races a huge crowd gathered calmly, without ropes or other barriers. The young riders formed circles and sang a song called 'Ghingo', summoning up the speed and endurance that made their forefathers extraordinary horsemen. The boys and girls, who had been riding since before their legs could reach the stirrups, got last-minute instructions from their fathers. They were dressed in their finest silks, red, yellow, blue and orange, with a number on the front and back of red cotton vests worn over their jackets. The girls tied back their hair with brilliant scarves and the boys donned silver and gold-trimmed caps like the warriors of yesteryear. And then, with great whoops from the riders and crowd, several hundred horses walked off to the starting line in the low hills thirty kilometres away.

I passed the time meeting the locals who were curious about the foreign film crew in their midst and delighted to see how our telescopic lens could spot the racers from afar. Exchanging names with the Mongols was a lot of fun. Most of them only used one name because they all seemed to have names as long as their illustrious history. One of my companions in Ulaanbaatar, a presidential spokeswoman, was named Dugersurengiin Suhjargalmaa. 'Call me Jarlma,' she said.

There were excited shouts from the crowd as the leading riders came into sight. The sound of many hooves thundered across the steppe. The young riders were high in the saddle, waving their whips in the air and yelling war cries to make the horses go faster. Watching these tough little horses, lathered in sweat but still galloping strongly after such a long journey, I could see how they had carried the Mongol hordes across the world.

In the front bunch was the twelve-year-old son of the herdsman who had invited me to the family *gher*. He came in second and I saw him later ambling around the camp on his pony, proudly displaying his blue ribbon. The first five placegetters shared the adulation. The winning steed was presented with a gold medal and as victory songs were sung by the crowd praising the horse and the herdsman who had bred such speed and stamina, that now familiar libation, *airaq*, was poured on the horse's forehead.

I was standing near the finish line talking enthusiastically to the television camera when the effects of the *airaq* suddenly kicked like a mule, or should I say mare. Great pains shot through my body from top to tail. Although the colour was fast draining out of my face, the cameraman, Phil Donoghue, and sound-recordist, Mark Brewer, were amusing the producer, John Little, by taking turns to call for 'just one more take'. I could have killed them but I felt like I was dying. As the race tailenders and a few riderless horses trotted home, I walked quickly away from the crowd trying to find a hollow to crawl into, because there were no latrines. But the plain was flat and there was not a tree or any other object to hide behind. As the irresistible tide of dysentery moved through my body I dropped my trousers in the open field. The Mongols riding away on their horses surely must have been thinking, 'Who is the barbarian now?'

*Kazakhstan's capital, Alma-Ata, 'the place of apples', is
nestled below a spectacular snow-covered mountain
range. We drove into the mountains in a battered Russian
van, brakes gasping on the descents, engine straining to
get us to our filming rendezvous with key members of the
Anti-Nuclear Movement. I met a poet, a scientist and a
mother and daughter who said that thousands of people
here were seriously ill with various kinds of radiation
sickness. Their story was chilling. The Russians had tested
most of their nuclear weapons here and had used the
Kazakhs as guinea pigs. According to the poet, ground
zero at Semipalatinsk was now 'the land of the mutants'.*
                                             (JOURNAL 1993)

When the first truly enlightened leader of the Soviet Union,
Mikhail Gorbachev, called a moratorium on nuclear testing in his
country, I seized the chance to investigate one of the grimmest
secrets long hidden in the darkness of communism, a nightmare
place called Semipalatinsk that I visited just once but never want
to see again.

I learned that from 1949 until Gorbachev's moratorium in
1990, there had been 470 nuclear devices detonated in this area
described by intelligence agencies as a 'secret citadel' in the far
north of Kazakhstan. I had heard of the place a decade earlier
during filming trips to the Soviet Union, but it was then forbidden
to go anywhere near Semipalatinsk. It was not shown on most
Soviet maps. After the failed Communist Party coup in Moscow
in 1991, many of the Soviet Republics like Kazakhstan began to
assert their independence and to hold the Communists responsible
for the hideous abuse of their land and people. In 1993 my *60
Minutes* team entered Kazakhstan with the help of anti-nuclear
campaigners and a few well-placed Kazakh officials. For the last
four decades the Kazakhs had been so oppressed in their own
country that they were not able to tell anyone the frightening
story of exactly how the Russians had become a nuclear power.

They wanted us to show the world how the carelessness and callousness of the Russians had contaminated vast areas of the country, irradiating numerous villages and causing a plague of nuclear illness.

The Soviet Union became a superpower on 29 August 1949, when it detonated its first atomic bomb, a 20-kiloton blast that scattered a vast plume of radiation over surrounding Kazakh villages. This tragedy, I was told by Dr Gusiv, a Russian specialist at the Radiation Institute in Semipalatinsk, was due to a last-minute change of wind, not the ineptitude of their nuclear geniuses. He admitted, however, that 116 of the nuclear explosions above ground often had irradiated several large cities as well as many small villages. He insisted that only two of the 'underground' tests had been so clumsy that they blasted away whole hilltops and showered still more radioactive fallout over a wide area. The Kazakh government officials disputed this and claimed scores of the tests went horribly wrong and furthermore that the Kazakh villagers had been used as guinea pigs over many years of nuclear testing.

You can imagine why they chose Kazakhstan and not Russia for these 470 weapons tests. It is the same reason the French opted for the South Pacific, the Americans went out west and the British were invited down to 'isolated' parts of Australia, irradiating some troops, Aboriginal settlements and other people. I have filmed the consequences of these weapons tests as well and come to the inescapable conclusion that the men who have been planning nuclear war are insane. There is no other way to explain the violence they already have inflicted on the earth and its people, particularly the Kazakhs.

Kazakhstan is about a third the size of Australia with a population close to ours, roughly eighteen million. I discovered that it was difficult for the newly independent nation to gauge the full extent of the nuclear damage because so much of Kazakhstan looked like an environmental disaster. A uranium-processing mill and lead smelters had heavily polluted some cities. The Aral Sea was full of pesticides, drying up and blowing another deadly pollutant across the land. This too was damaging the immune systems of the Kazakhs. It had been a slow and difficult task for an official Health Commission to investigate just how much of the cancer and other illness could be attributed to the massive nuclear fallout.

> *I filmed at two hospitals in Alma-Ata today. The cancer clinic was overflowing with children. A seven-year-old boy named Artov who lived near Semipalatinsk had been sick for three years. The doctors told us that most of these kids would die. The leukaemia clinic was under even greater stress, thirty children to a ward, some lying on beds in the hallways. They had that sickly, sallow look and seemed to be fading before our eyes. A Russian scientific adviser told us that illnesses relating to immune deficiency were in epidemic proportions among village children and that this appeared to be a kind of 'nuclear AIDS'. So even the Russians admit that the radiation damage here is widespread. Fallout also had caused 'numerous miscarriages, birth defects and genetic damage that would be long lasting'. It is astonishing that such horror could have been hidden from the world for so long.*
>
> (JOURNAL 1993)

After our initial meetings in Alma-Ata there was considerable trepidation among most of us in the film team about the dangers ahead. The very word 'radiation' made our hair stand on end because we could not see it and yet we all knew the results at Hiroshima and Nagasaki. None of us in the crew had fathered a child as yet, although it was something I for one looked forward to and was not anxious to jeopardise by further irradiating my sperm. I had been to Chernobyl after that nuclear accident and watched the Russian military officers scrambling to get their wives and children onto any available transport to a safer place. My film crew understood then that quite possibly we had eaten irradiated food after the widespread fallout in the Kiev region. On top of that, I no doubt had received another dose of radiation when I was allowed to film the United States' nuclear bomb plants and the dumping grounds for that superpower's nuclear waste, a store of poison that would be lethal for another 250 000 years.

It seemed, however, that the only way we could arrive at the truth was to go to Semipalatinsk and see for ourselves. The western world had seen no evidence, but it appeared that the Russians were guilty of a nuclear catastrophe far greater than Chernobyl. After carefully assessing the situation in Alma-Ata, we took a vote in our usual democratic fashion even in the land of the Red Army. Our unanimous decision was to take the risk and go to ground zero. Our Kazakh supporters had already shown faith in us by booking our flight to the north.

The testing grounds for the Russian nuclear arsenal were spread over a lonely, treeless plain with a few barren hills and a now massively irradiated river carrying its deadly poison to other hapless victims. The Red Army had built its version of human civilisation, multi-storied concrete buildings, military bunkers and steel bridges, all to be blown to smithereens by nuclear weapons. Old aircraft, tanks, military trucks and even a locomotive engine and freight cars were blasted to pieces here. This is the military mind. They call their wargame 'MAD' for Mutually Assured Destruction. If you want to slaughter millions you have to test your weapon of mass destruction and the best test of all is on real people.

As we drove in Red Army four-wheel-drives deep into the nuclear test zone, the occasional radiation warning sign the only relief from the mind-numbing isolation, a Russian colonel warned us that parts of the 'hot zone' had readings of radioactivity one thousand times higher than the safe level. We would not be permitted to stay long. I assured him that there was not much chance of that, but the Russian offered us no protection at all and made it clear he was only escorting us under orders from the government of Kazakhstan, which suddenly was getting a little respect.

We came as well prepared as one can be for such madness. We packed radiation meters and another device that would measure our accumulated exposure. Our plan was to don light cotton radiation suits and masks that could be quickly pulled over our clothing while we were at ground zero and then dumped before we left the site. There would still be a risk at the hot spots that we would ingest radioactive dust or pick it up on our boots. We planned to airbrush and vacuum the camera equipment before we left the area.

My red-haired Russian driver scoffed at the radiation danger.

'Oh, really,' I said, 'and how many people do you know who have died of cancer out here?'

He glanced sideways and said, 'My brother, my uncle, an aunt ... and my father. But we all have to die of something.' There was an uncomfortable silence for many kilometres.

The Kazakh anti-nuclear campaigners had shown us old black and white films which appeared to confirm that the military men and scientists who conducted these weapons tests were ignorant or just plain foolish. As in western test zones, observers had been positioned dangerously close to the nuclear explosions. The film showed some of the Red Army soldiers (mainly Kazakhs, we were told, although it was not possible to tell from the grainy images) emerging from the bunkers after the nuclear blasts. Incredibly, they walked across the irradiated mock battlefield with nothing more than ponchos for protection. Even Dr Strangelove could not have imagined a horror movie like this.

Our eerie drive brought us first to Atomic Lake, a variation on the usual MAD experiment but one that went horribly wrong. To convince the Soviet population that atomic bombs had peaceful purposes, one was exploded underground in 1965 to link two rivers and create a reservoir. Atomic Lake, of course, is completely useless because the shallow blast heavily irradiated the soil and water, providing a long-term source of nuclear pollution in the rivers. Even worse, this 'peaceful' atom bomb vented a massive amount of radiation over villages downwind.

The four-wheel-drives bumped and creaked over rough ground as we edged towards the huge crater-lake. We had our radiation suits on, hoods up and masks across our faces. The radiation meter was going berserk and so was my mate, Phil Donoghue.

'For Christ's sake can't you go any faster? Pull us up to that high rim,' he said.

We leaped out of our vehicles and began to film. It was like a moonscape. No sign of life, just the pockmarked crater and the chemical blue-green water staring at us like the eye of a giant. The radiation meter was frantic after just a few steps towards the edge. We got our film extremely quickly, and reluctantly I lowered my mask for about forty seconds to talk to the camera. I now know what they mean about talking through clenched teeth.

As we made a rapid exit, I pestered the Russians with questions. How could anyone think the Atomic Lake would ever irrigate the land or support livestock when it would remain dangerously radioactive for God knows how long? Who was responsible for this craziness? Were they put up against a wall and shot? There was another long silence on our drive back to our lodgings for the night. In the rooms of the hostel we ran the radiation meter over the dust on the telephone, the windowsill and the doorway. It was 'hot'! Semipalatinsk was glowing and would be for a very long time.

Day three. Semipalatinsk. We filmed in three frightening villages surrounding the test site. It is criminal that these impoverished Kazakhs were not moved. They showed us walls cracked by the force of the nuclear explosions and older folk described seeing the mushroom clouds of the above-ground blasts. One woman claimed her family was told by the Russians to stand outside their house to watch the bomb go off. The anti-nuclear campaigners insist that the Russians did not evacuate the villages and wanted these people here to measure the impact of the radiation. They certainly were tested after the bombs went off. Many women told us they had lost babies through miscarriages in the years of the underground tests. A Health Commission doctor claimed there was a

clear link between the radiation and a horrific number of
birth defects. There is mental retardation in every village
and some terribly deformed bodies. We saw too much of
this today. As long as I live I will never forget Berik, the
boy with no eyes.

(JOURNAL 1993)

A handful of dirt scooped up from the Kazakh village set our radiation meter flashing. The hundreds of families in these miserably poor shanties in front of us were living with radioactivity, huge unnatural doses of it. Downwind of ground zero, the village had felt the brunt of many of the nuclear explosions. Berik Syzdykov's mother was in the early months of her pregnancy when the ground trembled from another blast. A Health Commission doctor and a Russian scientist confirmed from the records that there had been a deadly venting of radioactivity the year her child was taking shape in her womb.

I walked towards the crumbling mudbrick house, crudely stuccoed and white-washed. Berik's mother, a solid woman, wore a cheap Russian dress, her hair tied back in a Kazakh scarf. Her gleaming gold earrings contrasted oddly with the sadness of her face. She beckoned for my translator and me to come inside. The family had little, but the house was clean and tidy, sparsely furnished with a wooden table and chairs, and a Russian-made sofa covered with Kazakh blankets. Hanging on the wall was a traditional rug with a strange geometric design, symbols of the life of the herdsmen on these desolate plains.

I heard music coming from the darkness of the next room and then Berik suddenly was standing in the doorway. The thirteen-year-old boy's face was so disfigured by large tumours that his features were barely recognisable as he shuffled towards us.

'He has no eyes,' my translator whispered as Mrs Syzdykov led the boy towards me. As I gently shook Berik's hand I could see the tumours that encrusted his face, covered his eye-sockets and continued over his forehead. He was crowned with them.

'The bomb did this to my child,' said Mrs Syzdykov. 'His eyes are closed forever. He will never see.'

The house was so gloomy we recorded Berik's story outside in the yard. Painfully aware of the horrified reaction his face usually drew from strangers, Berik kept his head bowed as his mother explained that there was a plague of birth defects, crippled bodies, blindness, deafness and mental retardation in the village. We knew she was telling the truth as we had visited some of the other twisted cripples, many helpless and bedridden, hidden away in the backrooms of houses, others leering with idiot grins from doorways and windows.

I felt a surge of sadness and empathy but knew that it would be pointless and patronising for a stranger to take the child in his arms. The boy would never go anywhere without suffering torment. It was doubtful he would live long enough to become a man. My tears were not going to wash away all he had been through.

'Do you enjoy listening to your music?' I asked, remembering my meetings with other blind people who drew so much solace from sound. Berik listened to the translator and then looked up and smiled.

With no help from his mother, the boy guided me into the backroom of the house where we sat down by an antique gramophone. Expertly he placed a record on the turntable and lowered the needle. A Russian classical symphony filled the room. Berik was now in his own world, in a land of the imagination far from the horror of his everyday life. He looked peaceful and happy. Old records were the only music Berik's family could find out here on the nuclear range where transient Russian military personnel easily outnumbered the Kazakhs. Before we left the country we surprised him with a big red ghetto blaster and an armful of new music from all parts of the world. I was sent a photograph of Berik, sitting in his chair, finger on the play button. Some good came out of telling Berik's story to the world. He has been 'adopted' by the Italian town of Albanella and surgeon Renato Joska has performed two plastic surgery operations on his disfigured face which have made a small cosmetic improvement.

In a nearby village we filmed what looked like a boy about the same age as Berik. But this scrawny, curled up figure had been lying in bed for the last forty years, tenderly nursed by his family. The elderly mother, while pregnant, was one of many locals who witnessed a dark mushroom cloud rising from the test site.

A nuclear explosion creates super-high temperatures and a brilliant flash of hot ionised air. This fireball, even at a distance of 100 kilometres, is many times brighter than the midday sun. The flash of light affects people and the environment even before the blast because of a range of radiation in the visible and infra-red spectra. Sometimes a firestorm is generated. The blast then moves out in a shock-front from ground zero. The initial radiation has a terrifying penetrative power and then comes the deadly radioactive fallout that may threaten the Kazakhs for several hundred thousand years.

As our four-wheel-drive pulled into one of the most isolated villages for our meeting with a Kazakh field doctor, I noticed goats and horses grazing on the few stubbles of grass that sprang from this barren plain. Presumably the animals and any crops grown around the area were irradiated too. I asked our host this question as we sat down to lunch. He smiled and shrugged. The radiation was now part of life and death here. The birth defects were hundreds of times higher than anywhere else. The long-term genetic damage would show up for years in the offspring of these people. They were getting very little help from the Russians now that Kazakhstan had chosen independence, and there was nowhere for these sick people to go.

As lunch was being served it was too late for me to escape the stomach-turning dish that suddenly appeared before me. The eye from a horse's head and some sliced meat from around the fetlock had been set before me as guest of honour. The doctor passed me the horse's eye on the point of a long carving knife. For the Kazakhs, like most nomadic people, it is considered extremely bad luck to turn down such hospitality. As I nibbled at the nag's head and the fetlock, trying also not to think too much about the radiation levels, I heard a scream from outside. Phil Donoghue and Mark Brewer had excused themselves from lunch, sudden converts to vegetarianism, and had gone walking around the village. Mark rushed back inside, breathless and white-faced. 'Phil's been bitten by a wild dog. He's a mess!'

A large mongrel that was more wolf than dog had leaped up and taken a huge wedge out of Phil's upper arm. It looked like someone had hit him with an axe. He was still standing, but in shock.

My thoughts immediately were of the danger of radioactive dust getting into the wound and into his bloodstream. But our host, the Kazakh doctor, was worried first about rabies. Many of the local animals carried the disease but the closest place we might find an anti-rabies shot was Semipalatinsk, 100 kilometres away.

I poured Phil a glass of straight vodka as the doctor got to work on the wound. Still calm and behaving very bravely, Phil asked the doctor to scrub up thoroughly before he tackled the stitches. Others looked away as the needle went in to close the gaping hole in Phil's arm. A lot of men would have fainted right there from the pain. He was still on his feet at the end, walking out with his arm in a sling. At the edge of the road I poured everyone a shot of vodka for a hasty toast. We wished one another luck, waved to the doctor and his friends, and then sped off towards Semipalatinsk.

It was dark when we reached the military town. I pressed a few hundred American dollars into our driver's hand and told him to go to the local black market to buy the strongest antibiotics he could find. The doctors at Semipalatinsk had none. With the help of the Russian colonel we got Phil into a hospital of sorts, a sanatorium where the officers came for rest during their lonely exile in this hellhole. A very large nurse with a row of gold teeth comforted Phil, but a Russian doctor told me that his condition was extremely serious. As well as the huge piece missing from his right upper arm, he had other bites including a nasty one on his chest. There were no anti-rabies shots in the sanatorium or anywhere in Semipalatinsk. It was a sleepless night for every one of us.

*Day six in Kazakhstan. Phil is still in great pain. The
doctor here cannot do any more for him. No chance of
getting an anti-rabies serum here by aircraft. Phil wants
Mark to pick up the camera and try to finish the last vital
parts of the shoot before we get out of here on a flight to
Moscow. Donoghue, you are a tough bastard. We will
book tonight's flight to Moscow and see how much more
we can get done.*

(JOURNAL 1993)

I have seen camera crews fall apart, turn around and run, even
quit in the face of great stress or danger, but this did not happen
in Semipalatinsk. Mark completed the film work. Phil made it to
Moscow, where a doctor pronounced that it was the worst
mauling by a dog he had seen, that Phil was lucky to be alive and
was still in a very serious condition. They unpicked the stitches,
cleaned the wound again and gave him a massive needle for
rabies, another jab to prevent tetanus and, for good measure, one
more for hepatitis. There was more treatment in London and then
extensive surgery in Sydney where they had to graft skin from
Phil's leg to patch up his arm. He did not complain or seek
compensation from the network for this injury, because this
prince of his profession believed that the story of what had
happened to the Kazakhs was of far more importance.

The chamber of horror we entered on our last day in
Semipalatinsk contained the strongest proof of all, long hidden
from the world, of the madness let loose in this place. After
heated argument with the Russian colonel and more persuasive
appeals by Dr Gusiv of the Radiation Institute, we were given
access to a locked military laboratory documenting the mutations
caused by the radiation. For decades the Russian scientists had
been testing blood, studying leukaemias and cancers and noting
birth defects, blindness, deafness and retardation. There were
reports on hundreds of cases of people who had died of radiation
illnesses and some like Berik who still lived and suffered.

There was worse to come and I warned viewers when we began filming. Turn away if you must.

The glass cabinets held shocking sights, almost too gruesome for words. The wooden shelves were lined with bottles preserving the legacy of forty years of nuclear testing. We could hardly believe what we were seeing. Floating like dolls in a clear liquid hideously deformed foetuses and stillborn infants screamed silently of the chromosome damage caused by radiation. Staring at us from a large jar was the single eye of a Cyclops child. In the centre of the room, almost dancing in the light, was a mermaid baby, a child with no legs but a fish-like tail. The chamber held more jars than I could count.

CHAPTER NINE

I SPY ... A BIG LIE

*I travel across the snow-covered Russian countryside on
the Moscow Express, full of sad souls going nowhere fast
as the communist world collapses before their eyes. The
old Russian Empire is breaking up and first Gorbachev
and now Yeltsin are powerless to stop it. After seventy-
five years it is clear to almost everybody here that only
terror, violence and suppression of freedom have
preserved the totalitarian state. When I reach the* dacha *of
George Blake, even the British master spy is forced to
admit that communism is a miserable failure.*

(JOURNAL 1992)

George Blake, the British double agent, has lived a life
straight out of a James Bond novel. For almost a decade
he was a KGB spy, betraying his family, his country and
democracy itself, while working as an officer in Her Majesty's
Secret Service. As Blake came skiing towards me with his Russian
wife, Ida, he looked remarkably fit for a man of sixty-nine ... or
was I confusing the bearded spy with Sean Connery in the Bond
films? The real life of spies is much less romantic, full of treachery
and deceit. In the world of espionage, the truth is hidden by a
prism of Big Lies.

The Blake I met at a snowbound *dacha* in Russia was a pleasant
man who said that he had no reason to lie anymore because the

great communist experiment had failed in the Soviet Union. It is possible, of course, that some of the intriguing revelations he made were complete fabrications, under instruction from his masters of the previous thirty years. In the same month that I was meeting Blake, January 1992, I was also exploiting the chaos in the Soviet Union to rendezvous with former KGB chiefs and other spies who were ready to discuss some of the darkest secrets of the communist era. It was difficult to fully trust anyone in Russia at that time. As I listened to George Blake's incredible story of three decades exiled in Moscow, I kept reminding myself that this was one of the most infamous traitors of my lifetime, who, according to a judge in Britain, had 'undone most of the work of British intelligence since the war'.

When Blake was unmasked in 1961 and convicted of espionage, the judge sentenced him to forty-two years in prison. At the time it was the longest sentence in modern British history and thoroughly deserved, the judge said, because Blake had betrayed about forty British secret agents. Not so, said the spy, it was more like several hundred that he outed and he had no regrets. Many British intelligence analysts have claimed that some of those exposed by Blake were assassinated, including an agent who was thrown into a blazing furnace. Poker-faced, Blake said that there was no evidence that any of those he had named had been executed. Imprisonment to him was just part of the spy game. The double agent still was very proud of his most famous exploits for the KGB.

In 1953 during the early years of the Cold War, British and American intelligence agencies dug a tunnel from West Berlin into East Berlin to tap telephone lines running to Moscow. It was the kind of daring plan, brilliantly executed, that led the western spies to believe that they had a jump on every move the Russians made. George Blake, however, was stationed in West Berlin and tipped off the KGB about the tunnel. This allowed the Russians and their East German allies to feed three years of useless and erroneous information to the western sleuths. In another brazen stunt, Blake introduced the British secret agents to a Russian economist named Boris who agreed to spy for the west. In fact, Boris was a KGB man who did more damage to western intelligence.

Over the days I spent with Blake out in the countryside and in the old KGB 'safehouse' he occupied in Moscow, it struck me that perhaps his most revealing betrayal was not of one of his fellow spies but of his first wife. This Englishwoman whom he always professed to love bore him two children but was ignorant of his secret life. Spies commonly argue that they lie to their partners to protect them, but the fact is their double life constantly risks exposure and shame for the entire family, not to mention prison or assassination for the spy. The partners, even the children, usually are pawns in the spy game. If the double agent finally crosses to the other side, inevitably he or she is provided with a 'companion'. Blake's Russian wife, Ida, seemed genuinely fond of the famous traitor she had married. They had a son in Moscow. About twenty-five years after fleeing England Blake caught up with his two grown English sons, one born while he was in prison. Blake claimed that while his sons did not approve of his treachery they understood that he sincerely believed his choice was noble. I told him that seemed hard to believe when the communist world he had abandoned his family for was in chaos. Blake can never leave Russia to spend time elsewhere with his British sons without risking going back to the prison where he pulled off a sensational escape in 1966.

After serving less than six years of his long sentence, Blake masterminded a jail break without a shot being fired. An Irishman and two British friends had smuggled a walkie-talkie to him in prison and on a dark, rainy night he hid in a niche of the outside wall of the main block. The Irishman threw a rope ladder over the wall and Blake climbed it slowly, quietly and then dropped to freedom. He spent nine hours hidden inside the false compartment of a camper van as the British couple and their two young children drove from London and crossed the English Channel by ferry. They made their way to Berlin where Blake walked into the arms of the East German police.

Blake insisted that he had no help from the Russians to pull off one of the most daring prison escapes in British history, arguing that if the bust had gone terribly wrong it would have been an international embarrassment for the communists. Nonetheless, the master spy turned up in Moscow just in time for the celebrations of the fiftieth anniversary of the October Revolution. In Red Square the British traitor was hailed as a Russian hero.

It was another traitor, Donald MacLean, who arranged Blake's first job above ground in Moscow, as a specialist on the conflicts in the Middle East and Persian Gulf. Keen to see how defectors ended up in the workers' paradise, I visited Blake's office at the Institute for World Economic and International Affairs. MacLean's portrait was in pride of place above Blake's desk. They were kindred spirits, simple in their tastes and passionate in their belief in the communist ideal.

Blake's British employers claim that he crossed over not for love of communism but love of money. Blake does not deny that his conversion occurred around 1950, after the outbreak of the Korean War, and after he had been captured by the North Koreans while working for the British in South Korea. The British version of events is that he negotiated with the communists for various privileges to make his imprisonment more tolerable and so became a prime target of the Russians. Blake says it was the great drama of the times, the clash between east and west, communism and capitalism, that focused his mind on the ideal of a classless society with equality and justice for everybody. While in prison he read Marx's *Das Kapital* and Lenin's *The State and the Revolution*. Curiously, he believed that it was his sense of Christianity that led him towards communism, a kind of idealism not unlike his boyhood desire to be a minister in the Dutch church. Blake was born in Rotterdam to a Dutch mother and Turkish father and his early rootlessness may have contributed to him betraying the country of his citizenship. As I watched him sipping tea from his delicate porcelain cup, beard neatly trimmed, listening to the BBC World Service on radio, he still seemed distinctly British in some ways, with only a few Russian friends.

The biggest jolt to Blake and other British defectors like Donald MacLean and Kim Philby was discovering that communism was a variation of prison. Philby was a secretive man who kept to himself in Moscow, but Blake said they shared a loathing for the Soviet restriction on the movement of citizens. To force people into the straitjacket of socialism, to intimidate them with violence, was the Soviet state's biggest mistake, for it was contradictory to the idea of equality.

The exile took me to his favourite places in Moscow, walking through the snow-covered grounds of the monasteries that now were museums to the old mysterious Russia, a country with soul, unlike the crushing conformity of the totalitarian state. I asked him why he believed the walls of communism had come crashing down so quickly. It was Russia's 'Vietnam', he said, the unmitigated disaster of the Soviet invasion of Afghanistan that undermined the tolerance of the Russian people for the use of force against the Soviet Union's client states. When the Berlin Wall was being torn down, Gorbachev recognised that Russians would not allow the Red Army to intervene as it surely would have in the years of Brezhnev. At home everyone knew that the Soviet state had not delivered prosperity. The economy was in a constant state of crisis. The lines for basic food items were growing and people were bitterly disillusioned. Everyone agreed that communism was not working.

Blake said that taking away private property and putting ownership of everything in the hands of the state had not changed the mentality of the people. He had not found a New Man or New Woman in the communist world, only bickering Russians who argued over their worldly goods when they divorced just as people did in the west. He admitted that people needed the incentive of private enterprise to build an economy as efficient as those in western countries. It did not seem to me that there was much of his communist theory left to cling to, but Blake said he blamed the failure of the leadership and the disappointing greed in the hearts of most people. It was propaganda to portray the Soviet Union as a workers' paradise, he said, for the classes of power were never dismantled. The state did not recognise the dignity of all people, but rather had become a mindless, inefficient bureaucracy, increasingly more powerful but unable to deliver bread, milk or heat in this bitterly cold winter. There was a great melancholy surrounding Blake because the famous double agent still desperately clung to his belief that some day, maybe in a thousand years, the world would experiment again with socialism and perhaps get it right.

THE SPY

He betrayed his country
for the belief in an ideal,
and when he crossed over
he admitted it was an illusion,
but who can say
the spy is true to his heart,
when he has betrayed the woman
he said he loved,
perhaps he also lies to himself.

(JOURNAL 1992)

As I climbed the stairs of the old KGB headquarters in Moscow I noticed a steel net strung across the stairwell. It was intended to stop screaming prisoners from attempting suicide. I turned down a dimly lit corridor and my KGB escort pointed to a cell where Gary Francis Powers, the American U-2 pilot, had been held and interrogated for over three months after being shot down over Siberia in 1960.

'Were other captured American pilots, those shot down in Vietnam, also questioned here?' I asked.

'It is possible,' the KGB man said. 'In the USSR anything is possible.'

In late 1991 and early 1992 as the old order symbolised by the KGB was falling apart in the Soviet Union, I was part of a small team of investigative journalists who exposed one of the most tragic Big Lies since the end of the Vietnam War. President Richard Nixon's insistence in April 1973 that there were no American servicemen left alive in Indochina after the end of the war was an unforgivable lie, and worse, the United States had considerable intelligence indicating that certain American pilots secretly had been handed over to the Russians.

I worked on this world scoop that made front-page news in the *New York Times* and other newspapers, as well as leading to highly dramatic testimony in the American Congress, with several of the most determined journalists I ever teamed up with, including my friend of almost thirty years, the American documentary filmmaker Ted Landreth, and John Little, the Australian journalist and author. Landreth had uncovered new high-level intelligence sources with extraordinary information about the fate of some of the 2267 Americans still officially listed as Missing in Action (MIA) in 1991.

Looking for MIAs had always seemed like looking for ghosts until I heard Jerry Mooney tell us about the 'voices' he had heard. An electronic eavesdropping specialist with America's top-secret National Security Agency (NSA), he had been stationed in Okinawa, Japan, and in Thailand, monitoring Vietnamese radio transmissions. Mooney, a highly decorated specialist, had managed to crack the enemy code. What he heard was that the Vietnamese were flying captured Americans to areas where Soviet 'advisers' were stationed and, even more startling, that the Russians were transporting some of the Americans to the Soviet Union. Terry Minarcin, an eighteen-year veteran of the NSA, also had intercepted coded messages about American pilots. Their conclusion was that between fifty and seventy-five of these POWs had survived interrogation and been flown to the Soviet Union. Both of these intelligence experts had impeccable service records and risked harassment or worse from American authorities, but they could no longer live with their own silence on what they described as their government's abandonment of its fighting men. After two decades of subterfuge and intrigue, they had the chance to bring out the truth about the MIAs.

If you are inclined to see the debate over the fate of the MIAs as an endless series of cruel hoaxes and myth-making by obsessive American servicemen, you must examine the historical evidence from the aftermath of the wars of our century. Men were captured, brutally interrogated, sometimes forced into collaboration with the enemy and at other times imprisoned long after the wars had ended. Spies were traded secretly. Men with war-making powers and vital technological knowledge were snatched by the victorious side. Great numbers of ordinary footsoldiers were virtually enslaved and forced into hard labour, building roads and railways for their captors. To understand the context of the American MIAs after the Vietnam War, remember that France got back only about one-third of the POWs it claimed were in the hands of the Vietnamese after the 1946–54 Indochina War. Even after the Vietnamese said they had returned everyone, many French POWs came home several years later. Amid great embarrassment the Frenchmen were branded as 'collaborators' by their government, but one of the POWs, denied his military pension, successfully sued the government of France. He proved that he and many others were held by the Vietnamese as genuine prisoners and cruelly used as bargaining chips until France made secret payments, almost US$30 million a year. This was ransom disguised as aid, such as payments to maintain French military graves on Vietnamese soil.

In the Soviet Union our team drew on wide-ranging sources and found evidence from some of the most senior Soviet officials indicating that Americans had been interrogated in Vietnam by the Russians and then flown to the USSR. George Blake told me in the kitchen of his Moscow apartment that Americans had been 'grilled' by the Russians after the Korean War, and he knew of attempts to obtain high-tech information from American flyers after the Vietnam War as well. Blake would not go into detail about what had happened to the Americans but suggested that men were 'turned' all the time and usually given a new identity, female companionship and a place to work where they would not be conspicuous as foreigners. Blake seemed a bit puzzled that I found this a shocking disclosure and said it was a common occurrence in the world of espionage.

It also became clear in the Soviet Union why the Russians had wanted to interrogate certain American flyers. They were not interested in pilots, it seemed, unless they had astronaut training or some other specialist knowledge. The Russians wanted the back-of-the-plane men, the electronic warfare officers who were successfully using radar-jamming technology to penetrate the SA2 (SAM) missile defence systems in Vietnam. The top-secret American aircraft such as the RB-47, the F-4 'Wild Weasel' and the F-111 were carving up the very system that protected the Soviet Union, to the extent that the Russians felt vulnerable to a

NATO attack. Jerry Mooney calculated that more than fifty of the Americans transported to the Soviet Union had expertise in electronic warfare.

In Moscow, as usual, we were shadowed everywhere and so any Russian who agreed to be interviewed before our *60 Minutes* cameras was taking a considerable risk. Yuri Pankov, a courageous young Russian journalist who had come to prominence during the democracy movement, was warned by the KGB that by helping our investigation he was breaking Russian state security laws. Late at night, away from our hotel rooms, we held strategy sessions, Landreth, Little, Pankov and I, trying to arrange meetings with the key Soviet military men who had handled the MIAs.

As we filmed in a wooded area outside Moscow, the KGB had an agent standing in the trees videotaping us. If it had been possible for them to detect the conversation they would have heard the first brave Russian to speak up about his country's real war in Vietnam, a secret contest between the superpowers over supremacy in missile systems and electronic warfare.

Pavel Ponomaryov, a former Soviet air force navigator, showed us his log books for more than one hundred and twenty secret missions in Indochina. His crew had dressed in civilian uniforms and flown unmarked transport planes. They were not only carrying rice (as they told the Soviet people) but North Vietnamese troops, munitions and captured American flyers. Pavel's plane had transported two of the Americans from the Tchepon base in Laos to Vinh, North Vietnam, where he said that they had been secretly interrogated by a KGB agent named Gorlanov. He also had seen another captured American pilot on a later occasion. Incredibly, this had happened in 1962, in the early years of the Vietnam War and had continued, he believed, into the 1970s. In the context of the Cuban Missile Crisis, America's U-2 spy flights and the escalating nuclear arms race, the superpowers were using Vietnam as a duelling ground.

Even before we arrived in the Soviet Union there had been several indications from high-level American officials that Washington had been pushing its Big Lie about the MIAs ever since Nixon was in the White House. The head of the Pentagon's own MIA investigation team, Colonel Millard Peck, who had fought in Vietnam, resigned in disgust early in 1991, suggesting that important information was being withheld. The former head of the American Defense Intelligence Agency, General Eugene Tighe, testified publicly that he believed that Americans had been left behind and that he had seen intelligence as late as 1986 indicating some may still have been alive. In secret testimony before a Congressional investigation, a North Vietnamese defector confirmed that the Russians had been interrogating captured flyers in Hanoi.

Our challenge was to find top-level confirmation of this in the crumbling Soviet Union without being arrested or thrown out of the country. Our protection was the chaos in the country and the deep divisions within the old Soviet power structure, allowing us unprecedented access to senior officials.

While Mikhail Gorbachev always denied any knowledge of American MIAs in the Soviet Union, senior Russian officials who had allied themselves to the democracy movement were rifling the KGB files and coming forward with some extraordinary claims. General Oleg Kalugin, a former Chief of KGB Counter-Intelligence, told me that he had supervised the KGB interrogation of captured Americans *after* the end of the Vietnam War. As late as 1978, many years after the Vietnamese had claimed that all American POWs had been sent home, General Kalugin's men were questioning fifteen Americans in Hanoi. It was clear that General Kalugin, like then president Boris Yeltsin, was anxious to discredit the old guard and especially Mikhail Gorbachev who remained the most respected Russian in the west. I kept factoring in the possibility that perhaps some of this was a Yeltsin-backed disinformation program. During two conversations with General Kalugin he was noticeably nervous when I asked my most pointed questions about the fate of Americans brought to the Soviet Union. He would not, or could not, say what had become of the men.

To try to confuse the Russian spooks a bit, we changed our tactics and instead of travelling to meet the military men we wanted to interview, we flew them to our safe locations. A Soviet air force colonel told us that he had been given orders in Vietnam to 'flak trap' the most sophisticated American aircraft, to try to gain access to their radar-jamming technology and the electronic warfare operators. Jerry Mooney confirmed that this technique had been mastered by the North Vietnamese anti-aircraft batteries. Russian experts helped the Vietnamese draw in the American planes by directing heavy anti-aircraft guns around the fringes, until lighter guns could target and bring down the aircraft without destroying them. The Vietnamese and Russians have a great number of photographs displaying their success.

A KGB colonel (who would not allow us to identify him) claimed that he had interrogated captured Americans at three secret locations along the Ho Chi Minh Trail. His most disturbing disclosure was that nine of these Americans had had their throats cut by the Vietnamese because they refused to give up vital military information to the Russians. This may explain why none of the 592 American POWs who came home at the end of the Vietnam War had been interrogated by the KGB. If the few Americans selected for special questioning by the Russians did not crack, they were executed. America's own intelligence specialists, including Jerry Mooney's NSA team, had warned the White House that Americans were being executed in this fashion. Mooney said that he and others were ordered not to alert the American combat teams who still were flying missions over North Vietnam. The men went off to war without being told that they could fall into the hands of the Russians and face the risk of execution.

After my first *60 Minutes* report on the Russian–MIA connection made headlines around the world, it was screened on Soviet television, an extremely unusual event. It again suggested to me that President Yeltsin was exploiting these disclosures to undermine Gorbachev, and what happened next confirmed those suspicions. In my first report, I floated the suggestion to General Kalugin that he show his sincerity about moving forward from the dark days of the Cold War by agreeing to testify before the American Congress. Washington sent an invitation and General Kalugin flew there, answering questions from the American politicans and explaining how he had been given his pick of captured flyers to interrogate. Again, he gave no information about the ultimate fate of these men.

Back home in Sydney, I was awoken early one morning by a telephone call from the American billionaire and presidential candidate, Ross Perot, who doggedly had kept searching for definitive proof of the fate of the MIAs. He congratulated me and my team of Landreth, Little and Pankov for bringing to light the strongest evidence the public had seen of the shameful conduct of the great powers. He agreed that Washington, Hanoi and Moscow were all part of the Big Lie. Perot said our investigation was 'the single biggest break in ending a twenty-year mystery'. He offered any assistance we needed to find Americans possibly still alive in Vietnam or the Soviet Union. I told him that we had found no proof that any of those captured were still alive, but there were strong indications that they had been alive long after their own government said they were dead.

In June 1992, President Yeltsin dropped the bombshell I had been expecting when he gave perhaps the most dramatic speech of his life before the United States Congress. As President George Bush nodded in agreement, Yeltsin said it was time to disclose some of the darkest secrets of the Cold War. He revealed that the Kremlin secretly had given orders for the downing of a South Korean passenger airliner in Soviet airspace in 1983 when 263 people were killed. The old Soviet leadership was fully responsible for this tragedy. There was loud applause in the Congress, but then a hush. There also were secret files, Yeltsin claimed, that clearly showed that Americans had been captured in Vietnam and brought to the Soviet Union.

'Our archives have confirmed that some of them were transferred to the territory of the former USSR and were kept in labour camps,' Yeltsin said. 'We do not have complete data and can only surmise that some of them may still be alive.' The KGB archives also indicated that '2800 captured Americans had remained in the Soviet Union after World War I and World War II'. Yeltsin also claimed that twelve American pilots on spy flights had been shot down in the 1950s and imprisoned in labour camps or psychiatric clinics.

It is possible that President Yeltsin was fabricating his part of the MIA story as a ploy to persuade some reluctant American congressmen to approve billions of dollars in desperately needed economic aid. If that were true his entire speech to the Americans would be an incredible slander of his countrymen. The momentum of Yeltsin's disclosures soon produced more evidence, even from the American side. In September 1992, two of the most senior officials in the Nixon Administration admitted publicly that Americans probably had been left behind at the end of the Vietnam War. James Schlesinger, former CIA director, said there was a 'high probability' that men were left in Laos and a 'medium probability' that some were held in Vietnam. The former American defense secretary Melvin Laird said that there was clear intelligence indicating that at least twenty Americans were still being held in Laos when he left his job in 1973.

One of the heartening calls I received after these film reports were shown around the world was from the New York columnist Sydney Schanberg, who was the real-life inspiration for the journalist character in the film *The Killing Fields*. Schanberg had deep sympathy for the military men who were used by their governments and then abandoned when the course of the war changed. He praised our effort to uncover the Russian connection. I also was contacted by a Californian, Bruce Brown, whose father was a F-111A bomber pilot, downed in 1972, captured alive according to the Pentagon, but never seen again. The son now believed his father, Lieutenant Colonel Bob Brown, was a prize catch for the Russians.

'My dad had three things that the Russians wanted. He had been a project scientist for the US anti-ballistic missile program. He had knowledge that could update their space program as he had worked on the Mercury and Gemini space missions. He also was flying in the most advanced combat aircraft of that time, the F-111A, which we were told by the Pentagon was brought down remarkably intact. The Vietnamese had him alive and I really think it would be ridiculous for the Russians not to take him.'

As I read Bruce Brown's anguished letter, I thought of my father, the airman, and his father, the footsoldier. Who goes looking for these men if they are captured? Who cares when the war is over? It is their families and their comrades in arms who are left with the agony. Despite President Yeltsin's disclosures, neither he nor his successor has provided any names or further details about the whereabouts of the missing men. After so much American secrecy I am not expecting the Pentagon to tell us all it knows. The Cold War may be over but the US government still has about seven million classified documents. World War I troop movements are still classified. Why would the government want to release highly sensitive MIA intelligence when so many weapons systems are involved and when such evidence would be final proof of a shameful betrayal of those fighting men?

Searching for the MIAs in the far-flung corners of the Russian Empire is a daunting task. Anyone who survived the isolation of the gulag is likely to be as mentally and physically shattered as the few who did come home from imprisonment after the Korean War. In George Blake's view, any captured American still alive today most likely has been 'turned' into a collaborator. If they were interrogated by the Russians and did not crack they were killed so that they would never reveal the presence of the KGB squads. If they clung to life by revealing anything useful to the Russians, they were indeed 'broken' men who could not return to the west. A Red Army major told us that there were many foreigners comfortably settled with Russian wives and children, just like the British master spy, George Blake.

CHAPTER TEN

GIVING PEACE A CHANCE

*In the American west, I toured the 'Valley of the Nukes'
where intercontinental ballistic missiles capped by nuclear
warheads were poised for action. In an underground bunker
designed to withstand nuclear attack by the enemy, two
American air force officers were on the doomsday watch.
Each had a key and they had to be turned together to fire
the missile. Each also had a .38 calibre revolver strapped to
his hip with orders to shoot if the other man went MAD!
I guess you would call this Mutually Assured Destruction!*

(JOURNAL 1975)

Civilisation has taken some of its boldest steps because someone, a man or a woman, had a conviction powerful enough to challenge the conventional wisdom. Visit Thomas Jefferson's magnificent home, 'Monticello' in Virginia, and you see the inventiveness of the mind that inspired America's Declaration of Independence. He was an architect, musician, man of letters, farmer and statesman. All of these talents are displayed in the splendour of Jefferson's estate. But at the other end of the scale of grandeur, the American philosopher Henry Thoreau chose the simplicity of Walden Pond for his meditations on political morality. It was from this rich American tradition of aligning life with conscience, challenging the state and demonstrating civil disobedience that a remarkable modern dissident was born.

Philip Berrigan refused to accept poverty, violence and especially nuclear war. He also refused to accept the orders of his Church. Berrigan was a Catholic priest and when he married a nun, Elizabeth McAlister, they were excommunicated. This humiliation pales by comparison to the suffering they endured in prison, the separation from their young children and a life of poverty as they pursued their highest ideals. This meant nothing less than trying to stop the Vietnam War and the use of nuclear weapons in that conflict.

A belief in peace and social justice ran deep in the Berrigan family. Philip's brother Daniel joined the Jesuit Order, and through his books, drama, poetry and public protest became one of the most inspiring leaders of the anti-war movement. Father Philip Berrigan chose the Society of Saint Joseph, working on the streets among poor blacks in Baltimore on America's eastern shore. The first of several dozen times he was arrested he was demonstrating against the unfair exploitation of blacks.

'At one point in the late '60s, about a third of the American combat troops in Southeast Asia were black,' Berrigan said when I caught up with him in between his visits to jail. 'This was simply because of the economic pressure on them to get combat pay, to get "jump pay", in order to help their families. There was a disproportionate number of blacks forced to fight for this country and its very vague and uncertain interests in Southeast Asia.'

Like Henry Thoreau, Philip and Daniel Berrigan believed that if you did not like the war machine, you did not pay your taxes. They were the first American priests to actively protest against the Vietnam War and they shared a conviction that one must be prepared to go to jail for one's beliefs. The Berrigans studied Mahatma Gandhi's non-violent tactics in India's campaign for independence and also drew heavily on Martin Luther King's strategy in the American civil rights movement.

'We have one of the strongest traditions of non-violence of any people in the world,' Berrigan told me. 'Paradoxically, on one side we are a very violent people and on the other hand we have this rich tradition of non-violent resistance to the state, to slavery, to militarism and corporate power.'

The American anti-war effort mainly involved enormous marches through the streets, people power that sometimes turned ugly and ended in violent clashes with the police. The Berrigans pleaded for non-violent protest, but they also sharpened the political message by adding symbolism befitting the United States' superpower status. They would use a hammer to tap dents in the nose-cone of a warplane or spill red paint on the steps of the Pentagon before condemning the contingency plans that were being made for the use of tactical nuclear weapons in Vietnam.

'Our high command contemplated using nuclear weapons in Vietnam several times. There was one instance in 1969. Back in the mid '60s there was another when we were besieged south of the DMZ [Demilitarised Zone],' Berrigan told me.

His most provocative protest, probably the most important single anti-war action in the United States, was using napalm to burn files taken from a military draft office in Catonsville, Maryland, in 1968. The destruction of the draft records inspired thousands of young men to resist the call-up to an unjust war. Berrigan paid the price by serving over three years in jail, but it was there that he was visited by the woman who would change his life.

From the age of twenty, Elizabeth McAlister had been part of a Catholic religious community. When she followed her conscience onto the same path as Berrigan, the Church did not approve of her behaviour on the personal or political front. Inspired by her activist friend, Sister Elizabeth started going to jail for her personal beliefs. She was stripped of her nun's habit after her marriage to Philip in 1973 made public a private commitment they had shared since meeting in prison in 1969.

'My sole reason for leaving the Sacred Heart community was that it would not accept married people,' said Elizabeth, watching their young boy and girl playing on the floor of their Baltimore home. 'I really had hoped that some day the Church might see the light.'

'I remember asking Liz,' said Philip, '"Have you ever felt that our relationship had any elements of evil about it?" And she said, "No, not at all." I had not felt that either and I wondered why, because everything in my education would say that I should be feeling guilty. We found out that mandatory celibacy actually had no New Testament basis at all. It was not introduced until about the fifth century.'

'I think I would have had to leave the nuns within a short time anyway,' added Elizabeth, 'because of my growing sense of what was required of every individual in any kind of community. It was this vision of non-violent resistance, opposition to war and nuclear weapons. I believed that we all had to stand up against the state to expose it. There was no support for that in my religious order.'

The Berrigans had come to the realisation that blind loyalty to the Church was the same as blind loyalty to the state. To resist the epidemic of violence that threatened the world, every individual had to find the strength of conviction to think clearly, to act honestly and, if necessary, independently.

Philip Berrigan's handsome, chiselled face became more serious as we discussed his growing differences with the institution of the Church. I told him how I had seen worker-priests enduring terrible poverty and even going to jail for trying to protect indigenous people from brutal governments. But I also had been horrified by the missionary madness that I had encountered in many places. It seemed to me that Christianity as a worldwide movement had lost its moral authority.

'People like ourselves look upon the Church now with its vast power, property holdings and investments and its silence towards the state, a silence that is meant to guarantee all sorts of advantages, and we say that this inner corruption is the basis of our downfall.'

'The Church must understand that it has a responsibility, that it's not only the political dimensions of opposing the war, it's the personal dimension too,' said Elizabeth. 'If we are talking about Christianity, the Church and its members must engage in a process of disarming themselves. We all must engage in a real effort to control or redirect what it is in us that is violent. This resistance must be ongoing on the personal and the public front.'

Here were a man and a woman who decided that each one of us can step outside the matrix of self-interest, of Church, of state, of corporate life and begin to question our destiny. At present it appeared that we were still on the path to the insanity of violence. If human beings were going to stop destroying human beings, then every thinking man and woman had to take action on a personal level. Philip and Elizabeth had decided not to be part of a MAD world. They wanted to change it. I found their intellectual clarity, their strength of conviction and personal action wonderfully inspiring.

In April 1972, Philip and Elizabeth were among seven people indicted in Harrisburg, Pennsylvania, for allegedly trying to influence America's Vietnam War policy with a bizarre plot to kidnap Dr Henry Kissinger and hold him for ransom. They also were accused of planning to blow up heating tunnels in government buildings in the style of the French Resistance. This did not sound like the Berrigans' non-violent civil disobedience. It looked more like another of the Nixon Administration's dirty tricks, another desperate attempt to crush the great conscience of the anti-war movement. Daniel Ellsberg, the man who leaked the Pentagon Papers in 1971 revealing American government deception over policy in Vietnam, spoke up in the Berrigans' defence, saying that all of the defendants (known as the 'Harrisburg Seven') had been framed. The Berrigans to this day deny that their protest ever turned to violence because that was the whole point of their activism.

'Within this war craze,' said Philip, 'we can see the real nature of violence. War is the summit of violence, fed by all other violence. We see a connection between the violence of American capital punishment and the bomb. Think about it. Do we accept human beings destroying human beings? When it comes to the inequality of women and violence against women, we know that war is the ultimate male adventure, the summit macho enterprise. It also happens to be the most economically profitable of all male enterprises.'

How profitable was the personal and political protest that the Berrigans had dedicated their lives to? How effective was the anti-war movement throughout the Vietnam War? While some members of my generation believe that they changed the world, Philip Berrigan was realistic and far more modest.

'We might have helped shorten the war somewhat, and in addition we might have had something to do with seeing that tactical nuclear weapons were not used in Vietnam. I'd let it go at that. I don't claim that we unseated Johnson in 1968. I don't claim that we forced the American government to quit Vietnam. The Vietnamese did most of that. The American peace movement exerted pressure and this was something we were morally bound to do.'

After surveying the march of history, from the day a caveman picked up a club in anger to the targeting of enough nuclear missiles to destroy the world, it is possible to conclude that violence is inescapable, an intrinsic part of our evolutionary journey. What can we do when most men appear to believe that war is our destiny, part of our genetic code? The Berrigans reply that for civilisation to advance we have to become truly civilised. Intelligent men and women have no alternative other than to individually resist this code of violence, no matter how strongly it pulses in our veins.

'Whatever our history might dictate to us we have to turn from this path if we are to survive on this planet, and we believe in the rationality of people,' Philip said, smiling. 'I remember a remark by U Thant when he was Secretary-General of the United Nations during the Vietnam War. He insisted over and over again that if the American people knew what was happening in Vietnam, Laos and Cambodia — and we didn't know too much at that point — then the people would stop the war. I have a great belief in people. If they know the truth and realise the evil and injustice and exploitation, then they will take some action. You can make choices against this. You don't have to bend your neck to this. You can become a human being. The question is, do you want to?'

> Fly with me
> to places
> no one has seen,
> to heights
> no man or woman
> has even dreamed.

                                                          (JOURNAL 1982)

To Richard Milhous Nixon, the anti-war movement was as much the enemy as the Viet Cong. He apparently despised Philip Berrigan more than Ho Chi Minh. For a man with a brilliant understanding of most of the world, President Nixon had a wretched appreciation of what made America a great society. The dissident voices, the questioners of the status quo, were at least as important as any rugged individualist in making Americans the most outstanding problem-solvers in the world. This president's paranoia at home consumed any prospect of greatness. Nixon certainly had delusions of grandeur. He spoke to his key aides of a 'revolution in foreign policy' and seriously anticipated that his secret tape-recordings of White House conversations would establish the Age of Nixon in world history.

You cannot blame Nixon or his Secretary of State, Dr Henry Kissinger, for getting Americans and Australians into the Vietnam War. But you can hold them accountable for the terms of defeat. The Nixon Administration's last major orders in the war were to bomb Hanoi and mine Haiphong Harbour. According to the House Speaker, Congressman Tip O'Neill, former president Lyndon Johnson had ruled out such tactics because he thought there was a genuine risk they could lead to World War III. Nixon, a deeply cynical man with no clear code of moral values, did not hesitate to inflict massive suffering on the Vietnamese and the loss of civilian life clearly was not justified.

Vietnam taught the Pentagon that it was pointless pursuing a war that the American public could not stomach. The protests did not halt the war and arguably the violence was more devastating towards the end than in the beginning. But a decade of vigorous reporting, using powerful words and images, had undermined government propaganda and steadily informed Americans and Australians of the futility of the uncertain military strategy. This was the first televised war and the public grew weary, then sickened, by the suffering of the troops and the cruel bombing of civilians. When that grandfather of the American nation, the anchorman of the CBS evening news, Walter Cronkite, told the dismal truth about Vietnam, the anti-war movement breathed a sigh of relief. Nixon's response was to step up the war at home on his political enemies.

The burglary on 17 June 1972 at the Democratic Party headquarters inside that birthday cake of curvy concrete, the Watergate Hotel, was a Keystone Kops bungle by Nixon zealots. It had little immediate effect as President Nixon was re-elected to a second term in the White House, winning 60 per cent of the popular vote and 97 per cent of the electoral college vote. As a crime, the Watergate burglary was far less serious than the abuse of the civil rights of those who opposed the war. Nixon's covert intelligence operations targeted courageous individuals like Daniel Ellsberg, the defence analyst, who by leaking the Pentagon Papers to the *New York Times* probably did as much as any man to end the war. The Pentagon's own study revealed that the Gulf of Tonkin Resolution, which led to massive American involvement in Vietnam, had been drafted months before the attack on an American vessel, the official excuse for escalating the number of US forces. The Pentagon Papers also revealed that the Johnson Administration had been committing troops to Vietnam while telling Americans there were no long-range plans for the war. Daniel Ellsberg and Philip Berrigan, because they disclosed so many official lies about Vietnam, were at the top of Nixon's hate list. The president and his men were fond of 'light at the end of the tunnel' speeches about Vietnam, but Berrigan knew that even within the government, the Pentagon and the CIA, most recognised that the war was a disaster. Nixon had lied to the country, but only those like Berrigan and Ellsberg, brave enough to incur his wrath, had spoken up about the truth. By 1973, however, Berrigan's nemesis was in full retreat, not because of the military defeat in Vietnam but because the Watergate scandal exploded. The central event around which all of American life was spinning madly was the political implosion of the imperial president. This was the biggest political story of my lifetime, Richard Nixon's final tumultuous year in the White House.

The breathtaking drama of Watergate was watching the American Congress wrestle with its conscience over a president who clearly had obstructed justice in trying to cover up a crime. Vital evidence was destroyed including the infamous eighteen-and-a-half-minute gap in one of Nixon's tapes of his conversations in the Oval Office. Ironically, instead of establishing Nixon's place in history as one of the greatest American statesmen, the secret tapes revealed a dangerous, delusional and vengeful president, and showed that his White House aides were involved in a staggering abuse of executive power, conspiring to use the CIA to impede the Watergate investigation.

By the 1990s, when America moved on to President Bill Clinton's scandalous affair with Monica Lewinsky, Congress was prepared to ignore or forgive personal lapses by the nation's leader, perjury included. By contrast, the impeachment proceedings against Nixon in 1973 were the greatest exercise of the democratic process in American history.

Ever since Lyndon Johnson had courted Australian support of American involvement in Vietnam, it had become increasingly important for us to have our own independent analysis of Washington policy. The ABC had three foreign correspondents covering America in the 1970s: Peter Barnett, Ray Martin and myself. We were all quite different but became friends for life. Barnett was a great wit, extremely popular in Washington and as much skilled diplomat as correspondent. Ray Martin, a talented young radio reporter, already was showing a populist touch, inspired by American journalists Pete Hamill and Jimmy Breslin. We were part of a new generation of Australian journalists fanning out around the world. Across the Atlantic in London were other sharp and energetic minds like Paul Lyneham and a kindred spirit, my great friend Roger Allebone. The contribution of this ABC generation was to give our country the first regular television coverage by Australian correspondents. We were reporting about a much wider world and about momentous events on our own terms, including an Australian view of the move to impeach the world's most powerful man.

To a foreign correspondent it was clear at a very early stage that unless Nixon resigned he was headed for impeachment. We did not know it at the time, but Watergate special prosecutor Leon Jaworski decided after his first six weeks of investigation that Americans had a criminal as president. When Jaworski's predecessor Archibald Cox had been stripped of his powers in

Nixon's famous 'Saturday Night Massacre' many people in Washington thought the appointment of the sixty-eight-year-old Texan conservative was a manoeuvre to save Tricky Dick. Instead, an honest and courageous man served justice well. The Democrats on the House Judiciary Committee also had to rise to the occasion, to establish the specific evidence that would convince a nation that their president was guilty of obstruction of justice, misuse of power, repeatedly abusing the constitutional rights of citizens and defying subpoenas. I felt disappointed that Congress did not agree to charge Nixon with illegally concealing the bombing of Cambodia. This seemed to continue a very old tradition of letting a president make war as he wished, despite the fact that such military actions constitutionally required approval by Congress.

Most Americans either loved or loathed Richard Nixon. As an Australian observer I was fascinated to see whether American politicians could fulfil the public's trust in them and rise to this momentous occasion by suspending their natural prejudices and judging Nixon fairly. Could a democracy arrive at justice when the man in the dock was the president, with so much power and tradition to support him? For those in Congress this was the ultimate test of personal and political principle. For a handful of magnificent Republicans and a few key conservative Democrats on the House Judiciary Committee who joined the majority to vote for impeachment, it was a long, gut-wrenching ordeal, one that left them drained and overwhelmingly sad. But in their commitment to the truth these men deservedly made history.

Watergate, close up, also was intriguing because it was the most critical test in my lifetime of the entire value system underpinning freedom of the press and the public's 'right to know'. In the beginning Nixon may have imagined he only had to worry about two young reporters, Bob Woodward and Carl Bernstein. But their tenacious investigation became almost a crusade at times by the *Washington Post*. Their editor, Ben Bradlee, guided and developed the coverage until everyone in the capital, and then the nation, slowly came to understand the truth.

The broadcasting networks also recognised their opportunity and responsibility, giving Americans daily information on the

Washington drama. We ABC reporters shared the CBS television studios in Washington, working alongside some of America's best and brightest journalists, including Eric Sevareid, Roger Mudd, Daniel Schorr and Dan Rather. These older men, who were in the fearless tradition of Edward R. Murrow, had far more influence on me than anyone back home.

I am mightily impressed with the integrity of Bill Moyers, whose thoughtful style of interviewing shows the importance of being a great listener. LBJ's old press secretary appears to respect other points of view, a mark of the man's intellect. How different to the grandstanding antics, theatricality and predictable aggression on Oz TV! Mike Wallace, on CBS 60 Minutes, possesses a sense of timing more often seen on a theatre stage, but that of course is how he began, as an actor. It seems American television journalism is being overtaken by showbusiness, to the dismay of strong newsmen like Walter Cronkite. Abe Rosenthal of the New York Times *is the journalist I most respect here, because he clearly sets the highest moral standards. He is like a conscience for his newspaper and for the rest of us. What a magnificent columnist, what a passion for freedom and truth. He has a concern for the dissidents in all of the world's gulags, including those here in America.*

(JOURNAL 1974)

During the Watergate hearings, John Lennon and Yoko Ono came to watch as the evidence mounted against Richard Nixon. They had good reason to view the president as 'old 666', Lennon's favourite nickname for Nixon, because he had authorised telephone taps and other surveillance on the former Beatle's every move. The Nixon Administration seemed determined to banish

Lennon from the United States by rejecting his application for permanent residence. The excuse given was a marijuana bust back in England in 1968, but the truth was that the grotesque FBI Director, J. Edgar Hoover, and old Tricky Dick himself feared that the youth idol who wanted to 'give peace a chance' was an anarchist. That all-American boy, Elvis Presley, had warned Nixon that Lennon was a real force for the 'anti-American spirit' building during the Vietnam War. After John and Yoko attended the Watergate hearings they slipped over to the embassy of South Vietnam to join one of the final demonstrations against the war. It was a struggle of ideals and values pitted against the awesome power of the presidency and the sheer momentum of the military in Vietnam.

'I am not a crook' sadly will be remembered far longer than anything else Nixon said about the Vietnam War, or about his grand designs for *rapprochement* with the Chinese and *détente* with the Russians. The Age of Nixon will be judged in terms of the damage he inflicted on his own citizens and on the office of the presidency itself. This was one of the saddest chapters of American political history, but also one that defined its enduring strengths.

In August 1974 the American leader told his nation, 'I would have preferred to carry through to the finish, whatever the personal agony it would have involved.' But in truth he knew that after the historic vote by the House Judiciary Committee to impeach him, he did not have the votes in the Senate to survive. After five and a half years in the White House, Nixon was finished. 'Therefore I shall resign the presidency effective at noon tomorrow.'

On his last day in the White House, Nixon looked more haggard than usual. The man who had risen from the grocery store to the presidency to fulfil his American Dream had come to a particularly melancholy end. He was shaking and stumbling as he said goodbye to his staff in a speech full of pathos and denial.

Writing the words to go with the image of this shattered man giving the thumbs up just before his helicopter lifted off from the White House lawn, I sensed that I would never again report a political story so grand and tragic. It was a self-inflicted tragedy and among Richard Nixon's final words as president were some he should have heeded: 'Always remember, others may hate you, but those who hate you don't win unless you hate them, and then you destroy yourself.'

At the edge of the fields of Gettysburg, Pennsylvania, where 50 000 men fell in that bloodiest of American wars, three leaders stood wondering about the chances of peace in the Middle East. Egypt's President Anwar El Sadat and Israel's Prime Minister Menachem Begin had been invited by President Jimmy Carter to visit the Civil War battleground during the Camp David peace talks in 1978. It was exquisite to watch men of great vision learn from the march of war and then attempt to change history themselves.

Jimmy Carter, a former Governor of Georgia, was never viewed by Americans as a great statesman like Richard Nixon. Ironically, the blue-jeaned former peanut farmer from the small town of Plains was given a chance in the White House because in the wake of Watergate he clearly was an honest man. He was also one of the best read of American presidents, with a keen interest in history. Carter had visited Gettysburg a few months earlier with Shelby Foote, author of *The Civil War: A Narrative*, the finest history of that American conflict, and later one of the eloquent voices in the memorable television documentary series *The Civil War*. Now the American president seemed to be sending the long-warring Middle Eastern leaders a message. Coming from the south, where about one-quarter of the men had been killed or wounded in the Civil War, Carter could understand how much Arabs and Israelis had invested and lost in four devastating wars in twenty-five years. He told his guests that 600 000 Americans had died in the Civil War. The White House press secretary, Jody Powell, believed that the president was trying to remind Sadat and Begin of the consequences of political failure and to suggest that reconciliation was possible even between bitter enemies.

From the first charmed encounter between Carter and Sadat at the White House in 1977 there had been a rare chemistry, the kind of warmth and intellectual respect that held out some promise when Washington proposed peace talks. Many other world leaders pessimistically had concluded that the Middle East never would bury its bitter differences. Carter and Sadat shared a more positive outlook.

Urged by the American leader to show the Israelis that Egypt wanted peace, President Sadat responded magnificently. In a dramatic and courageous move, Sadat went to Jerusalem and stood before the enemies he had faced on the battlefield. He talked about ending their state of war. This was the kind of personal action and commitment to peace that indeed could change history. The symbolism was breathtaking and Sadat's oratory left an indelible mark on all who heard his strong, clear message. But throughout the years of war, six Israeli prime ministers had offered to go anywhere to meet any Arab leader willing to recognise Israel's right to exist. It was not surprising that it would take more than Sadat's courage to make progress towards a peace settlement.

Next it was President Carter who made a bold move. After just a year in the White House he set out on a whirlwind overseas trip to build support for his peace plans. I was the only Australian reporter on this magic carpet ride through nine countries in eight days. As well as filing stories for the daily radio and television programs, cameraman David Brill and I filmed a *Four Corners* documentary. We could sense that some dramatic history was happening before our eyes.

In Iran, where President Carter met the Shah, Mohammed Reza Pahlavi, we walked out into streets swarming with the Ayatollah Khomeini's revolutionaries. They were demonstrating against American support for the Shah and calling for his overthrow. The young men wore scarves tied around their heads, clenched their fists, chanted and hurled stones at government buildings and the American embassy. They looked as though they would walk into hell for their ayatollah. Although the American president was inside the palace making a toast to the Shah, it seemed to me that

Carter could count on little help from this old ally. The next time I saw the Shah he was in exile, swimming at a beach on Paradise Island in the Bahamas. In Saudi Arabia there was some support for Carter's attempt to create the conditions necessary for progress, but the Saudis were committed to an independent Palestinian state. It was becoming clear that despite the weariness with war in the Middle East, no one else seemed capable of going that extra mile for peace.

Once more the man from Plains who wanted to be a peacemaker surprised everyone. He ordered the presidential jet, Air Force One, to head for Egypt, down the ancient Nile to a rendezvous with Sadat. We landed in a great cloud of dust at a military outpost near the Aswan Dam. It was a risky meeting for Sadat, inviting the wrath of the many Arabs opposed to negotiations with Israel. But this Egyptian leader was deeply fatalistic and despite all of the costly battles he had fought in the desert, the deep mistrust and suspicion, Sadat sensed that there was a unique opportunity for peace. It was a question of whether these mortal men could rise to greatness.

As Carter and Sadat huddled in secret conversation in the middle of nowhere, we could see missile silos on the horizon, relics of a previous Middle Eastern war, a reminder of how much was at stake. This is what drove the American leader. The price of peace may have seemed great, the diplomacy was exhausting and certainly won little public support back home, but the constant risk of another clash between the two most powerful Middle Eastern rivals also meant the grave danger of a limited nuclear war. Carter had been fully briefed on the chances of such a catastrophe, and had been educated about this risk as a submariner in America's nuclear-age navy.

After this desert encounter, Carter came up with another clever piece of diplomacy, a carefully crafted statement indicating that a true peace must recognise the legitimate rights of the Palestinians. It may not sound like much now but the former naval engineer was thinking logically, building piece by piece the solid diplomatic foundation for his greatest accomplishment. Carter's *communiqué* also stated very firmly that there had to be withdrawal by Israel from the territory occupied during the Six Day War of 1967. Ever so slowly Carter was manoeuvring the greatest of enemies towards the negotiating table.

I had a problem of my own that night as there were no communications available at the military airstrip to get out my story. Just before Air Force One and our White House press plane lifted off again, I paid an Egyptian 'runner' to carry a quickly typed report to a telex office in the village of Aswan, forty-five kilometres down the road. Journalism certainly was different before everyone had laptop computers and satellite telephones.

Within a few months the White House press corps was reporting another breakthrough, the acceptance by Sadat and Begin of Carter's historic invitation to try to negotiate a framework for peace in face-to-face talks at Camp David.

The presidential retreat, just thirty minutes by helicopter from the White House, is perched amid the peaks of the Catoctin Mountains in Maryland. Camp David has been a place of solitude for American leaders since the time of Franklin D. Roosevelt. Patrolled by a special Marine unit, it is extremely secure — and it had to be, given the fears of a terrorist attack on either Begin or Sadat. Carter also wanted privacy to remove the warring parties from the scrutiny and pressures they faced in public. For thirteen days they negotiated with a stressful intensity. At one point Sadat was so frustrated that he asked for a helicopter to go home. But in the end reason triumphed. Begin, a courageous Israeli freedom fighter, and Sadat, who had lost so much at war with the Israelis, agreed that a treaty between their nations offered a good chance of ending some of the bloodshed. Egypt and Israel ended what was virtually a three-decade-long state of war.

Look at what followed, as it says much about humanity. Begin seized the opportunity to walk in Sadat's footsteps and was cheered in Cairo by tens of thousands of Egyptians determined to show the world that they preferred peace to war. Begin will be remembered in history as a peacemaker as well as a man who had

Photo by Paul Boocock

60 Minutes producer Andrew Haughton and me during the Eritrean war.

This Eritrean woman had just lost her baby because the famine had driven her to the edge of starvation and she did not have milk in her breast. We offered her food but were helpless.

After meeting Javier Blancher, aged eleven, in Nicaragua's civil war, I discovered there are hundreds of thousands of child combatants illegally sent into combat.

In the Indian lands of the American West, Frank Lloyd Wright called Canyon de Chelly in Arizona 'America's masterpiece'. It was built by the ancient Anazasi Indians.

Russell Means, leader of the militant American Indian Movement, took over the trading post at Wounded Knee to seek recognition of the slaughter that took place here in 1890.

Photo by Janet Eastman

Some of the most unforgettable 'conversations' I ever had were with these Stone Age Amazon Indians, living along the Cuminapanema River. The *potoro* worn through their lower lip is the tribe's totem. Inserted during childhood, it is then increased in size as they grow older. The Indians on the Cuminapanema were beautifully adapted to live in the rainforest, but not to survive the threat of disease introduced by white men.

Photo by Ben Crane

With British archeologist John Romer, I flew into the Austrian/Italian Alps to investigate the secrets of the 5300-year-old 'Iceman' who thawed from a glacier at this very spot.

At Qumran, on the West Bank, Romer and I examined the caves where the mysterious Dead Sea Scrolls were found by a Bedouin shepherd boy. They tell us much about the age of Jesus but there is no specific reference to Jesus the man.

Near Ulaanbataar, Mongolia, the descendants of Genghis Khan race their horses for thirty kilometres as a celebration of their warrior tradition.

Phil Donoghue's brilliant camerawork at the Indian shipwrecking yard at Alang in Gujarat won a Golden Tripod Award (ACS) for cinematography.

As an eighteen-year-old ABC foreign correspondent I was sent to Papua New Guinea, where I roamed the country far and wide. I loved these feathered warriors in the Highlands.

A hot-air balloon ride over the deserts of India.

I enjoy myself in most places around the world and Carnival, in Rio de Janeiro, will put a smile on anyone's face.

My true companion. With Kim at the Taj Mahal.

fought for his people's survival. The great Sadat, as he had predicted, tragically gave his life for peace. This is the way of our world: an extraordinary man with a vision of a new Middle East was cut down by an assassin's bullet in his own land. His lasting, unforgiving enemies were those within his own borders. Sadat seemed to recognise that and accepted his own death as the price of peace with Israel. Carter, instead of being applauded for his commitment to world peace and his brilliant success as a negotiator that few have matched, ultimately was ridiculed by many Americans. The *New York Times* and other American media scornfully attacked Carter for committing American aid to support the Camp David Agreement. How short-sighted and shallow, how ignorant of history, how unappreciative of how much all three of these great men had given to the process of peace. I say all hail to those who walked the extra mile.

The Palestinians still are without an independent homeland, Israelis still refuse to give up some of the occupied territory and Arab militants still explode bombs and hope to destroy the state of Israel. The conflict that has burned in the hearts of these people since biblical times shows no sign of giving way to peace and true progress. Obviously there are limits to what was accomplished by the boldness of Carter, Sadat and Begin. The world, nonetheless, is a safer place with a peace treaty between the two major belligerents in the most unstable region on earth. That treaty hopefully will prevent nuclear war in the Middle East. Given the extraordinary negativity that surrounds this ancient battlefield, I prefer to celebrate the positive and praise the vision of these men who changed history. We need more like them: men of war who dare to become peacemakers.

In the morning light
men in white linen
touch the soil
hoping to feed
the people of the Nile,

I drift with the sails
enjoying the peace,
until the fire fades
behind the pyramids,
and a new moon rises
over the birthplace
of civilisation.

(JOURNAL 1985)

Individuals do not only determine their own destiny. We are not islands. We are interdependent. The statesman has the choice of inspiring positive change, encouraging the human longing for peace, or resorting to the military threat of confrontation. During the final climactic years of the Cold War, when President Ronald Reagan was describing the Soviet Union as an 'evil empire' headed for 'the ash heap of history', I was close enough to witness the power of his provocative rhetoric and the results of his military strategy. My wife, Kim Hoggard, was in the nerve centre of the White House from the beginning of President Reagan's first term in 1981. I was the ABC's White House correspondent, watching the exercise of power from both inside and outside.

'The Soviets,' said Reagan, in a speech just ten days into his first term in office, 'have openly and publicly declared that the only morality they recognise is what will further their cause, meaning they reserve unto themselves the right to commit any crime, to lie, to cheat' — and this was only the president's opening shot. Reagan was doing his favourite impression of John Wayne, twirling his guns and drawling about freedom. Americans felt reassured by his confidence and they loved the image of the president in the cowboy hat. The Soviet people, however, were terrified. Many were convinced that this American gunslinger was aiming his nukes at them with an itchy trigger finger. Reagan had ordered a rapid build-up of American military strength, convinced that this was the only way to negotiate with the 'evil empire'. The

Kremlin vigorously exploited his boast of the innate superiority of western democracy as the excuse to accelerate Soviet military spending.

In 1984, with most civil conversation between Washington and Moscow suspended, I joined fifty American physicians on a daring attempt to bridge the chasm of the Cold War. These were men and women who understood that a global nuclear war would mean devastating illness beyond cure or control. Their movement, International Physicians for the Prevention of Nuclear War, at that time had about 80 000 members in forty countries, including the Russian doctors who had invited them to Moscow. The Americans were led by a world-renowned Harvard cardiologist, Professor Bernard Lown, who had forged a strong friendship with Dr Yevgeny Chasov, personal physician to most of the ageing Soviet leaders and co-founder of the physicians' movement. These two men wanted to end the intellectual primitivism that allowed both superpowers to brainwash their populations into believing that only the enemy was capable of a nuclear first strike.

> *Twice I saw it along the way*
> *in the dust on the Tskaltubo Road,*
> *a calf fallen dead under the wheels,*
> *and the mother waiting, watching,*
> *walking out to the calf, unbelieving,*
> *in each small falling of life or leaf*
> *there is a reminder of our mortality.*
>
> (JOURNAL 1984)

The American physicians travelled extensively in the Soviet Union, from Moscow to Leningrad and then to Yalta to remind everyone that the two superpowers now locked in nuclear rivalry once were allies against the Nazi threat to the world. We went east and west, encountering everywhere the siege mentality of a nation that had lost twenty million people in World War II. One physician said to me that it was like wandering through an endless cemetery where those left alive felt that they could not escape their tragic past.

Some of the Russians, meeting an American for the first time, seemed shocked that they were not warmongers hungry for the destruction of the Soviet Union. The contest between the superpowers had reached such dangerous proportions that it was not possible to end the mutual suspicion even between physicians trying to warn of the consequences of nuclear war. The Russians kept pointing out that the United States reserved the option of a nuclear first strike. The Americans countered by pointing out the menacing scale of the Soviet intercontinental ballistic missiles. This is what I mean by saying that we live inside a matrix of self-interest. It leads to an acceptance of the MAD world where it is considered reasonable to develop enough nuclear weapons to destroy most of humanity.

In many ways the threat to civilisation seemed clearer to the world back at the dawn of the atomic age. Moscow and Beijing followed the Americans in building nuclear fallout shelters. I have walked down into the Chinese tunnels that you enter through the rear of clothing shops not far from Tiananmen Square. In New York and Washington you can still spot the nuclear symbols directing people to the shelters. During the Cuban Missile Crisis American children were drilled on what to do in the event of a nuclear attack. We seem to have forgotten that the vast nuclear arsenals are still there. The great marches for peace and various disasters involving the storage of weapons-grade plutonium focused some minds. But over time children came out from under their school desks and the fear of nuclear war slowly receded into a world amnesia.

Soviet physicians lamented the fact that they had to make do with inferior computers in their hospitals while the country's military machine, they believed, had state-of-the-art technology. The American physicians warned them that President Reagan would spend the USSR into the ground and that it was futile contemplating parity, let alone superiority. At times both sides became defensive and retreated to their own corners. But due to the persistence of Chasov and Lown the physicians concentrated on sharing the latest scientific knowledge about the effects of radiation on humans. They visited children suffering the kinds of cancers that would multiply to epidemic proportions if we subjected the earth to a catastrophic nuclear winter.

Curiously, while the Russian peace movement was often a tool of the Kremlin, these Americans were shunned by their own media and scorned by the White House. There were no other journalists along on this extraordinary journey except my *Four Corners* cameraman, John Hagin, and sound-recordist, Andrew Phillips. The American physicians knew that when they went home to report the results of their effort they would be accused of 'doing a Jane Fonda', collaborating with the enemy and fraternising with a totalitarian state. It was no good pointing out that there were almost one million people behind bars in the United States, a country still in love with guns and gruesome execution. You were not allowed to suggest that violence, poverty and racism still diminished the great American experiment with democracy.

Those of us who travelled widely throughout the Soviet Union understood that the monumental oppressiveness of totalitarianism and its chronic failure to organise an efficient and productive society would be its undoing. I secretly met many Russians who complained about the vast corruption that had spread like a disease. In this 'workers' paradise' the Communist Party elite had more money than everyone else, better apartments and *dachas* in the countryside. Among ordinary people, there was a longing for the simple conveniences most westerners took for granted, like plumbing that worked, bread on the table, meat and potatoes, heating in the cold winters, and roads, bridges and railways that were not falling apart like this whole rusting monolith. After a certain amount of vodka the sentiment would be expressed that it was the sinister power of the communist state that most Russians dreaded every day, far more than Ronald Reagan and capitalism.

The American leader's biggest impact on the Soviet Union was the timing of his sharp increase in defence spending when the Russians were particularly vulnerable economically. At first the grim faced Soviet generals were not cowed. Instead, the Soviet nuclear arsenal grew by nearly 30 per cent. The capitalists, more experienced at the enterprise of war, understood that they could keep on spending with their superior economic power until the communists faltered and had to negotiate significant arms reductions. On this assessment, President Reagan's Administration was correct, but he left the White House with the superpowers still holding about 25 000 intercontinental nuclear weapons. It was the sweeping reforms of Mikhail Gorbachev, and the Russians' growing need for peace that brought the major arms reductions under Reagan's successor, George Bush. Only then could Washington and Moscow declare that the Cold War was over.

In 1985, the year after our visit to the USSR, the International Physicians for the Prevention of Nuclear War won the Nobel Peace Prize. There is no evidence, unfortunately, that this thoughtful diplomacy or even the peace prize has had much impact on the Russians or Americans. There are more players than ever in the nuclear weapons game. President George W. Bush is fascinated with the idea of a nuclear missile shield, a Star Wars defence system. Hasn't he seen the movie? The bad guys always get through the shield until the heroes come up with a bigger and better weapon to blow them out of the sky. Who is making this movie anyway? Everyone knows that even a handful of terrorists could strike with nuclear weapons. And we still don't know what to do with our old war technology. The dangerous condition of some of the Russian nuclear weapon systems matches the decrepitude of the thinking that has landed our earth in such a predicament. It was a noble mission by the physicians to go to Russia, courageously expressing the civilising instinct, but maybe it is psychiatrists we need to end the world's state of amnesia.

The American who taught me the most on our journey for
peace in Russia was the psychiatrist Dr Robert Jay Lifton.
At the end of World War II he braved six months in
Hiroshima, studying the effects of the first atomic bomb.
'It's a tragic story. It was a very powerful experience,'
Dr Lifton said. 'No one who has lived in Hiroshima and
worked there can remain the same. I learned from that
one instant in time, from exposure to that first atomic
bomb, if one had the fortune to survive, one experienced
from then on a lifelong encounter with death. One was
immersed in fears and concerns about the after-effects
from that moment, for the rest of one's existence.'

(JOURNAL 1984)

CHAPTER ELEVEN

WOMEN OF THE REVOLUTION

Love sails through many skies
lightning, darkness
and full moon.
Who am I to understand
the softness
of love's lullaby?
Who am I to understand
all that mingles
in a look?
Who am I to understand
how two become one?

(JOURNAL 1982)

In a man's world a naked woman sometimes has the best chance of making herself understood. Nora Astorga knew that when she used her beauty as a weapon, and in the Central American war zones it made her a heroine, a *femme fatale* who showed that women were prepared to fight and die for the people's revolution. The struggle by the Sandinista women in Nicaragua also was part of the worldwide women's liberation movement.

It is a man-made myth that women are incapable of being warriors. In most western nations, war is a male enterprise that we like to keep to ourselves to help relegate women to positions of inferiority. We have hidden behind the excuse that we are saving women from the terror of hand-to-hand combat, the danger of rape and torture, and even resorted to the idealised notion of women rising above the instinct to make war. In my experience, some women can kill as readily as men.

Young, beautiful and wealthy, Nora Astorga did not look like a revolutionary. She could have lived far away from Nicaragua, dancing up a sweat in a New York disco with Bianca Jagger and other glamorous friends. Instead, she secretly joined the Sandinistas in the 1970s when they were a guerilla movement in the hills. Nora looked like a playgirl to everyone else. In the capital, Managua, the dictator Somoza and his army chiefs were unaware of her revolutionary role, until Nora heeded her call to arms.

One of the most hated *Somocistas*, General Perez Vega, a brutal killer nicknamed 'The Dog', had been hungrily pursuing Nora. She had resisted his advances for some time and it made him want her more.

On one of those hot Managuan nights when the men were lit up on rum and the beast in them all went stalking, Nora made a whispered phone call. A short time later, Vega walked into her house, savouring his conquest. Nora was a sultry, seductive woman even in a land of so many dark-eyed beauties. The general must have been thinking that soon his comrades would hear that he had taken what they all wanted.

To know a woman, a macho man will say, you have to make love to her. If that is true, it is why most of us men do not know nearly as much about women as we make out. On this night, Vega's conversation with Nora would remain unfinished, suspended in the folklore of the revolution.

At the very moment he unbuckled his pants in Nora's bedroom, armed Sandinistas sprang from their hiding place. She had been told he would be taken hostage and held for ransom. But the general did not surrender and he fought them, bellowing with rage. The Sandinistas said he went crazy because he had been made to look so foolish, falling for a woman's trap. Nora watched the struggle right there in her bedroom until her comrades killed the man she had seduced.

Word spread quickly of General Vega's death, as he had been one of Somoza's counter-insurgency chiefs. The army put a price on Nora Astorga's head and she was forced to leave Managua. Still worse, she was fighting in the hills carrying her own secret. She was pregnant with the child of one of her Sandinista comrades. After months of skirmishing with Somoza's troops, Nora went into labour out in the countryside. She told me that her baby was born under the moonlight, with another guerilla woman helping the delivery. A few years later, as I held that child on my knee, Nora explained that her man had left them both along the way to the Sandinista victory. She could see that for all of their talk of revolution and liberation, the Sandinistas were led by men who lived and breathed the code of *machismo*. Nora had been let down, abandoned, in the most commonplace way.

When the Sandinistas had their turn in power, Nora Astorga became a special attorney-general, prosecuting Somoza's officers and developing a new legal system. She acted as foreign minister and was later ambassador to the United Nations. She had responsibility and respect, but she spoke of feelings of loneliness and emptiness. After years of fighting, her country still was torn at the heart and so, it seemed, was Nora. She had her child to love but no partner to share the joy and the burden. Nora's beauty had not faded but she had developed an incurable cancer. It was not the fear of dying that troubled her most but the heroine status she had achieved because of a man's death. Because General Vega was so vicious, guilty of murder and torture, her entrapment of him was celebrated by leftist revolutionaries throughout Latin America, not to mention a few feminists north of the border. But there were murmurs of the heart, a trembling conscience, because Nora knew that she had used her body to set a death trap. Even in a state of war it was an extraordinary thing to do, but Nora wondered aloud if it was really much different to the role of a spy or double agent. Was she any different to the sniper who lay in wait for the ambush or the soldier who cut the enemy's throat? Nora believed she had a right, even a duty, to fight and to kill. In the last years of her life, she rationalised her personal military action by saying that it was lust that had killed Vega, his lust for her and also her comrades' lust for victory at any cost.

This revolutionary heroine recognised the shortcomings of a political victory won by war. She was modest about the inspiration she had given Latin American women in the wider struggle of the Women's Liberation Movement, because clearly throughout most of South and Central America women still were second-class citizens. Many women came into the workforce during the revolution, but even after standing shoulder to shoulder with men in war time, Nicaragua's women were no more liberated than any others. Sadly, Nora had to admit that although she gave her body and soul for the ideals of freedom and equality, the battle of the sexes was still raging. She died in 1988 at the age of thirty-nine.

> *I'm talking about the moon,*
> *you are wishing we had the sun,*
> *we walked a mile that night*
> *musing over so many things,*
> *what had changed in us*
> *and what we had done.*
> *There is a place lost in your eyes*
> *Trespassers Beware,*
> *the cost of passage is someone's life*
> *is that too much to ask?*

(JOURNAL 1982)

In Africa's longest-running war, that brutal grinding struggle between Ethiopia and Eritrea, I met many women who matched the feats of men in battle.

The strong, tall Eritreans were liberated, to some degree, years before the women of neighbouring countries where girls still were being brutalised by clitoral mutilation or 'female circumcision' as it was euphemistically called. Eritrean men were better educated and more progressive. The new society recognised that women had a right to control their bodies, their reproductive systems. This made the Eritrean women far more willing to give their lives to the thirty-year struggle against one of the most powerful armies in Africa.

The frontline in the 1980s was near the town of Nakfa, reduced to rubble by Ethiopia's MiG aircraft. Two of the poorest countries in the world were waging a gruelling trench warfare, dug in only a few hundred metres apart. If you listened carefully you could hear noises from the Ethiopian side. Eritrean men and women in khaki uniforms crouched in the maze of tunnels and shallow trenches. Occasionally they took sniper shots using mirrors so as not to present any part of their body in the narrow gun slits. Artillery positioned far from the trenches bombarded all of these hapless humans who endured years of hardship and danger to claw for any slight advance over this rocky wasteland.

There were whole communities living behind the Eritrean lines, with houses, schools and hospitals dug into the low hills. My camera team, Paul Boocock and Mick Breen, cautiously emerged from the bomb shelter where we had slept, scanning the sky for the Ethiopian MiGs before we went on with our distressing work. The producer, Andrew Haughton, and I watched doctors and nurses operate on a little girl, one of seventy people wounded and forty killed when they were caught in the open during a bombing raid. There was a canyon nearby that seemed to be full of the walking wounded. But in this war, starvation was the most gruesome weapon and some women experienced a particular kind of suffering only mothers could fully understand.

Driving through the desert of gravel and thorny scrub, Andrew Haughton and I were straining our eyes for enemy aircraft. An ex-RAF navigator, Andrew had described in detail what would happen to our four-wheel-drive if we were spotted on the road in daylight. But at this point of our journey there was an incident which made us forget about our own safety and took us to the heart of the Eritrean suffering and the cruelty of war. We came across a huddle of women sheltering under the gnarled roots of a tree in a dry riverbed. We walked over to them carrying some food and water. But this time we were too late.

An Eritrean woman, her face a sculpture of great beauty and terrible sadness, was crying over the small lifeless child who lay covered by a fold of her soft purple robe. The newborn baby girl had died that morning because through hunger the mother did not have the milk in her breasts to feed her. No words could comfort her, let alone make sense of her loss. This was the saddest face in the world. The woman would have given her life for her child but they were both victims of a man-made war and famine.

> *There is an eternal hour*
> *when mother has child*
> *pressed to her breast,*
> *and all the creatures*
> *of the Great South Land,*
> *are snuggled in their nest.*
>
> (JOURNAL 1994)

A woman in the full bloom of motherhood usually is a delight to behold. The moments when my own newborn children were raised to their mother's breast define happiness for me. The first exuberant cry like a magpie's morning carol, the tiny fingers clutching ours, the softness of skin and hair, are wonders to share and the source of a lasting joy. At once the love between two people miraculously expands to envelop the first child and then the next. And if you have a boy and a girl, as we do, it is impossible to conceive of valuing one more than the other.

A discovery that still astounds me, wracks my mind and troubles my conscience more than all other ethical issues is how the world accepts with such tolerance and passivity the practice of female infanticide. This is a terrifying part of the battle of the sexes that is systematically altering the very balance of males and

females in our most populous nations. In China there could be
about forty million missing women. India probably has lost thirty
million women. These estimates by western population experts
are conservative. Chinese and Indian doctors brave enough to
criticise this slaughter claim that even greater numbers of
newborn baby girls are sent to an early grave. This is not science
fiction but grotesque human behaviour that we have forgotten
through that collective amnesia about violence in our midst.

Population-control programs and commercial sex selection
using ultrasound technology are responsible for the termination
of many pregnancies when it is known that the foetus is female.
In China and India, however, it is female infanticide, the selective
killing of baby girls at birth, that has skewed the ratio of the sexes
so dramatically, so alarmingly, that now we are witnessing the
creation of a highly unnatural human order.

The natural balance at birth is 106 males for every 100 females.
This is an internationally recognised norm. In China official
statistics released in 2001 show 117 boys born for every 100 girls.
In rural areas the ratio often approaches 140 males born for every
100 females. In India, where sons are also valued more than
daughters, there are 110 boys born for every 100 girls. In both
nations the figures are believed to be understated by the authorities.

What alarmed me most when I began to investigate female
infanticide in the 1980s was that this ancient practice was
accelerating at such a rate that it could have profound
consequences for these huge populations which make up roughly
one-third of humanity. My fears have been well founded.
The latest census shows that of China's 1.2 billion people, there
are 41 million more men than women, up 10 per cent since the
last official estimate in 1997.

I began my investigation by reading the work of Harvard
University's Center for Population and Development Studies.
I also talked with Stephen Mosher, a highly experienced China-
watcher who had examined the harsh life in the villages where the
value of male labour appeared so much higher than that of
females. Afterwards I travelled to some of China's maternity
hospitals and secretly met several dissident doctors who estimated

that hundreds of thousands of baby girls were being put to death each year.

In disturbing detail I heard from doctors who did not inform parents when they administered fatal injections as infant girls 'showed' at the moment of birth. Sometimes they told the parents their girl babies were stillborn. Sometimes the parents went along with the decision because it was common practice. There was heavy pressure from the state for parents to have only one child but the doctors said if they let a newborn girl live the parents would keep trying until they had a boy. China's own newspapers, including the *People's Daily* and the *Southern Daily News*, reported that girl babies frequently were drowned, suffocated or simply abandoned under trees to die in numbers that over the decades amounted to tens of millions.

What a Brave New World! There are now so many women missing from the population, China's own official studies indicate that 80 million adult males alive today will never marry. This figure is expected to rise as younger generations face a crisis with up to 12 per cent of women 'missing'. How will men behave when there are even fewer women to be shared? Bigger brothels and more brutality is my guess, as there are already signs of an increase in prostitution and trade in sex slaves in nations where female infanticide is practised. The bargaining for child brides is increasing and it is not uncommon in India for girls to be taken at the age of twelve or thirteen by older men hungry for women. Chinese gangs are trafficking in women from Vietnam and North Korea. The social pressures created by female infanticide are certain to become worse unless we return humanity to its natural balance.

The unnatural order that has emerged in China and India also is showing in Pakistan, Bangladesh, Korea and Taiwan. Although infanticide is officially illegal the percentage of missing women is increasing. One possible explanation is the growing use of ultrasound machines to detect female foetuses and terminate pregnancies even in the third trimester. In the west, as well, sex selection after scanning has added a new dimension to the abortion debate. After listening to very poor Indian women in

Tamil Nadu describe how they had suffocated their newborn girls with mouthfuls of grain or hot curry, my own view is clear. The personal right of a woman to control her reproductive system is an essential tenet of equality. But sex selection during pregnancy or at birth which discriminates against females is unjust. The result of this injustice is a scale of female destruction unprecedented in human history. We should examine why this is still happening.

Female infanticide in the east is the consequence of a strong cultural belief that a boy child is an economic asset and a baby girl often a crushing liability. The historical explanation is that when the poorest agricultural countries suffered frequent natural disasters including floods, drought and devastating famine, farmers tried to survive by killing their female babies and saving their males. It was believed that men could work longer and harder, even though it is commonplace for women in these countries to labour in the fields and do other heavy manual work. China's controversial one-child policy placed even more importance on this old belief that it was better to have a male child. In Chinese families wealth is handed down from father to son.

In India and elsewhere, the difficulty of poor families finding a dowry to hand over when girls marry is another common excuse for female infanticide. This dowry system has led to much brutalising of women. But not all of the poor bury newborn girls in shallow graves. Having watched mothers in the midst of war and famine struggling heroically to keep their babies alive, girls and boys, it has been troubling listening to other women express a striking acceptance of the lowly place of the female. Many of the poorest women in China and India have come to accept the conventional wisdom that sons will contribute more to family farming, income and the care of parents in old age.

Here there is a real irony. Travelling through India and China I see women toiling in the fields, tending livestock, making fuel from dried cow pats, even carrying heavy piles of bricks on their heads. Then I notice that not only do women and girls do the cleaning and cooking at home (as most women do in the west), but they feed the men and boys first. Baby girls are often malnourished because they are the very last to be fed. In fact, women are always thought of last.

While females in most countries typically outlive males by at least five to seven years, women in China die younger. They suffer a lifetime of abuse and inadequate nutrition. The outcry from the rest of the world is barely audible. The selective culling of female infants, their higher level of infant mortality and the systematic denial of nutrition too often are dismissed as unfortunate, though effective, means of population control in dangerously overcrowded nations. The devaluation of the girl child, epitomised by this callousness and indifference, is a monstrous human habit and while it continues can any of us speak of 'human civilisation'?

> *Songs are sung*
> *before we are born*
> *and in the morning*
> *can be heard*
> *every small voice*
> *raised to sing*
> *the words of joy*
> *that lift us all*
> *with echoes*
> *remembered well*
> *beyond our evening fall.*

(JOURNAL 1980)

In Bangladesh, Dr Taslima Nasrin grew tired of seeing women crying out in the delivery room that their husbands would divorce them because they had given birth to girls. One of the most famous feminists in the east, Dr Nasrin led me to a young woman in Dacca who had been doused in battery acid and another whose hand had been surgically removed simply because their parents had not come up with the expected dowry. Their husbands or their husbands' families had taken revenge because they knew they would get away with it.

A writer as well as a medical doctor, Dr Nasrin used her pen to attack the social and religious customs that subjected women to this violence. Her confronting stories and angry poetic diatribe were aimed at the masses, demanding in the most provocative terms that men change their ways. As a result, Islamic fundamentalists put a price on Dr Nasrin's head, and like the writer Salman Rushdie she had to go into hiding.

In Dacca, thousands of male fundamentalists swarmed through the streets demanding that Dr Nasrin be buried to the waist and stoned, a traditional punishment for wayward women. They threatened to release 10 000 pythons and cobras unless she was tortured and then hanged publicly. Outrageous and ludicrous as these threats may sound, Dr Nasrin knew that she would die if these ignorant men got hold of her. She had investigated the deaths of many women — stonings, stabbings and bashings — where the men afterwards had walked free. After several months of moving from house to house, Dr Nasrin fled Bangladesh, shrouded in the traditional black *burka* that she despised.

In self-imposed exile in Sweden, where the government provided bodyguards for protection, this courageous woman continued to try to awaken the western world to what was happening to her countrywomen. While women and girls in the west have made huge gains in health and life expectancy, the majority of women in the east are discriminated against unfairly. Dr Nasrin helped me understand that it is poverty, as much as ignorance, that keeps women enslaved.

About 70 per cent of the world's poor are women and children. The so-called 'Third World' countries face levels of domestic violence, rape, sexual harassment, abuse in the media and restrictions on women's reproductive rights that suggest nothing short of a worldwide revolution will give women equal rights. From the early 1970s many brilliant eastern feminists, like India's Vina Majumdar, began to lobby the United Nations and campaign at home to end the oppression of women. There are strong grassroots movements in India trying to stop the bashing and burning of women. Mothers are being taught to value their girl babies and to give them the education that could make them economically productive. Women of the east also have found support at home from feminists who travelled from the west.

The American feminist Gloria Steinem told me that she had begun to write seriously about the status of women only after she travelled to India in 1956. Steinem discovered that hundreds of millions of people were living in poverty that was simply outside the consciousness of most westerners. For a young woman it was particularly disturbing to see how she would have been treated if she had been born and survived to adulthood in India. Once she had registered the fact that she was sharing the earth with a largely impoverished multitude of mainly women and children, either she could be numbed into the pursuit of self-contentment or, intellectually and practically, she had to take action until the world was truly civilised.

Steinem is a surprising Madame Liberty, deservedly as famous as that statue out on New York Harbor because of her extraordinary campaign to gain equal rights for women. Along those Manhattan avenues where businessmen in dark suits stride purposefully into their corporate towers, we once walked together to the offices of her publication, Ms. magazine, without anyone recognising her. She was the best-known women's liberationist in the United States (and still is) but with her glasses and her long brown hair parted in the middle like a 1960s schoolteacher, Steinem looked like a million other women. She was just turning fifty, healthy and poised, but so all-American she did not turn heads and appeared to like it that way.

It was the sheer injustice of the status of women, Steinem told me, that turned an ordinary young American woman into a radical feminist. She saw inequity not only in impoverished, class-obsessed India but at home in affluent America. Her mother had been a reporter but had felt compelled to use a male pseudonym because journalism was seen as an unfeminine profession. Then she had to end her journalistic career because of her husband's travelling. Deep frustration and lack of fulfilment drove her mother into a state of chronic depression, and after a complete breakdown her marriage fell apart. Gloria was ten years old and had learned the hard way that the same opportunities were not open to women as to men.

When Steinem became pregnant as a young woman, her mother's life was very much on her mind. Gloria decided not to marry her fiancé, and had an abortion overseas. A woman's right to control her reproductive system was far from established in the United States, as at that time abortion was illegal. This early experience would become central to Steinem's campaign for women's liberation.

In 1959 Steinem tried to get a job as a reporter in New York City. She discovered not a lot had changed from her mother's day and few women were being hired by the top newspapers. She freelanced for *Esquire*, *Glamour* and *Show* magazines. People began to take notice after she went undercover as a Playboy bunny to expose the exploitation and sexual harassment of attractive young women drawn to this work to make money. Steinem told me, laughing, that she felt like 'a complete idiot' wearing a bunny suit.

I was impressed that from her earliest years as a reporter Steinem was able to combine her writing with the advocacy of women's rights. This, ultimately, was her greatest achievement. Writing for *New York* magazine, she helped create the 'New Journalism' with Tom Wolfe and Jimmy Breslin, but to the dismay of her male colleagues she was drawn to subjects, like the abortion debate, that illustrated the discrimination against women. She gave many readers a new view of themselves and also of some very famous women often caricatured by the male-controlled media. For instance, Gloria met and wrote about Marilyn Monroe, whom she described as a woman who deserved to be taken seriously. In a 1980s essay on Madonna she praised the feminist qualities of this controversial performer who was determined to control her own life.

Gloria Steinem gave many other women, and men, the courage to change. She was the co-founder of *Ms.*, one of the first publications by women to look seriously at the spectrum of women's issues. The Australian feminist Anne Summers later kept this magazine firing the thought-provoking bullets of the women's revolution.

Steinem helped build several political groups important to the women's movement, including the National Women's Political Caucus and the Coalition of Labor Union Women. She has worked tirelessly to urge women to register to vote and to use their political power. Her bestselling books, such as *Outrageous Acts and Everyday Rebellions* and *Revolution From Within: A Book of Self-Esteem*, sometimes were criticised by other women as being written by an atypical individual who had not experienced marriage, motherhood or the maddening stresses of juggling career and family. Perhaps it was a surprise even to many feminists when in September 2000, at the age of sixty-six, Steinem married David Bale, aged sixty-one.

Instead of revelling in her fame and success, Steinem told me that she truly believed, as she had written, that her most outrageous acts ultimately were no more valuable to women's liberation than everyday rebellions. It seemed to me that her striking virtue was this plain common sense and the honesty with which she bared her doubts and frailties.

There are some women so beautiful that they render men almost speechless. Men imagine these women also have nothing to say. When a woman with a striking body should dare to show the same quality of mind, she is a challenge. Men respond to this threat, not by considering the female point of view, but by trying to conquer the woman. It is an age-old male manoeuvre aimed at maintaining ascendancy over the other half of our species.

Germaine Greer, that 'wild woman of the '60s' as the Australian media frequently portrayed her, was ignored by many men for the same reason they did not listen to Jane Fonda. The men were thinking of sex and not what these women had to say. Why bother reading *The Female Eunuch*... isn't Germaine raunchy? I wonder if Jane really is like Barbarella?

On the other hand, if it were a battleship like Bella Abzug, Betty Friedan or Andrea Dworkin sailing at you, feminists were dismissed as unattractive angry women. There was not much chance that men would listen to them either.

In this way, most of the fiercer spirits, resistance fighters, tacticians and real intellectuals of women's liberation have not been taken seriously by the majority of men. A few can thank their mothers or their partners for educating them about the female point of view. But during most of my lifetime the true emancipation of women has seemed years away.

When I met Germaine Greer on a visit to Washington in 1984 I was interested to hear her assessment of the latest political strategy adopted by American feminists. Betty Friedan, Bella Abzug and others, in a bid to bring about real change, were urging women to use their electoral power to vote for politicians who agreed to target women's issues. Greer, a great strategic thinker, just did not buy it.

'By now, according to my calculations, feminists should have become downright revolutionaries,' Greer told me. 'Men just refuse to give up power and I don't believe it can be done by taking aim at the so-called "gender gap" in a presidential election, somehow exploiting female voting power. It can't be done. Not here, not now, not in our lifetime! Maybe it's meant to be done a hundred years from now. I mean all of us have the privilege of serving the revolution.'

Greer, independent as always, was correct about the 1984 US presidential election when women helped re-elect Ronald Reagan over the Democratic candidate, Walter Mondale, who bravely had chosen a woman, Geraldine Ferraro, as his vice-presidential running mate. In my view, Greer's pessimism about the timetable for female equality is well founded. That great bastion of conservatism, the United Nations, came up with a study during International Women's Year predicting that it would take 'more than a millennium' before women achieved equality around the world. It seems to me that approximately half of the human species is quite accepting of this staggering injustice.

There are a few cautious optimists. The late Katharine Graham, the American publisher, once said that women had made more progress in the twentieth century than over the previous millennium. If Gloria Steinem set the standard for all women reporters who would follow, Graham certainly proved that women could be successful managers in those media boardrooms traditionally ruled by men. Boss of the *Washington Post*, *Newsweek*, television stations and cable networks, Graham climbed the *Fortune* 500 rankings to become the most powerful woman in the United States for several decades. But she was not deceived by the success of a small but significant minority of women powerbrokers.

'Although women have made gains, we still have far to go when it comes to real power. By and large it is the men who hold power, men who wield power and men who bestow power. Contrary to popular belief I do not think the small number of women in top positions today is surprising. Large numbers of women have been in mid-management positions for only a few years. These women who are mostly in their thirties are now just paying their dues and gaining experience. When they reach their forties and fifties they will have earned the right to exercise power in senior management. By that time the current generation of powerholders, men in their late fifties and early sixties who are still unsettled by women in senior positions, will have retired. A new more enlightened generation of men and women will hold the reins. This generation will be more comfortable with women at the top.'

Although certainly there is more 'enlightenment' today, women are still oppressed, violence against women shows no signs of decreasing even in the most advanced industrial nations and female infanticide continues in the world's largest countries. Women have been surging into the workforce since World War II, improving their education and employment prospects, but the feminisation of poverty even in the developed nations has kept hundreds of millions of them second-class citizens. Most women still earn less than men do. Typically, a man's income rises after divorce, but a divorced woman not only sees her income drop, she usually has the duty of caring for the children. Towards the end of their lives women discover that three-quarters of our elderly poor are women. It is still a man's world.

There has been a backlash against women's liberation because many men are reluctant to share power and privilege. Our worldwide economic system is based on the subservience of women and at times their enslavement. Giving women true equal pay would mean a fundamental redistribution of wealth and most men are not willing to see that happen. I suggest that the lives of men and women will be much happier when we recognise the full potential of human beings based on equality. Many men and women fear that the family as we know it would become obsolete if there was support for women who go to work, by choice or dire need. But 60 per cent of women are in the workforce and are somehow expected to cope with two jobs, at home and in the office, without just reward. We have to give women real choice.

The dissatisfaction many men express over the imbalance between work and home life indicates that the time is right for men to be more involved in raising our children and sharing the work at home. In affluent nations, women and men can have it all but you can't have it all at once. We need a balance in our lives. It is time the advanced economic countries started paying women fairly whether they work at home or in the office. Yes, that will mean a redistribution of wealth, power and opportunity, but I am eager for it. I was raised by a woman who believed that social justice was the most important human value. I want my own daughter and son to believe that and to join the revolution in thinking that could bring equality, without waiting for another millennium.

CHAPTER TWELVE

A WAR OF WORDS

It is not surprising that Australians have been among the leaders of the women's revolution and among the first women in the world to win the right to vote. When I look at the role of ordinary women in the battle of the sexes, I think of so many genuinely liberated 'working mothers'. They were convinced of the nobility of raising a family, saw the economic value of this hard work and at the same time made their way in whatever profession they could manage. My mother was such a woman.

A country girl, Joyce Shaddock grew up under the red tin roof of a settler's cottage at Singleton in the Hunter Valley of New South Wales. Her grandfather had watched the Great Flood of 1893 sweep away the family farm. He moved downstream to a smaller property and started all over again. Joyce's father also had reason to wonder about the cruelty of nature. Within a year of giving birth to her seventh child, Joyce's mother died.

At the age of four, with no mother at home, Joyce would run barefoot along a path to a mansion on the hill. 'Baroona' is still a grand place. The champion racehorse Peter Pan, winner of two Melbourne Cups, is buried there. One of Singleton's benefactors, A. A. Dangar, then owned 'Baroona', and was very fond of Joyce and her six brothers and sisters, allowing the family to live on the property for about twenty years. Joyce and the other children were well looked after, and their father found solace in the orchards, garden and vineyard, with the rich river soil on his hands, watching those early Hunter grapes ripen towards greatness.

Regardless of fate or fortune, my mother said that it was the values developed in country life that gave a family strength. One did not need much to live graciously, she said, just a white tablecloth and a single red rose. She encouraged her three sons to look for answers in the books that she loved so much. Even when her purse strings were tight she found money for books. When times were hard Joyce made her boys shirts from old parachute silk that Jack brought home from the air force. Some days there were colours bright as butterfly wings fluttering through the bush. She would say you don't need much to be happy. She was right. But she always wanted more for her children.

As a teenager she rode a bike around the country roads to cut hair, an early hint of the enterprise that would drive her to educate herself and establish her independence with a business career. She also had a way with words.

Both of my parents had a love of conversation that some say is inherited. While Joyce surely had kissed the Blarney Stone, that tongue turned to poison when she was riled. And the one person who could so easily raise her anger was the man she married.

As a child I clung to the happiest memories of my father, Jack, because he was away so often. At home he would sing in a bad baritone until my mother teased him and we all rolled about laughing. Jack loved to make us happy, often by telling stories.

In the air force he was known as 'Throbber'. The story goes that a servicewoman had walked into the barracks as Jack lay with an enormous erection beneath the sheets.

'Oh my, what a throbber!' she exclaimed and the nickname stuck.

Always the larrikin, the lad from Branxton who had ridden a pushbike from the Hunter Valley down to Sydney 'just for a good weekend', Jack was demoted a few times in the air force. He told us that it was for insubordination. He was a 'man's man', extremely popular throughout the ranks and quite a legend in the bar. But my mother knew the truth. Jack was busted so often because he was a drunk.

There was a time in their romance when drinking was associated with pure gaiety. Party hats, twinkling eyes and flashing smiles, old black and white snapshots caught them dancing cheek to cheek. But as the children came along Joyce saw Jack's fondness for the bottle as a weakness that jeopardised her sense of family security and threatened her considerable aspirations. She had become a successful businesswoman, running a lingerie store to ensure that her three sons had a first-rate education. She invested in land in the mountains, by a lake and in a well-to-do suburb because she was confident together she and Jack could build the life she wanted for her family. Jack could stand on the mountaintop and with her hand in his share the dream of the grand homes they were going to build and the travels they would enjoy after he retired from the air force. But he was a dreamer, not a man of action. Joyce was clearly pining for that strength of character she remembered in both their fathers. Jack wanted to run with the boys and come home when he pleased.

When he did come home drunk, it was war. Staggering down the hallway he had to run a gauntlet of verbal abuse. He would try to charm Joyce, plead for forgiveness and then ultimately concede that he had become a lousy husband and a pretty poor excuse for a father.

Watching them from a doorway, standing there trembling as a child, I felt sorry and afraid for them both. I always loved my father, even at his lowest, and could see him struggling for happiness. But my mother's pain was the greater because over the years she sensed that she was losing all that she cherished the most.

Even as a very small boy, as the middle child I took the role of mediator and would step between my parents to try to stop the fighting. I hated the shouting, was puzzled by my father's pathetic incoherence when drunk and was shocked to see the look of cold hate come over the face of a woman usually so full of love. Just once I saw my mother lift a cricket bat and strike a glancing blow across my father's brow. Blood trickled down his forehead but he never laid a hand on her. I can still see his look of stunned disbelief. I can still hear her cries of anguish.

The battle of the sexes drags on because men and women are afraid of one another. Men are afraid of losing the power that we associate with freedom. Women fear that they will lose their identity, their true self erased by selfish men. How many times have you watched as men and women slash away at the other's sense of worth? It seems only a matter of time until this negativity destroys all the hard work, all the glorious shared history, all the love. When it gets to that stage where they are incapable of affirming anything positive in what the other does or says, the writing is on the wall. They might as well call it quits.

Joyce never spoke of divorcing Jack. She simply suffered. Her only relief was during his absences that grew longer and had little to do with his air force duties. But then Throbber would return and try to charm us all once more.

When he retired from the air force, Jack's drinking grew heavier. I was in my early twenties then and could talk to him about life, but he seemed to be searching not so much for answers as a worthwhile riddle. He liked the company of men who drank themselves into a state of oblivion. His binges were getting longer and more frequent. I knew I would soon find him in a gutter or face down in a pub, but I never expected to see him in a state institution.

After one monumental bender his alcoholism almost destroyed him. He was seriously ill, delusional and had damaged his near-term memory permanently. My despairing mother consulted the same doctors she had before, through all the painful but failed attempts to counsel Jack. She was heroic considering all he had put her through but she knew that alone she could not save him. Jack was admitted to a detoxification hospital where he spent almost a year slipping in and out of our world.

Joyce seemed resigned to the fact that Jack would never regain full health and she chose not to visit him in that sad place behind high stone walls. I went there with some trepidation.

The corridors of the hospital were lined with lost souls. A woman sang to herself, staring at the tiles on the floor. Another old enough to be a grandmother rocked an imaginary baby in her arms. Broken men shuffled about silently and I felt concern and a twinge of shame that my father was reduced to this company. I paused to ask directions from a fellow with a face you could read like a blood-vessel map. Another heavy drinker, he knew my father and pointed towards the gardens. I walked along the path through the bloom of bougainvillea, wondering what I would say to a father who might not know his son anymore.

My heart leaped as Throbber came bounding across the lawn towards me with that wide, winning grin. He had made an amazing recovery. He looked rested, even fit. The man had a resilience that suggested he was living out his blues as a kind of adventure, believing he could always haul himself back from the edge. I have met many other talented but troubled men with the same dangerous delusion, their judgment addled by booze or drugs.

When I told him that Joyce was not really counting on him coming home he looked dejected. In fact Joyce did not believe she could handle him anymore. But his face brightened when I promised to try to arrange a final reconciliation, a homecoming that would be the last.

Another month passed as the doctors undertook thorough health checks, and after much talking into the night Joyce agreed to take him back. This time it was not only an errant husband she was accepting, it was a full legal responsibility, as Jack had surrendered control of his affairs to the state. I met him again just days before his release. For the first time I heard him recognise his alcoholism and the damage it had inflicted on his family and himself. He was no longer cocky but understood he would need Joyce to make even simple decisions for him because he was not capable of remembering what he had said or done the day before. This near-term memory loss is a common scar of alcoholism. True to character, Jack was still dreaming of spending the golden years with the woman he had never stopped loving.

After almost a year in a coma, Joyce opened her eyes in hospital. Before her car crash, she was a woman in her prime, just over fifty but still beautiful, independent and strong. The terrible head injuries that she suffered when she was flung from her car have aged her prematurely. Her hair now is silver, her skin almost grey, her blue eyes wide open and full of anxiety.

(JOURNAL 1971)

In the very week that my father was to come home, my mother was the innocent victim of a multiple car crash in Sydney. She fractured her skull and had to struggle for life itself. Her family too went through hell. I could see the distress on the face of every visitor. They knew that during one of several crises I had been the one to sign the medical papers authorising brain surgery to remove life-threatening blood clots. I did this because I was certain my mother would have chosen to cling to any chance of survival, no matter the odds or the agonising consequences. Now she was paralysed down one side of her body. Her speech was slurred and worst of all for such an intelligent woman her mind was slipping back to yesteryear.

'How was school, my dears?' she asked her three grown sons at her bedside. My brothers and I looked at one another. My father stared at the floor. None of us said a word for some time.

'You look wonderful,' she said, turning to Jack. My father gave her his bravest smile.

He sat with her for hours, just holding her hand or stroking her hair. It was cut short now, the way she used to wear it as an eighteen-year-old girl riding her bike around the country towns. Over the months, Joyce became more childlike. Perhaps she was drifting back along the path towards the red-tinned roof of her father's cottage at Singleton. Addled though her brain appeared to be, she left a half-written letter on her bedside table. It was addressed to her brother who had been dead for some years. I read it aloud to my father. Were these tender words the ones she had left unspoken? To us now she could say little that made much sense. How I longed for another of those family nights where we told one another everything, where we sang and argued and solved the problems of the whole damn world.

Like a ghost in a nightgown, Joyce somehow wandered out of the small private hospital where she spent her last year. That night, the police searched the local streets and even a creek bed in the nearby bush. The next morning she was found in a rocking chair on someone else's verandah. Perhaps she was trying to find her way home.

I imagined that Joyce was looking for signposts to somewhere in her past. All she found was the pain in her forehead. She complained often about it and I was worried that despite her broken mind she still understood that she was leaving us, heading for a tragically early grave. We could never really tell how much she understood or remembered. So much of our love, appreciation and deepest gratitude was offered in whispers.

Poor Jack could no longer stand to see her in pain. In some ways, he suffered as much as she did knowing that his drinking had broken her heart. On the last day we saw my mother alive, I led my father away in tears.

'She had the warmest laughter in the world,' Jack said. 'We should remember her that way.'

CHAPTER THIRTEEN

THE NIGHT IS FOR SINGING

Fifth Avenue was full of Saturday afternoon. Yellow Checker cabs moved in an endless stream down vast corridors of gleaming glass and stone, a new edition of civilisation. Pages of the *New York Times* were blowing on the wind, past the statue of Atlas with the world on his shoulders. The towers built on the dreams of ten million people reached even higher than the grand spire of St Patrick's Cathedral. This was a city so much larger than my life. As I wandered from the ABC's bureau on Rockefeller Plaza in the heart of Manhattan, a newly arrived foreign correspondent in the winter of 1972, I felt I had found my own *Metropolis*.

*Times Square, with the pimps and dopers, skin-flick
gropers, wigs in curlers, cops on horses, high heels and
leather haunches, ice-cream parlours, juice-squeezers,
alley-teasers, peep show peelers, wallet stealers, all of us
daytime surrealers, waiting for the nightlights or the end
of another war. Walk on Broadway, lines of faces buying
tickets, winners, losers, gamblers dealing. It's showtime in
the street. Blind man with a German shepherd. Beefsteak-*

houses, giant burgers. Man in the bin looking for food.
Dude singing. Saxophone crying. Plastic Jesus in the shop
window dying. Horns screaming. Big smoke-rings curling
up from the billboard above the square.

(JOURNAL 1972)

When I asked John Lennon why he loved New York City he gave
an answer that echoes still in the avenues of my mind.

'New York, man, it's the place to be!'

He could have lived anywhere but Lennon wanted the city that
had a dynamo for a heart. Arriving at the start of the 1970s, like
I did, he discovered the freedom and exhilaration of so much
creativity in the air.

I had never experienced the sheer brilliance of so much original
music. It was the age of the singer-songwriter. On any given night
I could listen to Howlin' Wolf singing the blues at Max's Kansas
City, Richie Havens in the cafes of Brooklyn, Bob Dylan at The
Bitter End in Greenwich Village, Nina Simone across the road at
The Village Gate, Al Jarreau at Sweet Basil, a cowboy like Jerry
Jeff Walker at the Lone Star Café, a rock poet like Lou Reed or a
Beat like Allen Ginsberg. All the legends and many thrilling
newcomers played here because it was the place to be.

Exuberant and self-indulgent, New Yorkers knew they were
living at the creative centre of the universe. Manhattan was one
big theatre set, with performance artists of every type stretching
the boundaries, dreaming up the unexpected, fashioning new and
important works. Talking Heads were discovered at the New
Wave music club CBGB's and Philip Glass had begun to rehearse
his avant-garde musicians for surrealistic shows like *Einstein on
the Beach.* The playwright Sam Shepard was making a name for
himself and I gave a bed to a talented young English writer, David
Hare, who was trying out one of his early plays in New York.

In late-night haunts like Elaine's and the Odeon I met novelists,
poets, dancers, artists and astronomers. All taught me so much
I did not know. I spent every available hour at the Museum of

Modern Art or the Film Forum, a cinema for foreign films right below my Soho loft. New York was certainly the place to be educated. Every day I passed small galleries, music stores and bookshops that introduced me to something new. Still in my early twenties, it was in New York City that I fell in love with music, with art and with women. I went home with flautists, actresses, painters and sculptors of fog. The city made love to us all and we could not get enough of it.

My favourite hangout was Kenny's Castaways on Bleeker Street, where one night a young guy with a guitar named Bruce Springsteen drove in from New Jersey to play songs that were so raw and powerful the crowd was hushed. When his E Street Band joined in, the house was rocking until the early hours of the morning.

'How did I do, Pat?' Springsteen asked at the end.

'Great, kid,' said Pat Kenny. 'You and your hornplayer will be immortal.'

Pat Kenny was a New York Irishman who gave more talented musicians a start in his club than even he can remember. What I loved about his place was that rock-star egos got left at the door because the music always came first. Any new song was given respect whether we were listening to raw talent like Steve Forbert and Willie Nile, or journeymen like Paul Siebel and Loudon Wainwright. Fine British performers like Bridget St John and John Martyn found an intimate place for their exquisite talents. Many of America's best songwriters, like Doc Pomus who wrote hits for Elvis, would come in to support the new kids on the block. On so many nights that seemed made for singing the music in Kenny's was inspired. I made friendships in that bar that I will treasure for the rest of my life and they grew from a shared love of music. People from different corners of the globe came together to draw on the magic from the same well. The more quality singing, songwriting and playing you were exposed to, the deeper your appreciation of each individual talent. I developed a great love of this kind of human expression, the combination of individual poetry and hands on the strings. In the years ahead, after some of my darkest hours, I always found music to be a great salve of the heart and mind.

When the band packed up at Kenny's, people stayed for the conversation. A lot of great musicians from out of town would congregate there because it was a small club where even the famous could kick back or go wild. So when John Lennon was going through his hell-raising years with Harry Nilsson, they often ended up at Kenny's.

> *John and Yoko in the flesh are smaller and more fragile than the rock god image created by the music industry and magnified by the media's hype and big-screen projection. She is tiny, like a little genie who will jump from the bottle, perform her avant-garde number and then disappear. Lennon is slight and quiet. But when his curiosity is aroused that charmingly musical Liverpudlian accent reveals a mind that wants to turn everything in life into something useful. That's what I pick up from him. Don't waste a breath.*
>
> (JOURNAL 1973)

John Lennon told me that after the break-up of The Beatles he felt free in New York to be himself. Yoko Ono and her performance art also were right at home there. They both loved the idea that Madame Liberty could open her arms to all types of people, and it seemed heartless and even politically pointless that Richard Nixon would try to have them thrown out of the country. Bob Dylan summed up the feelings of most New Yorkers when he wrote a stirring appeal against Lennon's deportation: 'They inspire and transcend and stimulate and by doing so only help others to see pure light, and in doing that put an end to this mild dull taste of petty commercialism which is being passed off as artist art by the overpowering mass media. Hurray for John and Yoko. Let them stay and live here and breathe.'

Norman Mailer, Kurt Vonnegut and Fred Astaire added their eloquent voices and eventually, with Nixon gone from the White House, the US Immigration Department granted John and Yoko permanent residence. Although his old English conviction for possession of marijuana had been used to hound this wonderfully creative man, Lennon's later New York years marked a transition from drug and alcohol abuse into a period of healing. There were some lost years in the city, but his underlying artistic ability led him to music that explored his pain and then helped him recover. Given the depths of his alienation and drug-addled depression, the therapeutic power of music for Lennon was extraordinary. It is a terrible irony that a healthy and balanced Lennon would be gunned down on the streets of the city that he loved so much by an obsessive fan from out of town.

The man's life and music speak for themselves, but after meeting John and Yoko there was one overriding impression I was left with that does not seem to be adequately acknowledged. It was the widely despised Yoko Ono, the woman usually blamed for breaking up The Beatles and distracting John from his collaboration with Paul McCartney, who inspired much of Lennon's most powerful work. While few men have been able to 'turn on' the young the way The Beatles did, it was Yoko who 'turned on' John, showing him how to step outside the *Sgt. Pepper's* cardboard cut-out of The Beatles and to use the full power of his enormous talent.

First there was the honeymoon 'bed in' for peace. But Yoko inspired far more than media stunts and encouraged John's political instincts. Instead of surrendering to his alienation, Lennon began to write about it. His extraordinary artistic curiosity responded to Yoko Ono's challenge. Lennon's music began to confront universal issues and themes, and at the same time became more personal and potent. 'Working Class Hero', an anthem of anger and class-consciousness, is his most honest self-portrait. His cry for female equality, 'Woman is the Nigger of the World', was co-written by Yoko. That universal hymn 'Imagine', John later admitted, was inspired by Yoko's existential poems. And has anyone written a better anti-war line than 'All we are saying is give peace a chance'? That was another song from the years shared with Yoko when they both campaigned against the Vietnam War.

Obviously these songs struck a chord with millions of people and still do. Such music has an almost immeasurable humanising force. For this reason I have tried hard to understand and appreciate what musicians like John Lennon go through for their music.

The evolution of modern music is a thrilling story because it is about human spirit. Out of the struggle to survive a harsh world comes the sound of hope. In the deadening conformity of the technological age we hear an expression of individuality. There is pain and loneliness, disillusion and despair. But this is *our* story. There are also songs of joy, the whispered words of love and the merry dance that sets us free.

> *In a club called The Golden Casino, in Cherry Hill, New Jersey, a thousand pairs of hands clapped in unison.*
> *It was like being in a church down south. People were dressed in their Sunday best and hooting and hollering, most of them on their feet from beginning until end. This was a double bill the likes of which you only see once or twice in a lifetime. BB King, the 'King of the Blues', opened for Ray Charles, quite possibly the best singer I have ever heard.*
>
> (JOURNAL 1975)

The voice of Ray Charles in conversation is as rich and melodious as in song, a blend of whisky and honey. At the age of forty-five, with a towel draped around his neck like a prizefighter, he looked and sounded like a man in his prime. I went backstage to have a chat with Ray, not as an assignment but a personal pleasure that I knew I could share some day with someone who appreciated this musical genius as much as I did.

Ray is a virtuoso. He composes music, writes lyrics and is a masterful arranger. He plays piano, clarinet and alto sax. His voice is unique, soulful, heartbreaking, soaring, the sound of the church and the street. As a singer he is comfortable with jazz, blues, rock and country and western. He told me that he keeps about three hundred songs, words and music, catalogued by numbers in his head.

Ray was not born blind. He could see for the first five years of his life before the disease of glaucoma began to slowly close out the light and the shapes and the colour. The world of sound became more important. But Ray says he was never consumed by self-pity as his eyesight was fading because his was not the only pain in the family. The last scene he can remember, the indelible image imprinted on his mind forever, is that of his three-and-a-half-year-old brother drowning in a tub of water out in the yard, and his mother trying desperately to breathe life into the child. Her sadness grew heavier as Ray's eyesight deteriorated rapidly and he became totally blind by the age of seven. He was ten when his father died, fifteen when his mother died. It seems that if you need pain and suffering to sing the blues, Ray Charles had plenty to draw on.

'Yes, we were dirt poor in Georgia. I did have my share of pain. But I would have been a musician even if I hadn't suffered. Suffering contributes to understanding suffering. When I sing I can feel it in my soul. But I don't buy that tortured artist stuff that I had to suffer to express feeling. After those early days I've had great happiness too in my life. If I had never lost my eyesight I still would have been singing and playing. Music is just in me. And I want to say, I don't think I am good because I am blind. I'm good because I'm good. You don't need eyes for everything in the world. I was trying to sing even as a very young boy, as long back as I can remember. The sound just fascinated me.'

As a child, Ray would always come running when he heard the boogie-woogie piano playing in his next-door neighbour's house. Old Wiley Pittman became his first piano teacher. If Ray started banging on the keyboard, Wiley patiently would explain, 'Not like that, try your hands like this,' and he would show the child how to pick out simple melodies. From the night of our first conversation, a quarter of a century ago in the Golden Casino, whenever I heard Ray Charles play I would find myself thinking about that stranger, Wiley Pittman, who guided the young boy's hands on the piano. According to Ray, it was kindness, not pain, that led to his discovery of his extraordinary musical talent.

So many of the wonderful musicians of our time seem to burn brightly and then flame out like shooting stars. Perhaps they believe that they have to suffer to play the blues or maybe it is the insatiable appetite of the audience and the media for another tragic hero that keeps alive the myth of the tortured artist driven to self-destruction. After Elvis Presley, Jimi Hendrix, Janis Joplin, Jim Morrison, Duane Allman, Keith Moon, Brian Jones, Sid Vicious and far too many others, haven't we seen enough rock gods die? Why should the world expect them to suffer when they give us so much and when the music they are capable of has such extraordinary redemptive power?

Perhaps instead of adulation and hysteria some other type of appreciation, like true respect, might have sustained these flickering souls destroyed by their alienation from a world that supposedly worships them. So many of these tortured artists said that they felt their lives were cheap or worthless measured against the unrealistic expectations created by the myth machine. If the business world that so ruthlessly exploits such talented people had real respect for them, they would have been helped long before they self-destructed.

Whenever I hear the glorious music of Ray Charles, alive with improvisation, no song ever sung the same way twice, uniting us, inspiring us, I find myself hoping that he goes on forever, or at least goes out like Duke Ellington, still playing and loving it. I was thinking of them both when I joined a huge crowd of New Yorkers in the magnificent St John's Cathedral to say goodbye to Ellington. The stone walls of the cavernous church echoed with hymns from a huge gospel choir and people wept thinking of the joy the Duke had given the world with his music. I remembered Ray Charles's words and smiled. 'Nobody owns the notes. We just catch them in the palms of our hands, use them and let them fly free.'

The great American bluesman BB King is another who taught me how to find pure joy. He sings the blues not to celebrate sadness but to relieve it. When BB King took to the stage in the Golden Casino that night, he was like a preacher in church, hands held high, urging the congregation to find salvation in music.

The blues was the music of BB King's great-grandparents who were slaves in the American south. One man in the cotton fields had the role of 'shouter' to alert the other workers when the boss was on his way. *Hey, Hey, de Boss is on his Way.* This 'field hollerin'' became so popular with the slaves and their owners that by the time Riley B. King was picking cotton in Lexington, Mississippi, he could hear it sung on the radio. He had been singing in church since the age of five but when he took his guitar to town on Saturday evenings and played on street corners, there was not much money in the hat for gospel songs. It was playing the blues that earned him real wages. In one night he could double the $22.50 a week that he was paid on the plantation. It is no wonder that he went to Memphis where they introduced him as the Beale Street Blues Boy, BB King.

'When I was young the white boss of the plantation was sheriff, judge and jury,' the big man told me. 'Everything in life the boss decided, and you did not complain if you wanted to stay out of trouble.'

All of the old taboos had been drummed into King since childhood. Coloured kids were not allowed to ride on the bus with whites and so he and his friends had to walk eight kilometres to school. Sometimes as the bus passed, the white kids would throw things at them. At school they talked about this with a sympathetic teacher. He told them that it would not always be this way and that some day they all would ride on the bus together. Stand with your head up and look forward, he said. Not all white people were like those who were holding up the changes that were surely coming. As a result of that wise advice, King said he grew up not hating all white people but focusing his anger and considerable talents against the racism that kept blacks and whites apart.

The 'King of the Blues' played benefit concerts for Martin Luther King's crusade for civil rights and in his own distinctive fashion became an ambassador for racial harmony. It was the healing power of his music that built bridges between blacks and whites, with a sound that seemed to touch the deepest places. Even in his seventies he was sharing his blues in concert at least 250 nights a year. With the guitar he called 'Lucille' and a pull-out bed on a big tour bus, he rolled from town to town in over ninety countries. King belonged to an old tradition where you did not give up or throw life away. The bluesman kept hollerin' his stories, shoutin' about the bad old days and the better ones to come.

'If I sing, "And nobody loves me but my mother, and she could be jiving too," well that is the pits, ain't it?' he said, roaring with laughter as we sat backstage. 'But if I sing, "I've got a sweet little angel, I love the way she spreads her wings," well I am not blue at all. I'm having a ball,' he said, with a smile so wicked I can see it today.

BB King's great love of the blues has inspired many white musicians to take up his cause. Eric Clapton told me that, for him, BB King and Muddy Waters were about as good as it gets. Waters's playing and singing was all about pure power and simplicity. King's guitar was about sophistication, taste and economy, a refinement of the blues.

The great British guitarist told me that he always felt it was his burden to pass on the blues because it was the music that had given him strength. He felt the blues deeply, as if he were born to play it. Abandoned by his father even before he was born and raised mainly by his grandparents, Clapton picked up a guitar while still a young boy and for the first time felt connected to his inner self. When his fingers made those sounds with the strings, his usual fear and self-loathing disappeared. Long before he began to make a name for himself, in fact with the very first blues song he learned, Muddy Waters's 'Honey Bee', he felt truly happy for the first time in his life. While many people go through their lives without thinking much about what might bring them fulfilment, Clapton discovered that secret quite early. But for almost thirty years he mistakenly believed that he had to suffer to play the blues. This he managed first through heroin addiction and then by losing himself in alcohol, as if pain were the only path to self-discovery and artistic achievement.

It was an encounter on stage with the mesmerising talent of Jimi Hendrix that convinced Clapton that no matter what his fans said the insecure white Englishman was not God! Clapton had met most of his musical heroes like BB King, Muddy Waters, Bo Diddley and Robert Johnson through their records. But when Jimi Hendrix showed up at a London concert where Clapton was playing with his 'supergroup', Cream, he was an unknown quantity. The Howlin' Wolf song that Hendrix stroked and strangled from his electric guitar was so powerful that Clapton went into shock. He did not know how to deal with such breathtaking, original talent. Clapton was at an age when he was trying hard not to be impressed by anybody. He was known around London as 'The Man', after all. But in two minutes Hendrix took over the spotlight. Clapton felt he could have been swallowed up by such an enormous talent, wiped out right there on stage. He had no doubt that from then onwards he wanted to be black, to suffer and to feel the blues.

Clapton was in awe of Hendrix's talent, but the thing that ultimately impressed him the most about Hendrix was his humility, a quality you never hear fans or critics talk about. Hendrix, a gracious man, was sensitive to Clapton's insecurities and refused to be drawn into competition with him. The two became as close as brothers for the short few years they shared on this earthly stage.

Clapton told me how he brought a fine guitar home from the United States to give to Hendrix as a token of his love and respect. He went to see Hendrix in concert, taking the Stratocaster in its case. But there would be no show that night. Hendrix had died after a drug overdose.

After the deaths of some of Clapton's other musician friends, including Duane Allman and Janis Joplin, 'Slowhand' felt that he had been left behind. He did not care from that point whether he lived or died. He went on a journey into darkness, thinking that he was not suffering enough. Using heroin and all the other drugs was like throwing himself on a fire to feel what it was like to burn. He thought that alcohol helped him come out of his shell on stage, loosen up and play better. Now, Clapton says, he can recognise that the drugs and the booze were a self-defence mechanism that he, like a lot of artists, used to hide his lack of self-belief.

Although he is lauded as one of the greatest musicians of his age, Clapton believes that he wasted decades of musical development because of his surrender to the myth of the tortured artist. He used to cut short recording sessions because he did not have the confidence to work hard enough to refine the music. His writing, singing and guitar playing were limited by his lifestyle. The real test came when he sat down with a bottle of vodka, a few joints and some cocaine, turned on his tape-machine and started to play guitar. His perception at the time was that he sounded brilliant and everybody kept telling him that he was God. But, Clapton now says, a lot of that music was awful. With a clear head, he can see a big difference in his songwriting and hear an amazing improvement in his playing.

Another musical generation has come and gone since Clapton's self-destructive days. The world has lost Kurt Cobain, Michael Hutchence and Jeff Buckley, and it seems that not much has been learned at all. Kurt Cobain said that he did not deserve the roar of the crowd. He was just a piece of garbage and the fools would not like him if they knew the truth. Clapton understands that dark view, but is disturbed that young musicians still feel they have to burn their wings. They cannot see that self-destructive addiction holds them back from greatness; it does not set them free.

Eric Clapton, like Kurt Cobain, had frustrated the friends who tried to help him. Pete Townshend of The Who knew all about the strength of heroin's grip and with Clapton's loved ones he persisted, leading the troubled man to treatment. But then alcohol swallowed Clapton up. He still could not see through the fog. It was only after the death of fellow musician Stevie Ray Vaughan in a helicopter crash and the terrifying plunge of his four-year-old son, Conor, fifty-three storeys from a New York apartment that

Clapton decided he wanted to be healed. To end his painfully obsessive self-pity, he approached counselling seriously and used his songwriting as therapy.

I told Clapton that when he played his song, 'Tears in Heaven', everyone understood how he felt. He did not have to talk with me about the death of Conor. I wanted to offer him a chance of silence on this painful and personal subject. Clapton nodded, but went on to explain, eloquently and movingly, how Conor's death had made him feel totally alone, in a place no one could reach. When he had to go and look at Conor in a tiny coffin, Clapton was helpless.

I listened intently as Clapton told me how he had taken his little boy to the circus the day before his death. They watched the clowns and laughed together, father and son. It was their last time together and when you hear Clapton sing 'The Day the Circus Came to Town' you can feel him holding on to those precious hours and using the music to try to find a way through his life-shattering experience. First, he told me, he would just hold his guitar and play. With his fingers on the strings, he would reach places no other key could unlock. The music, Clapton said, disengaged his mind and made him stop thinking about how he *should* be feeling. It allowed him to just *feel*. He stopped feeling sorry for himself and was carried high on his limitless love for Conor. Almost whispering, Clapton said that the key thing he had learned about life from the death of his son was that we only had this moment. Anything could happen before the sun set.

Whenever that 'outlaw' Australian artist Brett Whiteley attacked a fresh canvas, he liked to turn up the music. With his shock of wild curls bobbing and weaving, there was a connection between the beat and the brushstrokes. The music connected the painter to his inner-self and this was especially true if it were Mark Knopfler's guitar that was playing in Whiteley's studio.

The Dire Straits frontman told me, during a break in rehearsals in London a few years ago, that he drew tremendous pleasure from knowing that Whiteley painted to his music. Knopfler said that he had met few people as brilliant as Whiteley, as adept at conveying so many ideas with such flourish and talking about his own art with such freshness.

I discussed with Knopfler the impact of Brett Whiteley's death from a heroin overdose, this interest of mine in the deep insecurity of artists and musicians, and how this contributed to so much self-destruction. A fine Whiteley painting graces the cover of one of Dire Straits's early albums, *Alchemy*. It was clear that there was mutual admiration. But Mark Knopfler told me that they had taken quite a while to get close after meeting during one of the band's tours of Australia. Perhaps it was Knopfler's suspicion and his own deep insecurity, he said, but it took time to knock down the walls. Once they struck up a friendship, they enjoyed the dance of ideas that is so pleasurable to artists of different mediums.

When Whiteley ended his life the way of so many rock 'n' rollers, Knopfler found himself regretting that he had not spent more time with the brilliant but troubled Australian. He said that it would never be the same visiting Sydney without Whiteley, whose passion and painting seemed to express what the English musician loved about the harbour and its light.

Knopfler told me that he could identify with Whiteley's long struggle. Watching the lyrical grace and poetry in the brushstrokes he understood that art was a place of light to escape to when the darkness of self-doubt descended. Knopfler said he had gone through a lot of years when he did not have a particularly high opinion of himself, because of doubts about his real measure of talent. Living was a difficult business, but it was his music that made him appreciate life. He now drew great pleasure from the fact that people used his music to live with, as a marker for different events in their lives, for weddings, anniversaries, births and even funerals. He had been crossing under the English Channel one day when a French boy working on the train told him that whenever his troubles got too heavy he put on Knopfler's music and those troubles disappeared. Another great player had found the secret of his own happiness.

In the kitchen of his mansion at the edge of London's Hampstead Heath, the musician the world knows as Sting opened his arms to cradle his brand new baby boy, Giacomo. This was a house full of joy and wonderful music, once owned by the great classical musician Yehudi Menuhin, and now by one of the finest craftsmen of modern songwriting. The child, Sting's sixth, was named after the Italian composer Giacomo Puccini. For a rock god, Sting's taste surprisingly ran to older traditions.

I first met Sting in New York in the early 1980s and always enjoyed swapping stories with him about travels in the Amazon and sharing his passion for music. I admired the intellect of this former teacher who had stretched the boundaries of the modern song. At that point Sting was trying to move on from the fame he had established in The Police, a three-man band he dismantled at the very peak of its success. Everybody in the rock industry had said he was crazy walking away from an act that had packed more people into New York's Shea Stadium than The Beatles. And yet here he was sane and happy, with a baby boy in his arms. We laughed about the merits of trusting your own instincts at the most crucial times in life.

Sting's gift to us in the rock age is a mercurial music that draws on and spills into different traditions, but comes together in a tantalising form that reaches millions of people in diverse cultures. Sting sees music as one language. He refuses to pay attention to artificial compartments. Rock 'n' roll, jazz, folk, African, Middle Eastern, Latin American and classical music, Sting loves it all and plays with musicians who have facility in all of these fields, who are able to move seamlessly from one form to another. Music, for this wonderful songwriter, is an intriguing, mysterious journey. He is still studying it and feels that he needs to know more.

Sting had achieved fame and fortune beyond the dreams of a milkman's son, played to the world on stage and screen, and been hailed by none less than Frank Sinatra as the voice most likely to carry on the tradition of modern music. Yet he felt the need to play the role of the angry young man, the 'King of Pain' as he described himself in song. Deeply introspective, he had long felt outside the social mainstream, angry about the injustices he found around the world and full of angst about his personal relationships. When he bared his soul in the album, *The Soul Cages*, expressing the pain of bereavement after his father's death, critics psychoanalysed his behaviour. Whether he was on a political rock tour for Amnesty International or campaigning for the preservation of Amazon rainforests, someone was always second-guessing his motives. Despite his great success Sting was uncomfortable being observed constantly and having his life summed up by others. The loss of true privacy only makes famous people feel more alienated.

Sting came to realise that success and happiness were not the same thing. He also rejected the conventional rock wisdom that to be creative he had to be in pain. He began to look for satisfaction in simpler things. With six children he felt he had to be optimistic about the future and this helped him find contentment. It made perfect sense to be with his family and to create music at the same time.

Watching Sting at home, in the recording studio, on a film set in Paris or catching up again backstage in Sydney, I found a man at peace with himself and the world. He played his wonderful music for anyone who appreciated it, but already it had healed him.

The voice is a wonderful instrument, so are the hands and the brain. But at the end of the song it seems that the heart is left in charge.

Walking the line
Between desire and a fall
It takes the breath away
But don't be afraid
Because in time
You will find your balance
Up on this old high wire.

(JOURNAL 1982)

CHAPTER FOURTEEN

DANCING AT THE WHITE HOUSE

The large Christmas tree at the centre of a grand room in the president's residence was dripping with tradition, golden ornaments gleaming like the eyes of the man who greeted us. Ronald and Nancy Reagan were hosting a party for those who worked at the White House, like my wife Kim. There were a few of the powerbrokers in Congress and a handful of diplomats present. I was known as that Australian correspondent Kim Hoggard had married.

'It looks like I accomplished one thing here in the White House,' Reagan chuckled. 'You're a lucky man.'

In the eyes of most Americans and especially those who saw him in the Oval Office daily, Ronald Reagan was a charming, good-humoured president even in the most testing circumstances.

When a deranged young gunman, John Hinckley, tried to assassinate him on the streets of Washington during his first year in office, Reagan shrugged off his painful bullet wound, telling his wife, 'Honey, I forgot to duck.' He muttered to one of the doctors about to operate on him, 'I hope you're a Republican,' and then the surgeons got to work to dig out the bullet that tore through his ribs, down through a lung, stopping less than a centimetre or two from his heart.

It was only the bravery of his secret servicemen that saved the life of the boss they called 'Rawhide'. As Hinckley opened fire, one secret serviceman flung himself in front of the president and was shot in the chest. Another pushed Reagan into the back of the presidential limousine and tried to shield him. A policeman took a bullet in the neck and one of Kim's closest colleagues, presidential press secretary Jim Brady, suffered a terrible wound to the head. It left the 'Bear', as everyone called Brady, paralysed and confined to a wheelchair.

Just one week before the assassination attempt Kim had carried out virtually the same task as Brady's, escorting Reagan to a speech in the same downtown venue, the Washington Hilton Hotel. As assistant press secretary she routinely directed the White House press corps and it was just luck or fate that she was not in that hail of gunfire as the presidential party stepped from the hotel's side entrance towards their limousines.

John Hinckley had been trailing the actress Jodie Foster around the country trying to tell her how he felt after seeing her in the movie *Taxi Driver*. Hinckley said the shooting scene in the movie gave him the idea of killing somebody to show his love for the actress. When I met Foster briefly many years later I was respectful of her strength in surviving so long in a Hollywood career knowing that she had been stalked by a dangerous, delusional menace.

I stood outside the hospital to which Reagan had been admitted, trying to explain to my television audience how even the leader of a superpower was not safe in the capital of a gun-crazy nation. I wondered how many assassination attempts it would take before Congress agreed on reasonable gun control. Jim Brady and his wife, Sarah, campaigned hard for the registration of handguns, but the fact remained that somewhere in the United States you could always buy the most lethal automatic weapons.

After the shooting, the secret service was reluctant to let Reagan attend some public events. He was asked more often to wear what he called his 'iron underwear'. My wife was not offered a bullet-proof vest and, like the rest of Reagan's staff, accepted the risk as part of public service.

It was easy to warm to Reagan personally because of his courage and his passion for the virtues of American life. The son of a shoe salesman had become an actor, the president of the Screen Actors Guild, governor of California and then president of the United States. He was tall, handsome and athletic even in his late sixties, a man's man who had played football, led the swimming team and ridden horses over the jumps. Out on his Californian ranch Reagan liked to chop wood and build fences. When he slid into the saddle Americans were comforted by his frontier spirit, especially as he had survived his own shootout at the OK Corral. Reagan drew so much from his movie career that reality sometimes was blurred and we were never quite sure whether his stories had come from an old script. But for a B-grade actor he gave a stunning performance before a live audience or indeed the whole nation watching on television. My only concern was that Reagan often seemed to be *acting* the part of president.

I was never convinced that Reagan was intellectually gifted enough to be the leader of the free world. My experience in Nicaragua dodging the bullets of the counter-revolutionaries led me to believe that when it came to foreign policy, Reagan was not in control of his major players. Those scandalous secret deals with the *contra* and the Iranians were the consequence of much intrigue and real chaos in foreign policy. Reagan later admitted that he had not been told by Colonel Oliver North that the National Security Council had promised the Iranians secret intelligence data for their war against Iraq. To the dismay of Reagan's White House chief-of-staff, James Baker, some of his foreign policy staff sometimes ignored the president's wishes until Reagan overrode them with his single-mindedness.

'He stayed his own man and that is one of the great strengths of the Reagan era,' Baker told me to support his view that although Reagan was not well served by his foreign policy staff, 'his presidency was the most effective in a quarter century'.

Baker cited the example of the contest between the United States and the Soviet Union which pitted Reagan against a succession of Kremlin leaders who 'kept dying on him'. After outlasting Brezhnev, Andropov and Chernenko, Reagan squared off against one of the intellectual giants of our time, Mikhail Gorbachev. The American leader, nonetheless, followed his instincts, convinced of the strength of democracy and the inherent weakness of communism. When Reagan got hold of Gorbachev's masterwork, *perestroika,* setting out his visionary reforms of the decrepit Soviet economy, he realised it was an epitaph for Russian-style communism. Reagan never wavered from his strong belief that democracy would triumph in the Cold War because it was based on freedom of the individual, not the power of the state.

'He is very principled. He does not change. You pretty much know where he is coming from and I think the American people like that strength,' Baker told me.

Like most of the powerful White House team under James Baker, Kim was chosen because she could handle a crisis. The president's men and women sometimes appeared overqualified for their jobs until the pressure was suddenly on and the execution of their duties demanded nothing short of excellence. There was the Falklands War (which I covered from Buenos Aires), the decision to send jets to attack Libya's Colonel Gaddafi, the invasion of Grenada, not to mention the unravelling of the Soviet Empire. All of these crises at the White House required a superhuman effort, weeks without the normal amount of sleep, a concentration and intensity of purpose that tested physical and mental endurance.

Kim believes Ronald Reagan was an effective president because he performed like a skilled chairman of the board. He understood his strengths and limitations but always had the respect of his most senior aides. He delegated power efficiently to those he came to trust, like ex-Marine James Baker, a brilliant lawyer and a master of detail. It was Reagan too who promoted to National Security Adviser the strategically brilliant Colin Powell, who later would direct the Gulf War and go on to become the first black Secretary of State under George W. Bush.

Never a right-wing ideologue, Kim disagreed with some of the Reagan Administration's views — on a woman's right to abortion for instance — but she believed it was better to be making her arguments as a young woman inside the male-dominated circle of power. She found most of her male colleagues contemptuous of feminism and occasionally patronising, but many came to appreciate and respect her talent, which James Baker described as 'always cool under pressure'.

Ronald Reagan's own view of women was expressed in his worship of his wife, Nancy, whom he called the light of his life. The devotion to Nancy and the way he publicly expressed it, standing on a stage and beaming up towards her in the gallery, had the familiar qualities of an old Hollywood movie. While Nancy was protective of her man after the assassination attempt, there is no evidence that she influenced Reagan's major decisions the way Hillary pulled the strings of President Bill Clinton. To Reagan, Nancy was his beloved co-star in the White House movie. His favourite lines about love and his other homilies on life often came from films. Relaxing at the Camp David retreat one weekend, Kim joined the president in his lodge to watch the current box office hit, *Splash*. It starred Daryl Hannah as a mermaid. 'Ah ha,' said Reagan when the movie ended. 'Boy gets girl. Boy loses girl. Boy gets fish.'

'Yes,' replied Kim laughing, 'and it's about time Hollywood made a movie where the boy leaves *his* world for the girl!'

During one of Reagan's campaign trips, *Doonesbury* cartoonist Garry Trudeau joined the entourage of journalists. He later wrote a musical satire that caught another distinctive feature of Rawhide's presidency. Secret servicemen shuffled onto the Broadway stage singing:

From 9 to 12, from Monday clear to Wednesday,
from 9 to 12, this cowboy earns his keep,
but counting commies can get a man plum tuckered,
so 12 to 5 old 'Rawhide's' counting sheep.

Old Rawhide wasn't afraid to acknowledge his age. With hand cupped to ear he often bent to ask someone to repeat what they had said a little more loudly into his hearing aid. Uncle Sam's electronic eavesdropping experts had to sweep the hearing aid to prevent foreign spies from bugging the president with radio waves. The only crack in his armour Reagan had no way of foreseeing was the onset of Alzheimer's disease. His rigorous medical examinations while in the White House detected no sign of the cursed affliction which crippled his mind after he retired, but the jury is still out on how age affected his power of reasoning. I wonder about the mental balance of some of the Kremlin's old men too, from Brezhnev to the vodka-swilling Yeltsin, and also how Richard Nixon's unstable, delusional mind affected his critical judgments.

It was an interesting and challenging life for Kim and me, the White House staffer and the foreign correspondent. The CIA officially categorised me as an 'alien spouse'. During their extensive background checks one agent wondered why my dog, Ned Kelly, had a rubber Ronnie Reagan doll for a chew-thing. In well-worn leather jacket and jeans I would shuffle past the secret servicemen into Kim's hotel room as we rendezvoused in foreign capitals on our separate missions. We had to be careful in our journalist–diplomat relationship, but it never presented us with an ethical dilemma.

You could assume that I was very well informed about foreign affairs but Kim respected her privileged access to classified information and never betrayed that trust. She also never expected me to be a source of information for diplomats. Once, after filming the dirty guerilla war in Mozambique, an American ambassador pumped me for information. 'Sorry,' I said, 'you'll have to get a report as my story goes to air.'

Over the years I have had approaches from several diplomats and government officials — American, Australian and British — and even the odd beautiful spy seeking information about events I have witnessed. The CIA was mainly interested in why I made so many trips behind the Iron Curtain. An agent asked me directly whether I had ever been 'compromised' by a Russian woman.

'What exactly do you mean, *compromised*?' I replied, enjoying the game.

'Ahh ... put in a position by a beautiful Russian woman so that you could be blackmailed into passing on vital information or even American secrets,' said the agent.

'Look, I am a journalist and I don't really believe in secrets but you ask James Baker whether he thinks Kim or I would utter a word to jeopardise her work. If you've been watching me in the Soviet Union you'd know it was a beautiful Estonian woman, not a Russian, who tried to *compromise* me.'

In the aftermath of the Chernobyl disaster, with a great deal of fear and radiation in the air, I had taken a *60 Minutes* film crew as close as I could to the nuclear accident. We went to a lot of trouble to try to shake off the Soviet spooks who shadowed us everywhere and we managed to secretly record some revealing sound-only interviews with ordinary people describing the panic after the reactor meltdown. The Soviets put forward that friendly old bear Joe Adamov, a rotund apologist for the Kremlin, to attempt to explain away the radiation spill, but they also tried a secret weapon. A dark-haired, bikini-clad Estonian goddess appeared at my hotel offering her services — as a translator, a guide perhaps, or maybe just a dinner companion. My crew and I were not eager to dine at all given that most of the produce in the Kiev region had been irradiated, and despite the fact that the Estonian's English was as perfect as her body we could hardly use her as a translator for our secret interviews. To underscore the obviousness of these Cold War *femmes fatales,* I received a note long after I had left the USSR saying that the Estonian beauty was still waiting to be liberated.

In Washington, Kim was named as the first spokeswoman for the United States Treasury, one of a number of appointments where she broke the gender barrier. But in 1986 we had a family crisis, the kind that can hit anyone but suddenly challenges people in positions of influence to make crucial decisions about their priorities in life. To the surprise of most of her colleagues in Washington, Kim resigned and moved to Australia with me. I will never forget how graciously and unselfishly she walked away from her successful Washington career.

We told few at that time but my father, Jack, was ailing with lung cancer. Kim and I agreed that after fourteen years in the United States it was time for me to go home and put a smile on his face. Jack always had drawn so much satisfaction from our wanderings about the world. He kept our letters, photographs and postcards in books that he would pull out to proudly show the doctors and nurses gathered around him.

The last year with my father was precious to us all. We listened to his stories and he was keen to hear ours, always passing comment with his distinctive wit and wisdom. When we visited him in hospital for the final time, he was still joking.

'Do you need more morphine, Jack?' a nursing sister asked him.

'No thanks,' he said with a twinkle, 'but I'd love a schooner!'

A fitting epitaph for you, Throbber, although no tombstone could ever bury so much spirit. I am thankful you were my father. I kiss your forehead now.

> Have you ever just watched the rain
> and wondered
> who gave us this day?
> all we really need
> falling down our way,
> a new flower,
> the beauty of the clearing sky
> and the sunshine
> warming every part of us
> with love and words
> that last through the coldest days
> and see us on our way again
> with hope and confidence
> and an old familiar smile,
> knowing there will always be
> sunshine.

(JOURNAL 1987)

From the day we first met on the lawns of the White House I saw a quality in Kim that I cherish. She is a woman who speaks her mind in a language I can understand. I didn't get to know her well until President Reagan made a trip to the Caribbean in April 1982. I went along on my last assignment as the ABC's White House correspondent before moving back to my favourite city, New York, to take up a commission as a roving reporter for *Four Corners*. Aboard Air Force One flying from Jamaica to Barbados was the beautiful woman I had met at the White House. As we walked on a white Barbados beach, it was very easy for me to be swept away. I told her she belonged to the south seas, as she was born in Hawaii.

At the first chance we flew south to a thatched hut overlooking a clear lagoon and the volcanic peaks of Bora Bora in the Society Islands. As we swam in the warm turquoise sea and dived on the coral reefs, I found a soulmate. We could sit on the end of the jetty and talk about any matter on earth with honesty, on the same wavelength. Isn't this what it takes to find a true companion? Two people must find suitable challenge and reason for respect. Natures must be compatible as well as lips. Kim and I met laughing in a beautiful place and it has been like that ever since.

Kim's finer qualities were remembered well in the White House. Soon after George Bush was elected president in 1988, I predicted that James Baker would be named Secretary of State and that Kim would be getting a phone call at our home in Sydney from the transition team. 'Do it,' I said, and she joined a second Republican administration. We began another phase of international commuting, with homes on two sides of the world. I have lost count of how many times we made that twenty-four-hour flight between Sydney and Washington, lines scribbled on the sky, thoughts flying to the other hemisphere where together we felt whole. It seemed a curious marriage to some in the White House and my journalistic colleagues. Why be married and spend so much time apart?

I could have replied, why be married and watch the love of my life wilting for lack of the same opportunities I enjoyed? I learned from Kim that a man could not spend his life talking about freedom and equality. It was better to try it with the woman you loved. Besides, anyone who knows about time spent apart knows also about the glorious homecomings.

After President Bush was sworn in, Kim was appointed to an exciting high-level position. She was the first woman to hold that mouthful of a title, Senior Deputy Assistant Secretary of State. This involved running a department of 140 men and women, most of them career civil service officers older than she was. As well as managing a good deal of the daily public affairs of the world's most powerful Foreign Office, she directed its historians, recording a time of great world change. Living in Washington we were surrounded by history. A young Senator John F. Kennedy once had lived on our street, and Ben Bradlee of the *Washington Post* was on a corner opposite one of the Watergate villains, Nixon's Attorney-General, John Mitchell. Washington is that kind of place.

The first home we shared in the old village of Georgetown was once owned by a Civil War doctor who had walked across our courtyard to the nearby hospital to tear out lead and saw off the mangled limbs of Union soldiers. It was sobering to sit by our fireside, reading of this terrible bloodshed that touched our own extended family. While Kim's mother, Claire Canavan, was a Yankee from New York, her father, William D. Hoggard II, was a southerner from North Carolina. The Hoggards, originally Welsh farmers and shipwrights, came to the colony of Virginia in 1654, built the first shipyard in America and fought in the Revolution against the British. But during the Civil War this huge southern clan was divided. Some fought with the Confederates, others opposed the war and secession from the Union. At a time when any southerner who stood with President Lincoln was condemned to execution if captured by the Confederates, some of the Hoggards captained Union companies and one led former slaves into the war in their own fight for freedom. Among the three million Americans who fought in the Civil War and the 600 000 who were killed there were many such stories, as neighbour literally fought neighbour, especially in states close to the 'divide' like North Carolina. We talked in our family about the violent past, and when we could truly say we were fighting for survival, or justice, or the common good. It has been a shared interest in learning from our own history.

During Kim's watch at the State Department, there were many extraordinary upheavals around the world. China's democracy movement defied the tanks in Tiananmen Square, black South Africans gained political power, the Berlin Wall collapsed, the Baltic States demanded independence and the Soviet empire, long held together by the force of totalitarianism, disintegrated into fractious states, ethnic rivalries and a great uncertainty about the future. The challenge for the State Department was to manage this sweeping tide of change.

The climactic experience of Kim's professional career was without doubt the Gulf War in 1991. As a member of the Secretary of State's inner circle, she travelled with James Baker in a final and futile effort to prevent the unleashing of Operation Desert Storm against Saddam Hussein. American diplomacy had succeeded brilliantly in building up an unprecedented international coalition, persuading Iraq's traditional allies to stay out of the war, drawing the Soviet Union into support of the United Nations resolutions approving military action, and getting Germany and Japan to pay for the build-up of a vastly superior military force. Yet it was equally important for political reasons for American diplomacy to make an earnest effort to find a peaceful solution.

History judges statesmen after every war. When we weigh up whether the bloodshed in the Gulf War could have been avoided, judgment surely will fall harshly on Iraq's leader. He not only invaded another country, he amassed enough weapons of mass destruction to delude himself into thinking he had an opportunity to control the region's oil fields and to rule the Middle East. Saddam Hussein grossly underestimated George Bush's willingness to use military force, believing that the Vietnam syndrome still crippled the American will. The patient American groundwork surely should have told Saddam that war was coming unless he withdrew his troops from Kuwait. But this was a man with a Nebuchadnezzar complex, bent on domination of the ancient tribes of his region. James Baker believes that Saddam could see the decline of Russian influence and the ascendancy of American power in the Middle East, and sensed that this 'perhaps' was his last chance for conquest.

There was a proposal that would have seen Kim flying with the Baker team to Baghdad for a face-to-face meeting with the Iraqi leader. But Saddam was a cunning, ruthless, unstable dictator and it was feared that he might not play by the rules but hold the team hostage as the United Nations deadline of midnight, 15 January 1991 rapidly approached.

Shadowed by a tense security squad, the Baker team flew instead to Geneva. Kim and others in Baker's inner circle negotiated with the Iraqis until 3 a.m. just to settle the protocol for the meeting with Saddam's Foreign Minister, Tariq Aziz. This was the moment James Baker described as 'the last, best chance for peace', but it was a moment entirely in the hands of Saddam.

When the ramrod-straight Baker sat down with the smooth Iraqi envoy, the American put on the table a letter from his president to Saddam. It was an offer of peace. George Bush had been influenced by his diverse experiences as a fighter pilot, politician, ambassador, CIA boss and now Commander-in-Chief. He expected war and was planning for it. But his political instinct told him to offer Saddam one last chance to avoid bloodshed. The Bush letter repeated a public guarantee that if Saddam withdrew his troops from Kuwait they would not be attacked, but it also warned very firmly that going to war would be a calamity for the people of Iraq. The letter to Saddam sat on the table.

Baker then increased the pressure. He bluntly told Aziz that this would not be another Vietnam War. There would be no stalemate, ceasefire or pause for negotiation. If war began, Iraq would be defeated swiftly and decisively.

After Iraq's relentless war of attrition against Iran, many believed that Saddam Hussein felt invincible, even divinely chosen to defeat the infidels from the west. He had a terrifying arsenal of chemical and biological weapons and the capability of launching them against the Saudis and Israelis. If you have wondered why this military madman did not unleash those weapons during the Gulf War the answer probably lies in James Baker's next menacing words to Tariq Aziz in Geneva. If Saddam were foolish enough to use chemical or biological weapons the coalition objective would become not only the liberation of Kuwait, but the elimination of the Iraqi regime. Baker says the Bush Administration had ruled out the use of tactical nuclear missiles or chemical weapons against the Iraqis, but the ambiguity of his threat apparently helped snuff out an even greater tragedy. After almost seven hours of tension, argument and circular debate, the meeting ended with a grim handshake between Baker and Aziz. In a fatalistic frame of mind and obviously under orders from Saddam Hussein, the Iraqi envoy walked out with the letter still on the bargaining table. The last slim chance of avoiding war was squandered.

On a military Boeing 707 that once had been President John F. Kennedy's Air Force One, Kim flew with the Secretary of State to the Taif airbase in Saudi Arabia where the fighter bombers and electronic-jamming planes were getting ready for war. Her unforgettable impression was that these American men and women seemed so very young as they sauntered across the swirling sands.

'Time is running out but the path to peace remains open,' James Baker told the anxious troops gathered in a large hangar, but there were loud cheers and whistles when he said they would not have to wait much longer. Kim wondered how many of this group would die in the war; how many allies and Iraqis would lose their lives because Saddam Hussein refused to back down and withdraw peacefully from the country he had invaded.

THE WAR

For days dark storms
have gouged this sullen sky
bending all that stands
in nature's path.
Across the pitch-black sea
the Gulf is on fire,
a man-made hail
crushes a man's last breath.

Death has pierced so many hearts,
erased all meaning and memory,
nothing learned from history
except that nothing's learned.
Appeasement or peace,
occupation or retreat,
a just war . . . but
just death.
Four billion souls are now bound tight,
lashed together with electric wire,
the nervous system of the world,
plugged into this hellfire.

(JOURNAL 1991)

The devastating force of the air war and the short, blunt ground assault produced remarkably few Allied casualties but a terrible slaughter of Iraqis. When Operation Desert Storm was over, Kim flew above a highway of death looking down at hundreds of burned-out Iraqi tanks and armoured personnel carriers caught in the open on the last day of the war.

Kuwait's oil fields were burning in a fury of orange flame and acrid smoke, but Saddam Hussein was still in power. Although some believe that the coalition forces should have driven on to Baghdad to destroy the Iraqi leader and what was left of his Republican Guard, few who understand the Middle East and the history of the Iraqi regime think that option would have improved the chances of a lasting peace. The American leadership believed it had smashed Iraq's major weapons of mass destruction and wanted to avoid the far greater civilian loss of life which would have occurred had Baghdad been reduced to rubble. Killing Saddam would have created a martyr and united people in hatred of the west. A war of liberation would have been recast as a war of conquest. One of the lessons bitterly learned from the American experience in Vietnam was not to waver from the clearly defined objective of forcing Saddam out of Kuwait and freeing the world's

My mother Joyce was a genuinely liberated 'working mother'. She would say you don't need much to be happy, but she always wanted more for her children.

My father Jack said she had the warmest laughter in the world, but he also knew he had broken her heart.

My wife, Kim Hoggard, briefs President Ronald Reagan at the White House. Kim found him a successful 'Chairman of the Board' who delegated power prudently and recognised his limitations. Kim worked in two Washington Administrations, for Reagan first, then for President George Bush.

Ronald and Nancy Reagan welcome me to their Christmas Party on 14 December 1983. I met Kim at the White House.

Photo courtesy of US Government

Kim was part of the inner circle as James Baker moved through some of the most important jobs in the White House: Chief-of-Staff, Treasury Secretary and Secretary of State.

Photo by Jeff McMullen

Claire and Will are pals as well as brother and sister. They are so full of wide-eyed wonder that they inspire me with optimism about this world.

'Go Cathy, go!' I met Cathy Freeman when she was a teenager and admired her natural grace and speed. I took her rollerblading in London's Hyde Park because she wanted to 'go faster'. She always loved the feeling of speed, of having the wind in her hair and just racing the other kids.

BB King handed me his guitar, 'Lucille', and said, 'Go ahead, play it.' He is one of the most gracious masters of music, humble about his talent and still enjoying 250 concerts a year, even in his seventies.

Photo by Jeff McMullen

My *60 Minutes* crew in radiation suits at the Atomic Lake in Kazakhstan where the Russians tested their nuclear weapons, irradiating the local population.

Photo by Mark Brewer

Cameraman Phil Donoghue was mauled by a wild dog out on this irradiated stretch of desert on the nuclear test range at Semipalatinsk, Kazakhstan. We had no anti-rabies shots so I gave him Russian vodka.

Australian war crimes investigator Mike Hourigan campaigned bravely to hold the United Nations accountable for its shameful role in the genocide in Rwanda. With weapons like these, up to one million people are believed to have died in just 100 days.

My crew, Julian Cress, Phil Donoghue and Mark Brewer, were overwhelmed at times by the scale of the killing in Rwanda.

Photo by Jeff McMullen

Vulcanologists Maurice and Katia Kraft pose with one of 'the bombs' thrown up by the volcano we climbed together, Mount Etna in Sicily. These lava lovers were later blown to pieces by a volcano in Japan.

Photo by Val Taylor

Diving with a ten-metre whale shark at Ningaloo Reef in Western Australia.

With a husky in Antarctica.

Anyone who knows about constant foreign travel knows also about the glorious homecomings. This time Claire and Will were ecstatic when I met them, for a change, at Sydney airport after they had been to see Kim's family in the United States.

oil supplies. The American generals and diplomats had thought carefully about what could be called victory.

While Kim was at war, I was shuttling between the United States and Australia, always concerned about her vulnerability, her potential exposure to terrorist attack and crazed assassins or, for that matter, to the perils of walking in the streets of the American capital where she was mugged by a youthful gang. She made some risky trips in the course of her career, including one to Bogota to negotiate with the Colombian government at a time when the drug barons were kidnapping and murdering at will. There still was no 'iron underwear' for her, just plenty of attitude. James Baker tells the story of how Kim led a party of White House journalists straight past a protesting guard armed with an Uzi who tried to block them from doing the work of the Fourth Estate. These experiences allowed Kim to trust my own snap decisions and considered judgment about the dangers I faced and we sometimes shared. One time Kim's party was meeting President Mikhail Gorbachev to discuss the new world order, while I was interviewing Russians predicting a military coup and massive upheaval. It made for interesting conversations. But for two people born two days (and quite a few years) apart, living under different flags never made an important difference.

After ten years of an exciting, albeit unusual, marriage, we decided to have a family, believing that it could only add to what we shared. Kim said goodbye to her family, friends and colleagues and this time they sensed she meant it. Together we flew back to our home by the sea in Sydney. Kim's parents, Bill and Claire, were delighted, but also in a state of shock, having thought that we would never settle anywhere long enough to have a child. But life was still full of startling surprises.

> We all come from the sea
> adrift in time and space,
> a speck of life
> washed ashore
> to begin the human race.

I sail like a submariner
blowing bubbles from my brain,
baby swims inside you,
we think of life
and pain.

Your muscles strain
as baby grows,
I lift my arms and legs,
deep breathing keeps us going,
why, only lovers know.

Baby's heart is pounding,
yours is keeping time,
close your eyes
and listen now,
the love you hear is mine.

(JOURNAL 1993)

With Kim pregnant, I was the one unexpectedly rushed into hospital. After diving off the coast of Tasmania to film the invasion of foreign starfish into our natural fisheries, I was struck by a dangerous case of the bends. The navy had me in a decompression chamber after diagnosing an embolism, a bubble of air in the brain.

The dive to the bottom of Hobart Harbour in midwinter had revealed the ghastly spectacle of thousands of ravenous seastars feasting on the local shellfish. The water was cold and murky and the cameraman and I had worked hard to get our pictures. Seastars as big as dinner plates would crawl onto the smaller native starfish or any cluster of shellfish and consume them at an astonishing rate. Off the eastern coast of Tasmania we dived again, watching just a handful of seastars devour the equivalent of sackfuls of juicy scallops, much to the horror of the local industry.

A leading marine scientist, Dr Peter Young, said that the seastars had been carried into Australia in the ballast water of the

Japanese ships that hauled away our woodchips. I watched these vessels pulling up to our shores, flushing their ballast tanks and taking on the huge piles of woodchips, thinking this was environmental lunacy. Not only were we destroying vast stands of magnificent old-growth forest, some of the biggest and most beautiful trees in the world, but this trade in woodchips was importing a new threat to our ecosystem.

On the way home to Sydney with my *60 Minutes* story in hand, we took off from Hobart, touched down briefly in Melbourne, and then my brain lifted into a very strange cloud land. I felt a persistent pressure above the frontal lobes but none of the sharp physical pain that one expected with decompression sickness. Once home I consulted my diving and medical books and noted some mysterious cases of the bends included these symptoms, so I called the Australian navy's School of Underwater Medicine, HMAS *Penguin*, at Middle Head on Sydney Harbour.

Lieutenant Robyn Walker first gave me a concentration test. I was not able to tell her that Paul Keating was Australia's prime minister. I laughed thinking what Keating would have made of that, but I realised my predicament was serious when a mathematics test had me stumbling to deduct two from 100.

I was rushed into a decompression chamber, a submarine-like vessel that simulated a dive to a depth of about eighteen metres, where I breathed pure oxygen for almost five hours. As my pregnant wife peered anxiously through the portholes wondering whether this adventure had stretched my mind too far, Dr Walker's expert naval team calmly reassured us that some day soon I would remember Paul Keating.

After three days of treatment in the decompression chamber the bubble in my brain slowly dissolved. Dr Walker's analysis suggested that although I had not flown home until thirty hours after my last dive in Tasmania, the vigorous exertion and possible slight dehydration had combined to produce the dangerous embolism. Young naval divers had been struck by the bends diving in extremely shallow waters and it was thought that their previous day's exercise, pumping iron in the gym, could have contributed to the inability of their bodies to dissolve the dangerous nitrogen that remained in their bloodstream. The Abalone Divers' Association asked me to warn the public that up to half of all professional divers could be wandering around with either the physical or mental after-effects of an untreated case of the bends. Trusting my instincts thankfully had led me to the naval professionals who may have saved my life or at least kept me from ending up with a mind like a jellyfish.

My close call in the icy waters of Tasmania did not slow down my wandering. In that same year I travelled to Japan, India, the Philippines and Kazakhstan, filmed in the minefields of Cambodia, interviewed gangs of IRA knee-cappers in Belfast and investigated China's prison labour camps.

Kim and I shared a memorable trip through India and a visit to the mighty Taj Mahal. As we walked through the plaza areas of this white marble monument to one man's great love, the Taj Mahal seemed to float in the clouds. With no other building visible from this graceful space the tomb was the essence of ethereal beauty. A place sometimes derided by travel writers and reduced to insignificance on postcards seemed to us one of the most wondrous works of architecture in the world.

Kim made her own film for television about the life of women in India, examining their colourful, individual expression of beauty, their daily life in the cities, the poverty of women in the villages and the nightmare of female infanticide. As a mother-to-be it disturbed Kim to hear women expressing guilt and sorrow for having put newborn daughters to death. But it stirred her heart to see the strength of other Indian women and to listen to the aspirations of young girls receiving a good education. The fragility, the delicacy, the miracle of human life experienced in India left indelible impressions on us as we approached the birth of our first child back home.

14 December. Kim's birthday. At 6 a.m. she wakes suddenly after a dream. But it is real. Her waters have broken with the baby at 28 weeks.

(JOURNAL 1993)

Few babies arrive on the date we mark on the calendar. But we were not prepared for this. It was just too early. We were in shock but did not panic. I had filmed stories about premature births and we never doubted that our first child would make it. We just knew it would be a battle.

After an emergency admission to the old Royal Women's Hospital at Paddington in Sydney, we were told that the baby was engaged head down and that labour appeared imminent. The unborn child was a tiny 1000 grams, with good odds of survival but so premature that an immediate birth could have a severe impact. Dr Leo Leader, famous for his pioneering studies of what babies hear in the womb, gave Kim a shot of a controlled steroid to try to improve production of surfactant in the baby's vulnerable lungs.

'If you can hang on until tomorrow,' Dr Leader said, 'we can give you another shot and it will make a big difference to the baby.'

'I'll be here,' said Kim calmly. She set herself that one small target. It was a frightening first twenty-four hours because everyone thought the baby was on the way.

Another of the hospital's leading obstetricians, Professor Michael Bennett, told us that after the waters break 85 per cent of women give birth within a week, most of them within a couple of days. Kim, with her usual logic and optimism, said that she would be one of the 15 per cent who grew the baby longer. Maybe she could give the child a few more days, perhaps even a week or more.

After a wonderful, healthy pregnancy to that point, with plenty of rest, daily exercise and a meticulous diet, there was no reason for Kim to be frustrated by a sense of failure. Of course we were disappointed and upset that the baby was in some danger, but none of the experts could say why this had happened. There was no point surrendering to negative thoughts. It was time to harness the power of motherly love and the extraordinary value of positive thinking.

Kim had never had the time for meditation, but she thought now was the moment to try it. The doctors were very encouraging, explaining that avoiding stress was the key. With a yoga-like relaxation technique, Kim calmed her body and her mind.

She played classical music and read pleasing, brilliant things like Shakespeare's comedies that put a smile on her face. Sydney was surrounded by bushfires that long hot summer, but Kim turned off the news. She tried to shut out the rest of the world and visitors were discouraged. We were fortunate not to have children already to care for and my employers helped by allowing me to come and go, to just be there with words of encouragement. Kim certainly appreciated the cheerful sisterhood of women awaiting birth, including some in trouble. There were cries of pain, frustration and tears, but to me, watching as a man, the women were all so impressive in the way they helped one another.

Dr Leader and many of the nurses were convinced that by staying calm and positive, just one day at a time, Kim was making an important difference to the unborn baby. If she felt even the ghost of a contraction, she concentrated her mental strength to massage away the tremor that threatened her child. That is how it seemed in her mind. It is hard to say physiologically exactly what was happening because the precise trigger for the moment of birth in such cases is still mysterious. At times it seemed like an eternity of waiting but Kim looked beautifully serene as she lay quietly in bed, day after day, then week after week. The doctors were ecstatic with her progress, because with each day the baby grew stronger, the brain developed fully and the lungs reached the point where they would operate without the help of a ventilator. After five and a half weeks of this horizontal meditation, our baby had developed to a point where Dr Leader said it would be fine for the child to arrive at any time. Within a day of that news, Kim went into labour.

Was it the baby who decided when to be born? Was it sheer good luck? It was uncanny that the baby arrived just when Kim felt she had done all she could. We shared so much with other couples in that hospital watching over babies who had come early that we felt no matter what you did, birth would have its own mystery and challenge. Every birth is awesome and personal. I only know that at that moment and to this day I felt that Kim's magnificent effort of focused concentration was the greatest thing she would do in her life.

15 January. 2.30 a.m. Dr Leader opts for a Caesarean
delivery. Kim has an extreme allergic reaction to the drug
in the epidural. Although numb from the waist down, she
goes into deep, cold shivers, trembling so much I wonder
how Dr Leader can make the cuts. I hold her hand and
urge her to draw even breaths. It takes fifteen minutes for
Dr Leader to get close to the baby. Kim is in a terrible
state but Dr Leader tells her to use her abdominal muscles
to push the baby into his hands. He has five minutes,
he tells me later, to clear the baby's head still caught
perilously inside. He uses two and a half of those minutes
and then lifts our new baby girl into the world. There is
a wonderful cry that says, 'I am here ... I have
arrived ... this is my world.' As Dr Leader checks her vital
signs I whisper, 'Welcome to Wonderland, little girl.'
Dr Leader looks at me and says, 'Alice?' 'No,' I say,
'Claire Mae McMullen.'

                                            (JOURNAL 1994)

Tiny, beautiful Claire, 1800 grams of joy, was lifted in a space
blanket close to her mother's breast.
   'It's amazing. It's amazing,' whispered Kim. 'She looks perfect.'
   'She is,' said Dr Leader, 'thanks to you.'

Your footprints wandered the Americas
through forest, prairie, high mountain and plain,
the eagle, deer, brown bear and buffalo
were the animals of your domain.

My tracks crossed the Great South Land
past grass trees, red gum, wattle and palm,
the kookaburra, kangaroo, koala and emu
are the creatures that give us charm.

One day, somehow, our paths crossed,
a glance at a stranger's face,
heaven's chance to fall in love,
a journey to the same place.

With a harvest moon, golden and full,
rising slowly from the sea,
and our bed bathed in moonlight,
you made love with me.

I heard the sound of her newborn voice,
so clear, so bright, so pure,
now our whole world belongs to her,
footprints on Eternity's shore.

(JOURNAL 1994)

CHAPTER FIFTEEN

COMING HOME

At Amata, in Central Australia, an Aboriginal woman was feeding her baby at her breast. She was sitting on a blanket in the red dust, a brown kelpie curled at her feet, swatting flies and waving at the stranger in the same motion. I smiled and asked how her baby was doing. She flashed a grin as big as Uluru. For longer than any European could remember, for longer than written history, for as long as the songlines and the dreamtime stories, Aboriginal women had been raising children here in the dry heart of Australia.

I walked on through the cluster of hovels our government called an Aboriginal 'settlement' and heard the sounds of young children in what looked like a hall or a schoolhouse. But there were no classes underway here, no music or dancing. Through gaping holes in the fibro walls I could see a gang of kids in the shadows, their faces buried in rusted tin cans full of petrol. They were sniffing the brain-damaging fumes to get high, to get wasted, to lose themselves in a tin-can dreaming.

Petrol sniffing by indigenous Australians was the subject of my very first story for *60 Minutes* when I joined the Nine Network towards the end of 1984. It was also my first film back in my own country after so many years as a foreign correspondent. After tackling racial injustice and the plight of indigenous people in many parts of the world, I now was confronted with our own sad record at home.

I am as satisfied with this report as any I did over the next sixteen years on Australia's most watched current affairs program, proud too that my first story was about the first Australians, and pleased that it established the raw, direct style that would be my trademark at *60 Minutes*. I kept my narration clear and spare. I wanted honest images, action that was uncontrived, interviews that were not choreographed or rehearsed, relying on thorough preparation, careful listening and improvisation in the questioning. I wanted to avoid the theatrical over-acting that was turning television journalism into predictable, low-grade farce and to break the addiction to confrontation as the favoured approach to every difficult or reluctant subject.

I had decided from my earliest days as a reporter to try to be fair and truthful. I worked hard at that against the usual pressures. I honed my style of narration to build the power of filmic images during eighteen and a half years at the ABC, from the early days on *Weekend Magazine* to my world-wandering *Four Corners* documentaries. With the greater reach of the populist *60 Minutes*, I tried to improve storytelling in the short-film format. I believe my contribution was to put a new stress on authenticity, to catch things as they really were, and to remove my 'fingerprints' from the film, letting the images have the maximum impact.

I soon discovered that *60 Minutes* had a handful of the gutsiest camera teams in the world. The cameraman in Amata, Vernon Moore, was a bear of a man, wild-eyed, with powerful paws, the kind you like on your side when you have your back to the wall. He was also the type of cameraman who did not lift his head from the eyepiece, no matter how threatening the danger. His sidekick, the sound-recordist Terry Kelly, a gypsy charmer with an earring and a dazzling grin to match, relied more on the gift of the gab to talk his way out of trouble. They were the perfect combination to capture for the first time on Australian television the full horror of the petrol sniffers lost in their dangerous dreamtime.

An Aboriginal woman in her twenties, completely out of her mind after sniffing petrol drained from a nearby car, lurched towards the crew waving a wheel wrench and screaming. Vernon stood his ground, the camera rolling. It soon became clear that he was not the target of her anger. She had become so deranged by the toxic fumes that she was crashing the steel bar into her own skull. Once! Twice! Three times! Then her hands went limp by her sides. She staggered and collapsed in the dust. The brown dog ran over and sniffed at her body but the young Aborigines ignored her, as most of them had their heads lowered to their own tin cans.

Day and night this madness raged, like a horror movie that tore at your sensibility, left you feeling as uncomfortable, as ashamed as the local elders who watched helplessly as children destroyed themselves. There were brain-damaged kids strewn across the tops of abandoned cars, under tin humpies and inside what was left of the shattered community hall. Vernon's camera floated through this place. You hardly knew he and Terry were there, but they captured scenes of dark, disturbing intensity.

A young girl of about ten, Ingrid, rolled her big brown eyes and flashed a crazed smile as I tried to find out whether she understood that the tin can pressed to her face could kill her. Petrol sniffing had killed several of her friends. There had been eight deaths in recent months. Yet Ingrid was drunkenly singing, 'I'm still standing ... I'm still standing,' as she sucked in more of the deadly fumes. My hand gently reached for the tin can to try to get her to ease off the petrol.

In the same squalor, another youngster, Peter, sat on top of a broken cupboard watching the others sniffing at the petrol. His eyes were clear. He sat with both hands cupped under his chin, staring at his friends. 'It wrecks their brains. They told us at school,' he said, 'and I've told these kids lots of times.'

There is always at least one, wiser than the rest, stronger than the mob. This young boy, Peter, gave the film its poignancy and the faintest glimmer of hope. With Peter

in one corner of the lens and Ingrid sniffing away in the
other, Vernon Moore exquisitely framed the problem and
the solution. The kids like Peter who still respected their
elders and listened to their teachers would survive, but so
many like Ingrid would not. In Central Australia we
showed not only the despair but the concerted effort by
many people, black and white, to stop the petrol sniffing.
A young nurse typified the spirit and the self-sacrifice of
the isolated medical teams trying to care for the children.
A blue-eyed activist expressed his anger at our national
neglect of a living, priceless asset, the first people of our
ancient land, the oldest continuous civilisation. The
Aboriginal elders conveyed their wisdom and a sense of
the underlying strength that has guided these people
through thousands of years of survival.

(JOURNAL 1985)

This story was praised by several Aboriginal organisations because it was honest and balanced, qualities that they found lacking in much of the commercial television coverage of indigenous issues. Later the report was included in a documentary circulated to universities to help guide budding journalists learning to cover sensitive and provocative Aboriginal stories. So many times current affairs television has managed to aggravate race relations by a confrontational approach, shallow stereotyping and plain ignorance of important cultural differences. There are so few Aboriginal storytellers given access to the Australian media — and there should be more — that the rest of us need to put ourselves in their shoes and take particular care as we tell their story. In fact, that is a useful motto for fair reporting everywhere.

As I left Amata some of the parents thrust a letter into my hands asking the federal government to help them save their children. These are *our* children, I thought. Have we done enough for them?

In pain the desert splits
where the heart is swollen
and the hands bruised,
the forehead creased
from ancient times,
crumbling near the ochre pits
where dreamtime dancers
have forgotten the
colours in their rainbow.

(JOURNAL 1980)

In a remote river gorge in the Australian bush a young Aboriginal man was poling a raft forward on a river, his arms and legs all black muscle, and a fierce scowl on his handsome face. At his feet lay a beautiful Aboriginal girl, eyes wide with fear or expectancy, not sure what he was going to do with her. He was a tribal man. She had been taken away from her family in the bush like many others and raised by whites on a cattle property. She was one of the stolen generation and the young man had stolen her back.

This is a scene from the landmark Australian film *Jedda*, made in the 1950s. That beautiful young girl in the starring role grew up to be one of the most memorable characters in the Aboriginal rights movement — Rosalie Kunoth-Monks. She is a woman I deeply empathised with after seeing the suffering my mother endured because of alcohol.

Rosie and some of her friends were not content to sit back while alcohol and petrol sniffing destroyed so many lives. The Aboriginal women organised a march right into the heart of Alice Springs, with many of the 25 000 residents lining the streets to see what all the commotion was about.

With white feathers in their headbands and bodies daubed with paint, the women were chanting, 'We have eyes. We have ears. We have mouths. In our mouths we have tongues. We will now speak on our own behalf.'

Tired of seeing their husbands rotten drunk around town, these women wanted the men back home and sober. They were desperate, believing that this was the last chance to save their families and their culture. For years the fringe dwellers from surrounding settlements had been cashing their government cheques at bottleshops in the Alice. They drank themselves into a stupor just like my father. Some bashed their women and their kids. Whole families fell apart under this wave of distress. Rosie remembered how her mother thought that a demon had got into the men, the demon grog.

In the old days only a few trusted blackfellas like the great artist Albert Namatjira were given dogtags that signified they had the special privilege of buying booze. But with the right to vote for the white man's government, in 1967 Aborigines also won the right to buy his poison. The famous fell just as quickly as all the forgotten in the dry creek beds of Alice Springs.

'What happened to your co-star in *Jedda*, Robert Tudawali?' I asked Rosie one night as we sat outside her home in the Alice looking at the desert sky.

'He was a magnificent-looking person. He was a fantastic actor. Bob was also a gentleman, always trying to please everyone. After *Jedda* he went back to Darwin but he was just one of the blacks there. Probably a lot of white people made sure he knew he was just a black and had to keep his place. He finished up drinking and sharing whatever he had with his people and eventually falling — or somebody pushed him — onto a camp fire and dying as a result of those burns. I appreciate now what the director Charles Chauvel tried to say in the movie *Jedda*. That story has really happened, especially in the Northern Territory. Aborigines were treated terribly. Our children were given to white people to bring up, so they could be assimilated into the white way. This happened, even if some people don't want to remember.'

A prime minister like John Howard could dismiss Rosie's story as more of that 'black armband' view of history and he would be supported by a significant number of Australians tired of hearing about Aboriginal 'victims'. I discovered that even if they were watching Australia's most popular television program in the 1980s, some people would not comprehend what was happening to the Aborigines. As well as their infant mortality, shorter lifespan and appalling state of general health, AIDS in Aboriginal communities was widely ignored. Many Australians refused to be shamed by the arrest rate and number of black deaths in police cells and prisons. We were quick to pour scorn on South Africa's white supremacists or the loathsome 'nigger' bashing in the American south, but we lacked the collective will to address the disastrous state of a far more manageable number of people.

We could unite on Anzac Day or applaud a sporting triumph, but it seemed difficult for some Australians to recognise that Aborigines had a legal right to justice. Was this conscious racism, benign neglect or a consequence of the bewildering changes in government policy towards the Aborigines? It has been a long and painful walk from the first disastrous experience of invasion and conquest, through separation, forced assimilation, a stolen generation lost and searching for identity, a civil rights campaign, land rights, court battles, confusion, bitterness and disillusionment.

To a traveller come home, it appeared that white Australia knew what was going on, but that a curious, convenient amnesia had settled over us. It was a common misconception that some 250 000 Aborigines had been given too much, not too little. The acid-tongued black activist Gary Foley made me understand, just as Russell Means had at Wounded Knee, that even documenting a tragedy was not going to stop it. The whole truth was not getting through, just bits and pieces of a very depressing story. Remarkably, most Aborigines, including Rosie, are full of extraordinary goodwill towards whites while still shunned in their own land.

'When you see the damage that has been done to your people do you ever feel like throwing yourself off a cliff?' I asked Rosie before I left her house.

'I certainly do, just like in *Jedda*, but that's a defeatist attitude. I believe, however small your light is, you've got to let it shine, so that people can see and become aware. If Aboriginal Australia could be made to feel that this is their home, this is their country and they are not second-class citizens, maybe then we will stop destroying ourselves ... in time, whites may understand.'

Rosie, I will not forget your cry. The bottles keep draining to empty. The glass is shattered. But the spell is not broken. All of these years later I hear my mother pleading with my father. It is these quiet tragedies of ordinary life that remind us we are really all the same.

To a town called Alice
I came to see
Aboriginal life on its last legs,
staggering the main street
on the fringes of white decency,
where there is no dreamtime
except on Wednesdays
when a welfare cheque buys a bellyful
near the New World supermarket
and the nightmare of Alice
recedes like a tottering drunk,
rituals of ancient times,
the dance and the hunt,
the squeal of birth
and cry of death
reduced to insignificance,
lives abandoned
with brown beer bottles
broken,
the sun tearing at the rooftop
of a car hurtling to its fate,
the windows smashed
and the hood raised
like a tombstone
for those laughing wretches
who have ended the journey.

(JOURNAL 1980)

I have learned that words do not always invite action. White men talking about Aboriginal infant mortality, black children stolen from their parents and even clear cases of mass murder in our history have never swayed public opinion to any great extent. In the 1980s I went looking for new ways to make the truth impinge. You have to do this as a journalist. If you see that people are not listening to the truth, find another way to tell the story.

In the typically middle-class suburbs of Brisbane we tried an approach that has since become a staple in current affairs television for exposing double standards and racial prejudice. We followed a young married couple, a black man and a white woman, as they tried to rent a place to live. You don't have to guess who got turned away and who got lucky in the house hunt.

Portraits of Aboriginal people made pleasant, acceptable viewing on television unless I introduced the critical views of the radicals like Gary Foley who made history by helping establish the Aboriginal tent embassy in front of Parliament House in Canberra. The truth is that television was very slow to acknowledge that there was a whole range of Aboriginal people with various political views — some radical, some conservative. When the celebration of Australia's Bicentenary rolled around in 1988, I argued for the inclusion on *60 Minutes* of Aboriginal views of the 'discovery' of Australia. As the history-conscious New South Wales premier Bob Carr has pointed out, it is an important and distinctive feature of our national days that many of us have mixed feelings about what we are celebrating.

One of my most effective stories on Aboriginal Australians back in 1987, one of those small breakthroughs that made people consider them in a fresh light, came from a simple, personal observation after having lived for so many years in the heavily African-American cities of Washington and New York. In Australia, blacks seemed to be invisible. At that time it was impossible to find a single Aborigine in a television commercial or on the cover of a fashion magazine. The agencies that hired models had no Aborigines on their books and imported blacks from the Caribbean or the United States rather than look for local talent. Companies that produced commercials said there was no interest in Aborigines because they would not sell the product.

To illustrate our invisible Australians, we filmed dozens of beautiful young black women and handsome young men who had no training at all before a television camera. I invited the advertising supremo John Singleton to look over these rank amateurs, assess their beauty and talent and then explain honestly why not one black had ever graced a magazine cover or appeared in a television commercial. 'Well,' said Singo, 'they're not exactly your Arnott's Biscuits family!'

After neatly erasing the face of the first Australians for so long the advertising industry and the media generally have changed, even if not dramatically. John Singleton was among the first to hire an Aboriginal person for a television commercial that went beyond tokenism and stereotyping. The Chadwick model agency signed a striking young woman, Elaine George, who went on to become the first Aboriginal model on the cover of *Vogue* magazine in September 1993. The warm and funny Ernie Dingo entered the television mainstream and made us laugh with his parodies. The late Charles Perkins became a regular on television chat shows. A young ABC journalist, Stan Grant, made it to primetime on commercial television despite encountering his fair share of frustration with some white ignorance and stereotyping.

The eloquence of Pat and Mick Dodson, the unsettling logic of Noel Pearson and the charm of Lowitja O'Donoghue began to be appreciated by a mass audience. White musicians like Peter Garrett, Paul Kelly and Neil Finn helped build bridges to the new Aboriginal bands like Yothu Yindi. We revisited the soothing voice of Jimmy Little and discovered the strength of Archie Roach and Ruby Hunter, the vitality of Christine Anu. In music, film, dance and opera Aboriginal stars were born, to join the pantheon of black sporting gods.

When Cathy Freeman entered Sydney's Olympic Stadium
for the final of the 400 metres I looked up at five-year-old

Will held high in my arms. There was awe on the face of
the child as in excess of one hundred and ten thousand
people raised their voices in unison. All hail Catherine the
Great! Our nation supports you. This unity of purpose is
something I have rarely experienced. Claire, now six,
waved an Australian and an Aboriginal flag, just like
Cathy had done so famously on the track. Kim and I were
roaring, urging her on as she accelerated past us on the
home bend. In her one-piece jumpsuit she stood out from
the rest, but it was her belief, her grace, her commitment
to the goal of so many years that switched on at that
moment. She ran a superb race tactically. Her two main
opponents had used up juice to go out fast. Now Cathy
was catching them, passing them, beating them. Over the
last fifty metres she showed her clear superiority, crossing
the line as the first Aboriginal athlete to win an individual
gold medal at the Olympics.

(JOURNAL 2000)

Almost a decade before the Sydney Games, as an innocent
sixteen-year-old helping our Commonwealth Games relay team to
a win in Auckland, Cathy Freeman had won over most of us. Her
natural grace, humility and carefree laughter simply charmed
people. It was a remarkable national romance as we began to
know and love this young Aboriginal girl with the radiant smile,
although many were not aware of the anguish Cathy had been
through.

After she returned to Australia with her first Commonwealth
Games medal, she did not join her team for the ticker-tape parade
in Brisbane. Cathy was attending the funeral of her sister Anne-
Marie who had been stricken with cerebral palsy. The flowers that
she had been presented with in Auckland were buried with her
sister and Cathy made a promise that if she had been given the
talent to run fast, then she would not rest until she had fulfilled
her destiny.

One of five children, Cathy was born in Mackay in north Queensland where her father was a legend on the rugby league field, a speedster the locals called 'Twinkle Toes'. Her mother, Cecelia, was born on a mission at Palm Island, off Townsville, after her own mother had been taken from her home, another one of the stolen generation. Cecelia remarried a white fellow, Bruce Barber, who spotted Cathy's natural talent and began to coach her using books he borrowed. 'In the beginning,' Cathy said, 'it was just racing the other kids "down to the fencepost and back".' When she won a scholarship to the International School at Kooralbyn near Brisbane, Cathy had a professional coach and over 400 metres on that high school track she was unbeatable. Even when she was still so young that natural balance was beautiful to watch. She simply loved the *feeling* of running, flying on the wind, powering off the bend and striding home a winner.

Australians were used to seeing Aborigines win at sport. One of the first decent television scripts I wrote as an eighteen-year-old kid at the ABC was about the boxing champion Lionel Rose. We watched Evonne Goolagong win Wimbledon. On the football field we saw the Ella brothers run magical patterns and admired the champion qualities of Arthur Beetson, Mal Meninga and Laurie Daley. Some Aborigines, like the Aussie Rules star Nicky Winmar, dealt with racial taunting by baring their chests and displaying black pride. Anthony Mundine left football in a rage and let his fists explode in the boxing ring. But Cathy Freeman was always on a different track.

Not everyone agreed that victory in the World Championships or at the Olympic Games was enough of an ambition for the rising star, and some of more radical temperament urged Cathy to become politically active. Instead, she focused on what she had to do first, to become faster and stronger and wait for the time when she could defeat the seemingly invincible Olympic champion, Marie-Jose Perec.

In London, where she trained for world class competition, I once took her rollerblading. The girl who loved speed had never tried this way of going faster. After making a spectacle of ourselves and scattering the crowd in Hyde Park, we collapsed laughing on the kerb and began one of the most serious of the many conversations we have had over the years. Cathy was physically trembling as she described how deeply disturbing she found old photographs and historical sketches of Aborigines in chains. How many times have we quickly turned the pages of that mournful history? For Cathy these were like the early pictures in a very old family album. She experienced the pain in the heart all Aborigines feel at some time in their lives.

Cathy told me that she always believed that she was running for herself. All the power she had was bound up in her talent on the track. But even as a young girl she understood that if she became the first individual Aboriginal Olympic champion, she could do more for her people than with a thousand political statements. Along the way there were wonderful milestones, like the Young Australian of the Year Award, and she became an inspirational role model for all children. Black and white, they claimed her as theirs and championed her cause to be the very best.

Instinctively, Cathy turned her victories into victories for her people. When she won gold again at the Commonwealth Games in Canada she draped her body in the Australian and Aboriginal flags, igniting a new passion in millions of Australians. History soon will forget the names of the humbugs who complained about her expression of true indigenous pride. Her bold and brilliant symbolic gesture will be eternal, a moment that will be celebrated as long as her people tell stories. It made many of us wonder if there was a way we could fold black and white Australia into one, a glorious possibility of an original fabric fashioned from appreciation and recognition that there is far more to unite us than divide us. Cathy Freeman believed all this was possible.

When in 2000 at Stadium Australia the Olympic torch was handed from one legendary Australian woman to another, and out of the darkness emerged a shining beauty, ascending, encircled by flames, our nation won a new image in the eyes of the world. We had good reason as Australians to feel proud and inspired. But the real challenge is still ahead of us all.

As the enormous crowd sauntered down the hill onto the northern approach to the Sydney Harbour Bridge, I was thinking about how long Aborigines had been walking to find what had been lost so long ago. Can you hear the voices from the Kimberley, from Broome and Cape York, from the Spinifex people wandering in the dry heart? I spotted faces we know, black and white, including brother Ron and wife Kerrie. 'Isn't this a great day,' they said, as maybe 250 000 people together joined the long walk. A skywriter was spelling out the word 'SORRY' large enough for the prime minister to see, if he had been home for the weekend at Kirribilli. A stranger said to Will, 'You're too young to know what sorry means.' Will looked at him and replied, 'We are sorry this government won't take care of the Aborigines.' Kim, Claire, Will and I held hands walking across the bridge with our friends from the beach. Sydney felt like home today. There is still so far to go, but if as many people as this feel this way in every city in Australia, we will get there together.

(JOURNAL 2000)

CHAPTER SIXTEEN

FREE THE SLAVES

On a badly rutted dirt track in the Sierra Madre mountains of the central Philippines, three runaway slaves appeared slowly from the jungle. They were short black men known as Dumargets, among the last of the indigenous people who had survived the Spanish invasion and occupation of these islands. They had run away from their *tabong* or slavemaster because he beat them and cheated them. There was fear in their eyes as they scanned the white men in the vehicles. Outsiders usually did not come here. As we continued on our way the track became barely negotiable and we knew that when the wet season arrived the Valley of San Miguel would be cut off completely from civilisation.

It was the fierce heat that led my film team to stop for water in the next small village, but uncharacteristically for the Philippines we found that most people seemed afraid to talk. A Catholic priest, Father Apollo de Guzman, explained that there were thousands of Dumarget slaves in these isolated mountains, people so wretchedly poor that to the rest of the nation they were subhuman. Slavery, he said, had gone on here longer than anyone could remember and each *tabong* was fiercely protective of his patch. They were also armed and not particularly friendly.

I am sorry to say that I have been to quite a few parts of the world where it is still possible to buy a slave, sometimes illegally as in the Sudan but in other places it has been perfectly legal. Slavery was not banned in Saudi Arabia until 1962. In the north-western African nation of Mauritania slavery was still allowed well into the 1980s. The Berbers, the indigenous Caucasians of North Africa, found it hard to give up this ancient trade which grew from the practice of selling one's conquered enemies. It was introduced on a massive scale in the days of the Roman Empire to provide the labour force essential to the agrarian economy. In their harsh exploitation of slaves the Romans were surpassed only by the later generations of Europeans who settled the New World using slave labour.

The scars are still there on the psyche of the 45 million descendants of African slaves sold onto American plantations. Despite Abe Lincoln, the Civil War and the overriding power of federal laws banning slavery, a few American states still had the old slavery statutes on their books until the 1980s. Afro-Americans have never been compensated for the fact that their ancestors were transported in chains to a foreign land to be bought and sold like animals.

Nowadays the cruelty and injustice of slavery often is dismissed as an unacceptable but understandable practice of the past. It was a jolting experience to discover that for about A$200 I could buy an entire family of human beings: a man, his wife and their children.

Day one. Valley of San Miguel. We slept in a raised wooden hut with pigs snuffling and grunting below the floorboards for most of the night. It took us all day in scorching heat to drive and then hike into the mountains where the slaves were living in camps. The Dumargets were barefoot, men, women and children dressed in ragged clothes, jet black hair, large staring eyes. They were all very hungry. The distended stomachs of the

children, a lot of coughing, and a few goitres probably
caused by iodine deficiency suggested serious health
problems. We gave them the only food we had and they
wolfed it down. Their camp seemed so pathetic it is
puzzling that more of them have not joined the runaways.

(JOURNAL 1987)

Trying to talk to the slaves was not easy. They had not seen white men before but our biggest problem was not their fear, it was the language. Father Apollo could not speak the native dialect but translated my questions into Spanish for a young Filipina woman who could communicate with the Dumargets. Slowly over several days spent in the jungle we began to piece together their history.

I got to know two brothers, Artemio and Heemi, who had been slaves for their entire lives. They did not know how old they were because they could not count, read or write. All they knew was that they had always been owned. Their *tabong*, Paulio, never paid the slaves for their work. He gave them just enough rice to keep them alive — most of the time. Artemio's wife had not survived this hard life and now the brothers were taking care of the children who were slaves too.

Father Apollo told me that each *tabong* owned fifteen to twenty families, or around one hundred slaves. No matter how hard the slaves worked they would always be in debt. As the Dumargets could not count and had only ever known the barter system, the *tabong* cheated them, keeping false or inflated accounts, and they remained trapped as slaves forever.

The daily work of these slaves was to climb the mountainsides to gather rattan, the long vine that they would cut into strips and give to the *tabong*. It was then made into cane furniture and sold to countries like Australia. We followed Heemi, Artemio and his young children up the steep slopes on their search for the rattan that appeared to grow in the most inaccessible jungle thickets. It was a real struggle for us. They did it in bare feet. Artemio's hands were as hard as leather and I watched him snatching at the vines covered in sharp thorns and stinging ants. His children worked equally hard dragging the vines down the mountain after long hours in the sun. There were cuts and scrapes and bleeding feet, the children seemed exhausted, but this was the only life the family knew.

> *Day two. San Miguel. Some of the slaves had a thirty-kilometre walk to haul tied bundles of rattan to the tabong's house. Most of the Dumargets seemed weak from lack of food and overwork. I asked Father Apollo about the illnesses the slaves were suffering. 'Malaria, dysentery, TB, serious diarrhoea, malnutrition in the children and early blindness in the adults. You won't see many old Dumargets,' he said.*
>
> (JOURNAL 1987)

We came across just one old man, lying in the dirt under a shelter of branches in a dry riverbed. He had been there for many days after suffering a severe wound to his leg. The producer, John Little, and I tried to clean out the wound and gave him some antibiotics and pain-relievers from our medical kit. But it appeared gangrene had set in and so we lifted the old man into the back of our jeep. It was a drive of almost a hundred kilometres to the nearest doctor.

When the slaves filed back into their camp after another hard day on the mountain I asked Artemio and Heemi why they did not run away from this misery. Their answer was simply that they must cut rattan and hope for some rice from their master. Otherwise they would soon starve. Artemio said that he had dreamed of running away, of finding a water buffalo and a plough to work in the fields. But when he awoke with nothing he knew that there was nowhere to run to, especially with young children who were desperately hungry.

Finding the *tabong*, Paulio, in the Valley of San Miguel was easy because he owned the only decent house. As I walked up his driveway, Paulio's cronies were slouching around smoking and laughing about our interest in the wretched Dumargets. Slavery had reduced the indigenous people to a status similar to that of the untouchables in India. You might think it was better than the outright genocide many similar tribes had experienced but in many ways slavery is a social death. The Dumargets had ceased to be members of the human race.

Paulio surprised us all by claiming that he loved his slaves like his own children and that indeed they were part of his family. When I laughed aloud his manner abruptly changed. I pointed out that he *owned* these families, they were enslaved and that the Dumargets felt ashamed that their children, too, had been forced into slavery. I told him how the runaways and others had accused him of beating them with sticks to make them work harder. They were only beaten, Paulio said, because they were lazy and, besides, he gave them rice. His cronies gathered around as Father Apollo supported my argument that the slaves were not only sick and sorry, they were on the edge of starvation. During four days spent with the slaves the only rice they got was from us. The old man with the gangrenous leg had been left to die like so many more of the Dumargets. The *tabong* made money from their labour, why couldn't he give them some medical care and a clean place to live?

The slavemaster had no answers. He was angry but not ashamed. His cronies smirked when I mentioned the old man and we never discovered how he came to have a deep machete gash across one knee. I kept coming back to the *tabong*'s claim that he treated these slaves like his children. Shouldn't these children be in school, as his real children were? Who gave him the right to force children to work without proper pay? Paulio shrugged and said that it had always been this way.

Day three. San Miguel. It is hard to know what to do for these slaves. Father Apollo says Paulio has books in town that no doubt can be fiddled to support his claim that the

Dumargets owe him money for rice. The government in
Manila has no interest in these tribesmen. The tabong *and*
his men seem to know they can get away with this
exploitation in a country that still has so many terribly
poor people. I gave Artemio and Heemi fifty bucks to buy
some large sacks of rice. The good news is that the doctor
who has treated the old fellow thinks he got to work on
the leg just in time. He should save the leg and the old
man will live.

(JOURNAL 1987)

Father Apollo believed that the only hope for the slaves was to
give them an education, particularly the children. If they knew
how to count they would soon understand how the *tabong* kept
them in permanent debt. They also needed huts of their own and
a patch of land to try farming. The slaves had never tried to grow
their food because they had no tools. From birth they had been
deceived and exploited.

On our final day in the Valley of San Miguel, Artemio, Heemi
and the children came to say goodbye, but something odd was
happening. Their mood had changed. Through the usual fumbling
third-hand translation we got the news that was conveyed as
much by their smiles and gleaming eyes. My lousy fifty dollars
had bought the family's freedom. Instead of buying enough sacks
of rice for the months ahead, Artemio and Heemi had struck a
bargain with the *tabong* who was embarrassed by his foreign
visitors. These slaves were free for the first time in their lives.

I really did not know whether to laugh or cry. The fifty dollars
was the kind of helping hand I gave anyone in trouble. Even when
the *tabong* had confirmed the going rate for a Dumarget family
was about two hundred dollars, I had never expected there was a
way to set free Artemio and his family. Who would take care of
them in the mountains when they had nothing of their own?
Father Apollo quickly stepped in with a solution, the kind of
practical action that makes some worker-priests the only friends

of the desperately poor. He arranged shelter with a Filipino family and the promise of a little work. Now that Artemio and Heemi were clear of the *tabong,* there was at least a chance they could earn enough money to eat.

My story about the slaves of the Sierra Madre, broadcast on *60 Minutes* and in scores of countries around the world, had an immediate impact. When people could see that fifty dollars could change the lives of their fellow human beings a great number wanted to help the Dumargets in the same way. A Catholic relief agency collected more than A$30 000 made up of mainly small donations of five or ten dollars and often from people like old-age pensioners who no doubt had the least money to share. Whenever I hear others talk about 'compassion fatigue' I remember this warm response when people could clearly see that their money would make a difference.

I recognise that there are opposing views on the merits of buying the freedom of slaves. There is always the risk that charity continues to fuel the slave trade. But in this case there was a hopeful result. Father Apollo used the money wisely to build decent huts and a school for the Dumargets. He wrote us a moving letter saying that we Australians had no idea just how much our money was worth in the Valley of San Miguel. He was able to negotiate the release from debt of a large number of the slaves. Some of the Dumargets began to live together in a village, getting soil on their hands instead of tearing at the rattan on the mountains. Imagine how those children must have felt to run free.

The joy of freedom is so natural for most of us that we spend little time celebrating it or even thinking about the ways in which we are free to choose, free to act, free to live our own lives. My sense of freedom, my daily delight in being a free man, certainly has been heightened by meeting some remarkable men and women who triumphed over various kinds of enslavement. Meeting Jews who survived the Nazi death camps in World War II, Australian survivors of the Japanese concentration camps and

Russian dissidents who escaped or outlasted the *gulag* has left me with the most powerful impression of the meaning and value of liberty.

Chinese-born Hongda 'Harry' Wu is one of the bravest men I know. As a young student in Beijing in the era of Chairman Mao, Wu was arrested in 1957 for 'counter-revolutionary opinions'. His 'crime' was to think freely and then speak freely about his opposition to the Chinese government's abuse of human rights. He also opposed the invasion of Hungary and suppression of freedom there by the Soviet Red Army. Harry was incarcerated as a political prisoner for nineteen years in China's own secret *gulag*, the *laogai*, a vast system of forced labour camps that still exists today and where millions of people endure another type of slavery.

If you visited China, you would have had to search carefully to find the prison camps. Unlike the Soviet *gulag*, isolated in Siberia, China's three thousand labour camps are scattered throughout the country and ingeniously camouflaged. The Shanghai Laodong Pipe Works, for instance, looks like a factory from the front, except that all of the unsmiling workers have shaved heads and are guarded by men in uniform. At the rear of the 'pipe works' are the cells that hold some of these prisoners of the *laogai*. The intention is to fool western buyers and trade officials who come to do business with the rapidly expanding Chinese economy. As many countries have laws against slave labour, the reality must be concealed. According to the US State Department, there were at the very minimum three million Chinese held in these forced labour camps in the early 1990s. Wu's personal experience, his decade of research and independent investigations by the Asia Watch human rights group suggest that the real number of prisoners is between ten and fifteen million. Wu says hundreds of thousands of them are political prisoners.

When I met Harry Wu he was a visiting professor at various American academic institutions. His life sentence was suspended when Deng Xiaoping came to power. At great personal risk Wu travelled back to China, posing as a western businessman wanting to buy goods made in the *laogai*. He took secret videotape of some of the twenty labour camps he visited, showing prisoners in appalling conditions, including naked men forced to wade in vats of an alkaline solution used to treat hides for the manufacture of cheap Chinese leather jackets. While prisoners in quite a few countries work as part of programs to give them useful skills, the Chinese prisoners are forced labourers. It is a brutal system.

Wu's own nightmare past came back to haunt him while he was in China. He told me how prisoners of the *laogai* had been tortured with electric prods, whipped in public until they bled, chained with arms around toilet buckets used by other prisoners and kicked unconscious by guards. Wu's mother had been so distressed after his arrest, knowing that he would be tortured, that she committed suicide. His brother too was branded a counter-revolutionary and was beaten to death by Beijing police. His father was arrested, tortured and lost everything the family owned. Through sheer human spirit Wu endured nineteen years as a prisoner after vowing that one day the *laogai* would stand condemned in history alongside the brutal concentration camps of Dachau and Treblinka.

Wu said that he literally was a slave for the communist system. While held in twelve different institutions, he was forced to dig canals, work in sweltering brick ovens, plough fields and go underground into iron and coal mines for up to fourteen hours a day. In 1975 he was buried under rubble after a mine collapse. Fellow prisoners dragged him out with a severely injured back and a broken arm and leg. When Wu was too sick to work, he was hung up by the hands on a wall and other prisoners were ordered to abuse him. This was the Maoist style of repression and so-called 'political re-education'. Wu told me that he was locked in a concrete, coffin-like box, the first three days without food. He thought then that he would die and could see no other way out of his misery, but from the frequent screams he heard he knew that many other political prisoners were suffering far worse.

This torture continued in China's slave camps long after the era of Chairman Mao. The Chinese authorities clung to their belief in terror and oppression as the most effective means of controlling one-quarter of the world's population, especially when the democracy movement began to challenge the old guard. One of the student leaders, Tang Boqiao, told me that he had been thrown into the *laogai* after the massacre in Tiananmen Square. He described in excruciating detail being tortured with painful electric shocks to the eyes, nose, ears and mouth. Professor Peng Yuzhang, a man in his seventies who supported the student sit-ins, was dragged off to Changsa No. 1 Prison and placed on the 'shackle-board'. This was the most feared method of torture and it screamed of the sadistic nature of the prison guards. The old man's hands and feet were shackled to a door-sized plank with a hole for defecation. Then he was subjected to the vilest brutality. This man, whose only crime was to dare to think of freedom, was kept on the 'shackle-board' for three months and then locked away in a psychiatric asylum.

After he was released from the *laogai*, Harry Wu witnessed one of China's public mass executions, the 'final solution' for many of its slaves. On 23 September 1983 in Zhengzhou City, the capital of Henan province, a huge crowd gathered in the streets to watch a chilling procession of police motorcycles and military vehicles escorting an open truckload of forty-five prisoners from a nearby labour camp. This was a blunt message about the consequences of challenging the communist system. On some flat ground outside the city, at least one hundred thousand people gathered for what had become an annual spectacle. Each province was given a quota for executions and around the country some twenty thousand took place each year. When the prison truck arrived the forty-five men were quickly lined up against numbered posts, with a shallow hole in front of them. On command, the military police kicked the backs of the prisoners' legs to drop them into a kneeling position. There was another order and forty-five rifle shots rang out as one. The blood and brain and life of these human beings trickled down into the holes in the dirt. The execution squad jogged away in a line, leaving the bodies for three days, just to make sure that everyone got the message.

The evil of these mass executions and the enslavement of tens of millions of people is excused by some for the same reasons that female infanticide is ignored in China. With 1.3 billion people to rule, the political leaders are forgiven for maintaining the last *gulag*. The world's largest nation surely has an equally large responsibility to treat every one of its people as citizens, not slaves.

Before the international community troops off to Beijing for its stage-managed celebration of universal values at the 2008 Olympic Games, every nation, large and small, should ask China to give amnesty to those imprisoned in the *laogai* for political 'crimes'. Such a display of mercy is possible if the world shows the will. The Chinese leadership must be reminded that the saturation media coverage surrounding the Olympics may well expose the shameful exploitation and brutality of the *laogai*, just as Harry Wu has predicted.

All of those who do business with these slave camps have blood on their hands. Before we buy goods marked 'made in China' (or 'made in the Philippines') shouldn't we ask ourselves whether they were made by slave labour? If Chinese ideology can modernise successfully to move the nation into the global economy, then its trading partners should insist that Beijing give up forced labour and mass executions. The truth, revealed by Harry Wu's courageous investigations, is that Chinese slavery makes so much money that it makes some officials rich. Even after prisoners serve their sentences, millions of them see out their lives in a cruel, almost Kafkaesque final act. They are categorised as *jiuye*, non-convicts, but they are forced to stay in the same labour camps, working for half the normal wage, until they die — still slaves.

CHAPTER SEVENTEEN

THE MAN AND THE MYTH

MANDELA'S CHILD

Is it the gleam of diamonds
in her lovely eyes?
I do not think so.
It is freedom
that makes her smile,
her bare feet free
to walk the final mile.

(JOURNAL 1994)

At Sharpeville, on the anniversary of the police massacre of sixty-nine South African blacks, the crowd of over fifty thousand was restless. They had been waiting for most of the day under the hot sun on this open field and they were nervous about attacks from their black and white political opponents. Gunfire crackled sporadically. Officials of the African National Congress (ANC) stepped onto the wooden stage to urge their armed supporters to stop shooting their guns in the air. Violence on this day could only mar the party's relentless march to victory in South Africa's first democratic election. For 342 years blacks had been voteless. For the past four decades the politics of white supremacy, the system of apartheid, had allowed a minority of 5 million whites to legally exploit the majority, the 30 million South African blacks. But this crowd knew that the balance of power was changing. They had the scent of victory and their liberator had come to meet them on the ground where blood had been spilled during the long armed struggle.

'Mandela, Mandela' the crowd sang, even before we could see the great man moving slowly like an African lion. At seventy-five he still looked strong and fit, the result of his daily dawn workouts that went back to his youth as an amateur boxer. Someone held an umbrella and he stood in its shade, surveying the crowd like a king awaiting coronation. There was a surge towards the stage and I saw several young children fall to the ground. 'This is death,' Mandela roared into the microphone as the crush of the crowd grew more dangerous. He turned, full of contempt and chastised the ANC officials who had so poorly planned this campaign event, letting everyone know that he was his own man, not a captive of any party.

One of Mandela's favourite catchcries on the election campaign trail in 1994 was to tell the crowds, 'If the ANC government is unable to deliver the goods, then you must overthrow it.' This endeared him to the armed activists who still wanted to slay the dragon of apartheid, to cut off its head or maybe 'necklace' it with a burning car tyre. Mandela was a master of playing with fire. After all he had been one of the architects of the ANC's armed struggle. But at Sharpeville I also saw Mandela the peacemaker, the politician and the visionary who had led his people to this wondrous moment of freedom.

He slowly raised his hands and calmed the throng with body language alone. In a firm, autocratic voice, he then warned the people firing guns to beware of playing into the hands of the 'third force', the security units he accused of fanning violence around the country. Only a democratic government could deal with the violence and crime from whatever quarter they may come, he said. Suddenly the African chief showed another facet of his complex persona. In the flat, drawling monotone of his anti-hero guise he said that change would come but it would take time, it would not be dramatic. Then the soothing peacemaker began to sound like a politician. 'The enemies of peace are also unemployment, poverty, illiteracy and bad living conditions.' The crowd cheered loudly as he hit his mark. Finally it was Mandela the consummate performer who smiled at the crowd and asked them to look at the voting cards for the letters ANC. 'Put an X alongside the old man who has grey hair because of the trouble you have given him. Make a cross next to that face.'

The crowd began to rock with one of those African rhythms that had become anthems during the twenty-seven years he had spent in prison. The watchful security forces and the ANC's black rivals held back their bullets and batons. A dream of peace was still alive. This was Nelson Mandela's South Africa. The children were held high on shoulders and people were dancing with pure joy and tears in their eyes. *Mandela, Mandela*. The great man was free. They soon would be free. On this day Mandela the man seemed to measure up to Mandela the myth.

At ANC headquarters in Johannesburg, Cyril Ramaphosa, the Secretary-General, told me that Australia's role in supporting economic and sporting sanctions against South Africa was 'crucial' in bringing an end to white domination here. Although the economic sanctions hurt the black majority more than the wealthy whites, this was the 'necessary medicine to get the cure'. The election itself will not end apartheid and it will take new laws and strong leadership to break down the racial barriers. The ANC looks strong enough to hold the army together and to avoid a civil war, but the hardest task for Mandela and his younger proteges like Ramaphosa and Thabo Mbeki will be to heal the deep scars after three centuries of oppression.

(JOURNAL 1994)

White supremacy, or *baasskap* as Afrikaners call it, was fostered by a secret society known as the Broederbond. In the way of such cults, only the *broeders* (brothers) knew which politicians, military personnel, police, teachers and churchmen subscribed to the Nazi-like belief that the chosen people, *herrenvolk*, should always rule South Africa. After the National Party was elected to government on a platform of apartheid in 1948, the real architect of this racist social engineering was Hendrik Verwoerd, prime minister from 1958 to 1966.

'Our motto is to maintain white supremacy for all time to come,' Verwoerd declared, adding the tragically misguided threat, 'by force if necessary.' It was this Christian zealot, presenting himself as a man of principle, who banned the ANC, jailed Nelson Mandela and created the police state responsible for the Sharpeville Massacre of 1960.

At the climax of the fight against apartheid I met Verwoerd's grandson, Wilhelm, a lecturer in political philosophy at the University of Stellenbosch, a haven of white affluence near the beautiful city of Cape Town. Wilhelm had spent thirty years trying to wash his hands of his grandfather's monstrous crimes and had become one of the ANC's young eloquent white supporters. He accompanied me to the Crossroads, the huge black shantytown on the sand flats just to the north of Cape Town. Here was the hideous contrast of apartheid. Instead of the bougainvillea-covered mansions of the whites, who had 95 per cent of the wealth and 85 per cent of the land, this black community was built on a garbage dump. About three-quarters of a million people were crammed into leaky shacks, with little sanitation. The Crossroads was one of the most depressing and violent slums I have ever seen, guarded by security forces in high watchtowers with huge spotlights that raked the sky at night.

'South Africa needs new houses for at least seven million people. This is a human crisis we are facing,' Wilhelm told me as we took in this miserable sight. 'The Crossroads has one of the highest tuberculosis rates in the world but we South Africans were the first to transplant a heart. This is apartheid.'

Wilhelm, like many white South Africans, had come to his own crossroads. He had chosen to tell Mandela personally how sorry he was about the black leader's long and unnecessary imprisonment. Mandela had replied, 'Let's not talk about the past, let's talk about the future.'

Nelson Mandela was the world's longest-serving political prisoner. From the age of forty-four until he was seventy-one he was shut away in the maximum-security prison on Robben Island, often in solitary confinement, but his mind remained free. He used to rise before dawn, exercising to keep his body strong, and apart from one bout of tuberculosis he remained remarkably healthy. This determination to maintain his prowess, a seemingly instinctive competitiveness and air of authority can be traced all the way back to his youth.

Mandela grew up as a fleet-footed child in the village of Qunu in the Transkei. A member of South Africa's largest tribe, the Xhosa, Mandela was twelve when his father died and he was raised by the region's most powerful chief. His Xhosa name, Rolihlahla, means 'a man who brings trouble on himself' and from his early days, as a law student and then activist lawyer he lived up to that description. In the 1940s, Mandela created the ANC's Youth League and later helped organise the ANC guerilla army. During his days in the underground movement, his legend grew, partly because of his success in disguising himself to elude the security forces. When Mandela and other ANC leaders eventually were arrested, the trial became a stage for one of the most magnificent speeches the world has heard about human bondage and liberation.

'I have fought against white domination and I have fought against black domination,' Mandela said, never bothering to deny the charges but explaining why he felt compelled to fight. 'I have cherished the ideal of a democratic and free society in which all persons live together in harmony and equal opportunities. It is an ideal which I hope to live for and to achieve. But if needs be, it is an ideal for which I am prepared to die.'

As Mandela and other ANC leaders served their life sentences, they directed the ANC struggle from within the walls of that prison on Robben Island. Although Mandela was never a Communist, most of his comrades hotly debated Marxism. The sheer force of Mandela's personality and intellect dominated the discussion of black consciousness and military strategy. Even during the 1980s many of the youngbloods in the ANC still imagined that they would seize power in a Cuban-style revolution. Mandela thought differently. Like the great Anwar Sadat and others who have come to see the limitations of armed struggle, Mandela decided to strike at the apartheid regime where it was most vulnerable rather than where it was strongest. Instead of the battlefield, Mandela chose the bargaining table.

Cyril Ramaphosa told me that the boldest political move in Mandela's crusade was secretly opening negotiations with the apartheid government in 1986 at a time when he was in solitary confinement and unable to discuss plans with the rest of the ANC leadership. The white politicians for years had tried to neutralise his influence by offering him freedom if he agreed to house arrest in one of the homelands where 75 per cent of South African blacks lived a life of separation, but Mandela always said no to this kind of surrender. According to Ramaphosa, the international sanctions, strongly supported by Australia, put so much pressure on South Africa's economy that Mandela could sense a unique opportunity. After years of the most extraordinary cat-and-mouse game, there he was sitting face-to-face with the most senior government officials, insisting that if they wanted to end the war, they had to lift the ban on the ANC and release all political prisoners.

When Mandela was released from prison in 1990 he described his negotiating partner (and Nobel Peace Prize co-laureate) President Frederik de Klerk as 'a man of integrity', but now he paints him as the mastermind behind the black-on-black violence. When I interviewed President de Klerk today he showed no bitterness towards Mandela, dismissing the cutting words as campaign

politics to diminish de Klerk's future influence. The right-
wing extremists like Terre'Blanche (looking pathetically
beaten and more absurd than ever in those old Nazi
costumes) keep yelling at our camera that de Klerk is a
'white traitor who has abdicated power without a fight'.
Mandela surely knows that de Klerk too has helped avoid
a massive civil war and kept his promise over the last four
years to surrender without bloodshed.

(JOURNAL 1994)

The legend of Nelson Mandela is of a saintly man who forgives all, never shows any bitterness or anger, and is kind to his enemies. The real man I watched over the extraordinary weeks leading up to his election was far more human. Depending on the nature of the audience, Mandela could be soft or hard, a moderate or a militant. He spoke of forgiveness and reconciliation with whites, then used President de Klerk as a whipping boy. His domination of ANC colleagues and mockery of his old Zulu rival, Chief Mangosuthu Buthelezi, revealed the steel within the velvet glove. He was still a boxer in the arena, feinting before a cruel attack, feigning weariness then enjoying the cheers of the crowd as he showed his superiority over his opponents.

Mandela's brilliance was to realise that he could be all things to all men. The Mandela magic was a unifying force that overpowered the greatest difficulties. The world's oldest political prisoner managed to change the world's oldest liberation movement into a government in waiting. A proud man who was the heart and soul of a revolutionary movement also was humble and wise enough not to become another African nationalist hero so dazzled by power that he mismanaged his country into economic ruin. When he stepped down from the presidency in 1999 he continued to be critical of the ANC, warning that the black administration was becoming as corrupt, intolerant and racist as the apartheid regime. Mandela said that people in power had to be clean to be credible. A government had to show tolerance, accept criticism and not personalise it, qualities he did not always exhibit himself when handling his political rivals. This great man's unassailable strength was not saintliness. In the end, Mandela had unquestionable moral superiority because of the justice and inevitability of his cause: the liberation of thirty million black people.

Wandering the world I met another remarkable man far more interesting than the myth that enveloped him. Like Mandela he was hailed as a living saint. In fact, to millions of his followers worldwide he was a Living God, the Ocean of Wisdom and Protector of the Snows. My own impression was that the fourteenth Dalai Lama, spiritual leader of Tibetan Buddhism, was more earthly than his disciples and even his detractors may have thought.

Our pilgrimage to Dharamsala, the Himalayan community of 100 000 Tibetans in exile, began with a two-day drive from New Delhi, twenty-five silver boxes of film equipment bouncing around a rattling bus that seemed to narrowly avoid a head-on collision with a truck about once an hour. The roads of India are full of 'miraculous' sights like the chassis of a truck rolling past your eyes in the opposite direction to its driver in the cabin.

We slept in the old medieval forts of the maharajas, always more interesting than modern hotels because the bedroom walls are lined with ancient armour and hung with paintings of the warriors of the past. At one palace we were admitted to an exotic chamber where the harem once lay. Even the four-poster beds have a way of conveying history in such places.

As we slowly climbed towards one of the old hill stations of the British Empire, the snow-capped peaks of the Himalaya appeared majestically from the clouds. The dusty village of Dharamsala was crowded with pilgrims and Buddhist monks with claret-coloured robes and crested saffron hats walking in single file towards the Namgyal Temple. Thousands lined the narrow road and suddenly all heads were bowed. A convoy of heavily guarded four-wheel-drive vehicles roared around the bend towards the gates of the Dalai Lama's compound. Through the dark-tinted glass of a Range Rover, I caught my first glimpse of the living Buddha.

It is not a simple task to arrange an audience with a god but I have had a little luck over the years. Several times I laughed with and even danced with the Indian Godman, Rajneesh, to the astonishment of some of his orange-robed followers. The Bhagwan was a wickedly funny provocateur, a mix of Woody Allen and Lenny Bruce, taunting his highly educated followers to enjoy life as much as he did and to overcome their need for a guru with ninety-three Rolls-Royce limousines. While the Bhagwan was insulated from the world by his 'queen', Ma Sheela, and a circle of devotees, the Dalai Lama was under the protection of the Indian army inside a virtual fortress on the highly sensitive border with China. After months of negotiation it took four more days in Dharamsala just to get an audience with the Dalai Lama's bright and articulate personal secretary, Tenzin Geyche Tethong.

My producer on this story, Julian Cress, is without doubt the most thoughtful colleague I have known. To borrow a Buddhist notion, perhaps his kindness produced *karma* at the Dalai Lama's door, because Julian's masterstroke was to mention that we had carried all the way from Australia a very special present for the Dalai Lama's sixty-first birthday.

As the sun began to rise next day, the sound of the *ratong*, the Tibetan long horn, echoed through the foothills. I walked into the gardens and handed the holy man of the Himalaya our own Australian long horn, an authentic didgeridoo. Well, you tell me what you would give a living god for a present! The Dalai Lama's laughter after he tried to blow a note established the tone of this unforgettable meeting.

I was curious as to whether this reputedly intelligent man literally believed in the Buddhist concept of reincarnation. If he did, he was not sixty-one that day but 605 on the spiritual calendar. Back in 1937, on the wordly calendar, wise old monks had identified him as the next god-king after viewing the traditional auspicious signs, cloud formations, and a 'corpse that moved'. I always remember

John Romer explaining that whenever people deeply believed in auspicious signs, stars in the sky over Bethlehem and the like, you could be sure they would appear. The Dalai Lama seemed to have accepted his destiny with very few tears and a surprising amount of laughter. He had a hilarious habit of chuckling, sometimes shrieking with laughter, at the oddest times. He explained this by saying that he was a very happy man and when he looked at human behaviour he felt like laughing. Yes, I agreed, we were a bit of a cosmic joke. He laughed again and said that practically speaking he knew that he was just an old man of sixty-one, but as a Buddhist his life was limitless. There was no beginning or no end. Now he was in an absolute fit of laughter.

One of the god-king's even more unsettling habits in the eyes of dedicated Buddhists is his way of playfully suggesting that he might be the very last Dalai Lama. It was not unlike the Bhagwan telling the Rajneeshies that when they got anywhere close to nirvana they would not need him. The Dalai Lama said that he did not have any wish to be temporal ruler of Tibet. Perhaps this was a tacit admission that the Buddhist theocracy had not provided the most enlightened rulers of the nation. He added that it might be time for a more democratic method of appointing a Tibetan spiritual leader and he might not be the popular choice.

Ending the line of god-kings after so many centuries may sound like sacrilege to his most devout followers or like the absurd ramblings of a man living in a fairytale kingdom, but the real wisdom of the Dalai Lama is his recognition that he is no more than a symbol of Tibet's cultural survival. If Buddhism is strong enough to survive it will do so without this mortal man. Tibetans survived the chaotic theocracy of the lamas and still have a chance of surviving communism.

The Dalai Lama claimed that Tibet had lost 1.2 million people during four decades of Chinese persecution. He said the Red Army had massacred about 400 000 Tibetans and the rest had died of starvation.

It is difficult to say for certain how many Tibetans have been wiped out since their failed revolt in 1959. Soon after that uprising China carved off about half of the territory traditionally claimed by Tibet and so the unreliable official statistics show just over 2 million Tibetans in an area designated as the Tibetan Autonomous Region (TAR). The Dalai Lama estimates that there are, in fact, about 6 million Tibetans but that they are now outnumbered by 7.5 million Chinese inside the traditional borders of the ancient kingdom. As a result of Deng Xiaoping's economic drive in the mid 1990s, the Chinese practice of transferring people to neutralise defiant minorities has accelerated to exploit Tibet's forests, gold and uranium deposits. The façade of Tibet may look much the same to outsiders, but the Tibetan exiles claim their culture is being erased.

The Dalai Lama told me that after so much senseless bloodshed the century of war had to give way to a twenty-first century of dialogue. The old guard in China slowly was changing and he believed Buddhist altruism could help the world's biggest nation make a transition to a genuine socialism based not on force but on reason.

In the Dalai Lama's view, armed rebellion against the Chinese was futile. He wanted Tibetans to absorb their enemy's worst blows and in time the Chinese would discover (as they had in the past) that Buddhist philosophy had much to offer. Listening to the Dalai Lama reminded me of Jesus saying, 'Turn the other cheek.' Do not be consumed by anger because it will destroy you. Rise above war and become civilised. Challenge your enemy to change. Inspire the world with your spirit.

Some Buddhists see the Dalai Lama as a sell-out because he has accepted China's unbending view that there can be no independence for Tibet. This man who had to flee his kingdom to survive knows that any form of autonomy that preserves the hope of cultural survival is preferable to what he calls the cultural genocide now under way. As Tibet is a landlocked country, he believes that it makes sense for his 6 million Tibetans to unite with the 1300 million Chinese, not through force but through reason and mutual respect. This is Tibet's only path to survival. If Tibetans can reduce their anger and hatred there will be a chance that the Chinese will slowly show them appreciation and then affection.

It may be the result of his lifetime of contemplation, of year after year of metaphysical meditation and pondering the meaning of life, but what struck me most about the fourteenth god-king was that he was not one bit god-like. He was an honest and wise man, with the time to think about what was best for his people and for the world. While many people appear to have a profound, sometimes life-changing experience after merely being in his presence, the qualities I remember were his impish delight in being alive and a calm, rather unassuming humanity. For the Dalai Lama, balance on this globe spinning in the heavens was to be found in altruism and simple human kindness.

At dawn in the temple we join a hundred or more monks, drums and long horns sounding. A bowl of Tibetan tea is passed along the line to the film crew having trouble closing orifices this morning. Ah, doesn't that bring you back to earth? The Dalai Lama waves me closer to the front and I sit cross-legged, shoulder to shoulder with the monks as I once did as a child in Penang. The prayer wheels keep turning. How much I have seen and learned on this journey. The monks bring offerings. Their slow, guttural chanting gets louder. The Dalai Lama rocks from side to side, holding a gold thunderbolt in one hand and a bell in the other. He addresses his people and at one point laughs heartily. No one responds. He flashes them a bigger smile and slowly it spreads until the whole temple is enjoying his joke.

(JOURNAL 1996)

CHAPTER EIGHTEEN

RIVER OF TEARS

*It was an eerie night of fitful half-sleep camped in the
ransacked Jesuit monastery in Kigali. The Rwandan
capital was only recently liberated by the Tutsi army and
troops surround the walls of this place where thirteen
Jesuit priests, eight nuns and an unknown number of
Tutsi workers were hacked to pieces with machetes during
the Hutu genocide. When I stepped briefly into the bush
I saw a decapitated corpse almost cut in half, shiny white
Reeboks still on the feet. It is impossible to sleep inside
the buildings because of the unbearable stench of the
slaughter here. In one room a prayer book lay on the
ground and the walls were riddled with bullet holes and
splattered with blood. We pitched our tents in the grounds
but awoke through the night when the Rwandan Patriotic
Front soldiers fired rounds at the dogs munching on
the corpses.*

(JOURNAL 1994)

As one of Africa's bloodiest wars was coming to a terrifying
climax, I went to Rwanda to investigate how as many as
one million Tutsis could have been massacred in about
one hundred days. This was the swiftest slaughter the world had
seen, faster than the Nazis or the Khmer Rouge. To most
outsiders this almost unbelievable spasm of violence in Rwanda

could be explained only as 'African tribal war' or 'black-on-black savagery'. During two unforgettable journeys into the darkness of Rwanda I learned that the genocide in Central Africa was the result of a master plan by a political elite that viciously exploited both the tribal hatred and the world's indifference to the massacre of black Africans.

Near the shot-up airfield, I walked among the wreckage of the plane of the Hutu president, Juvenal Habyarimana. It had exploded and crashed near the rear walls of his own residence after one or two surface-to-air missiles had hit the aircraft as it was coming in to land. The death of Habyarimana sparked the genocide. It was the signal for the Hutu political elite to implement a premeditated, systematic slaughter of the Tutsi educated class and even of moderate Hutus who supported a bipartisan government.

War crimes investigators I have talked to have various theories about who was responsible for lighting the fuse to this catastrophe. It is believed that the surface-to-air missiles used in the attack on the president's plane came from a French stockpile left over from the Gulf War. France has accused the Tutsis of firing the missiles from a hill near the airport, claiming that some troops of the Rwandan Patriotic Front (the RPF) had infiltrated Kigali. On the other hand, the leader of the Tutsi army, the West Point-trained General Paul Kigame, told me that he was sure the attack on the plane was organised by the Akazu, the Hutu president's small group of advisers. He claimed that their motive was President Habyarimana's involvement in sensitive negotiations to end the conflict and to share power with the Tutsis.

As General Kigame had been waging a bitter war against the Hutu forces openly supported by their French allies, it was clearly in his own interest to portray that side as totally responsible for the genocide that followed. Even some Tutsis have questioned why it took General Kigame's forces so long to halt this slaughter but his reply was that it was a difficult conflict and that ultimately only the complete rout of the Hutu forces stopped the bloodshed. The French role, General Kigame said, was very clear. The late François Mitterand had long had a personal interest bordering on

obsession with Rwanda. General Kigame alleged that the French
secret service not only supported the murderous plans of the
Hutus but directed some legionnaires to help train the death
squads. After its own inquiry into the Rwandan tragedy the
French government defended its behaviour as the normal support
a great power would show towards its allies, in France's case the
Hutus. General Kigame's strongest criticism was aimed at
Mitterand's son, Jean-Christophe, whom he alleged had been
involved in arms deals with the Hutu government. Again, Jean-
Christophe Mitterand does not deny they put weapons in the
hands of the Hutus but says they were helping them fight off the
Tutsis and had no idea the genocide was coming. General
Kigame's face was full of scorn at this suggestion. He alleged that
a year before he led the Tutsi forces south from Uganda, he had
made a visit to France, was briefly held captive, and threatened by
some senior foreign affairs officials. He claims he was told that if
he went ahead with plans for a military takeover in Rwanda,
'there would be no Tutsis left alive to govern'.

When my film crew pushed out into the countryside where the
fighting was continuing, French legionnaires refused us access to
parts of Rwanda where the Hutus were carrying out some of their
most terrible massacres. The reason given was that they were
trying to protect all civilian life in a 'safe zone'. I believe the
French military role in effect was to cover the retreat of the Hutu
army and protect the ringleaders of the genocide. Any
unfortunate Tutsi in the path of the Hutus was butchered and this
happened all the way to the Zaire border.

For all of the battlefields I have crossed I have seen only one like
Rwanda. It was more like a human abattoir. Wherever you went
there was the unmistakable stench of rotting corpses. It leaked up
from the latrines stuffed with bodies, from the burned ruins of
houses, in the corridors of the old government buildings and even
in the churches. In the 'land of a thousand hills' there was
nowhere the Tutsis could hide. Jean-Baptiste Kayigamba, press
attaché to the Tutsi leader, chillingly described how his parents,
brothers and sisters were among the estimated twenty thousand
bodies that made the rivers run red. The whole world was

watching terrifying images of corpses washing over waterfalls, but the international community took no action until it was too late.

A brave young Australian working with World Vision, Scott Kelleher, saw the immediate aftermath of the massacre of 800 people in a Catholic mission. The horror was written all over his face. For anyone from a peaceful country it was hard to believe that we were seeing roads lined with corpses tied up in grass mats. My friend and producer, David Hardacre, had never seen mutilated corpses and wondered aloud how much any audience could bear to see. It was a good point. The scale and savagery of this slaughter was almost beyond comprehension. There were so many corpses it was simply beyond the capacity of the relief teams to organise decent burials. The walking wounded fell by the wayside. The refugees kept flooding towards the borders in great straggling processions of hungry and forlorn faces. Children who had run away in terror lived like animals in the bush until they crept out of hiding when the Tutsi soldiers arrived.

I met a six-year-old boy named Cassius Niyonsaba who was among 5000 people herded by the Hutus into a church at Nyamata. This was a typical page from the Hutu master plan. A few armed Hutu soldiers stood guard on the perimeter. They lobbed grenades into the church to create panic and terror. Then a death squad, the Interahamwe ('those who attack'), armed with machetes and clubs began to slash and crush skulls with terrifying speed, screaming their frenzied war cries as they went. They cut down dozens of people and left them to bleed to death. The child Cassius saw his parents hacked just before he was bashed unconscious with a spiked club and then slashed with a machete. I looked at the deep scar across his head and then into the eyes of this little boy, wondering how he would ever recover from this trauma. Cassius had been one of only two survivors lying underneath the pile of bodies.

The Hutu Akazu had drawn up a plan for genocide that mimicked the Nazis'. They ran a radio station broadcasting the most racist propaganda, exploiting the old loathing towards the taller and wealthier Tutsis, the minority tribe which made up about one and a half million of Rwanda's seven million people. There had been great resentment of the Tutsis ever since the Belgians had patronisingly nominated this 'better looking' (or more European) tribe to fill the top administration jobs in the colonial era. The Tutsi highlanders measured their wealth in cattle. The Hutus had to scratch out a living as farmers in a landlocked country whose borders were artificially created by Europeans ignorant of the interplay of the dominant tribes in Central Africa's lakes area. Anthropologists claim that there is no evidence of genocide involving the Tutsis and Hutus in ancient times. The large-scale slaughter appears to be a modern phenomenon, a variation of class war expressed through the horror of 'ethnic cleansing'.

The Hutu announcers were fully aware of how much hatred they had to work with in a poorly educated population, and so they broadcast the lie that the Tutsis were planning to kill all of them. Hutu farmers were instructed to get their machetes, clubs and even garden hoes to join in the drills that took place around the countryside. Like Hitler's henchmen, the Hutu ringleaders made frequent tours to whip up hysteria. The ultimate goal of the Hutu Akazu was to kill so many Tutsis that the country would be ungovernable. General Kigame alleged that the French were then meant to help the Hutus regain power.

Just like the Nazis, the ringleaders of this genocide had drawn up lists of those marked for extermination. The workers were shown how to herd these Tutsis to open ground, how to trap them using only a few riflemen and then how to make sure that no one was left standing. They were particularly ruthless in hunting down pregnant Tutsi women to try to ensure that there would be no mothers giving birth to their future enemies.

At one massacre site, near a pile of 20 000 skulls and bones, I saw the evidence of a death so cruel it made me certain that we all must try to lead the world away from this violence. A slender teenage girl had a wooden stake jammed into her vagina, her hands clutching the weapon as she died a painful, hideous death.

In Kigali, a beautiful young Tutsi, Louise Mushikiwabo, wept softly as she told me that Rwandan women had not taken part in clashes of the past. It wounded her heart to think that Hutu women, some carrying babies on their backs, had picked up machetes and joined in the killing spree. Louise and her sister Anne-Marie had to bury seven members of their family including their brother, Lando Ndaswinga, the only Tutsi Cabinet minister in the Hutu government. A United Nations Peacekeeping Force of 2500 men was specifically instructed to protect Lando and other political figures, but many simply ran away when the genocide started. The procrastination at United Nations headquarters and the treachery of the great powers allowed the killing in Rwanda to build into a frenzy of bloodletting that will stain Central Africa for centuries.

I walked today in the midst of 8000 mass murderers, jammed into Kigali's Central Prison. With Mike Hourigan, ex-South Australian detective, crown prosecutor and more recently UN War Crimes investigator, we were allowed in for some rare interviews with men who had slain not just one but scores of Tutsis. Each of these serial killers was dressed in a bright pink cotton shirt so that he would stand out if he made a dash for the large steel gates of this old fortress. Because the system can't handle all 124 000 Hutus so far charged with crimes of genocide, the prisons are overflowing. The relatives of the killers are allowed to come here each day with baskets of food, some holding the babies of the Hutu fathers. They assemble outside the prison in parallel lines, kept in order by just a few men with bamboo canes. The Tutsis have executed a few dozen, but Mike Hourigan says they realise the international community would not allow them to execute the 124 000 moving slowly through the group trials. How ironic when the international community was so passive when the genocide claimed up to a million Tutsi lives.

(JOURNAL 1999)

I made a second trip to Rwanda after Mike Hourigan, the war crimes investigator, resigned in disgust when he uncovered the truth of the cowardly role of the United Nations and certain member nations in the death of so many Tutsis.

This South Australian is a brave man, a great detective and a fine prosecutor with a true sense of justice. What has compelled Hourigan to spend several years of his life, unpaid and largely unsupported, trying to establish the true anatomy of the Rwandan genocide is a deep sense of morality. Some others came across the truth but out of fear for their lives or their jobs chose not to disclose it. Hourigan could have been living the good life in Adelaide but he came to realise that only a few people knew the secret story behind the Rwandan tragedy. He told me that he simply could not live with his conscience unless he tried to tell the world how we all became part of this great crime of silence.

During his hunt for the ringleaders of the genocide, Hourigan discovered a secret cable from the UN Commander in Rwanda, the Canadian Major General Roméo Dallaire, to UN headquarters in New York with a clear warning of the Hutu plot to assassinate prominent politicians as a precursor to the genocide. As I sat with Hourigan behind locked doors in Kigali and read the message, we both could see that this was explosive evidence. It meant that the UN had two months warning but still did nothing to protect those politicians officially in its care, like Louise's brother Lando Ndaswinga, or the Supreme Court judge and other officials murdered in April 1994 when the slaughter began. Hourigan could not stomach this. How could an organisation as powerful as the UN not act when it had sworn after the Nazis there would be no more holocausts? The Australian and his team of investigators went on digging for more evidence of the negligence of those in charge of United Nations peacekeeping.

After the first twenty-four hours of ethnic slaughter, General Dallaire had given the bluntest warning to his superiors who included Kofi Annan, at that time head of peacekeeping operations and now the UN Secretary-General. Ten days later on 17 April 1994, Dallaire begged for a change of orders and additional troops to allow him to try to stop the bloodletting:

*The ethnic cleansing continues and may in fact be
accelerating... Bodies litter the streets and pose a
significant health hazard... The force simply cannot
continue to sit on the fence in the face of all these morally
legitimate demands for assistance.*

The UN continued to sit on the fence, and, shamefully, some of its
peacekeepers ran away. Hourigan says there is evidence that the
Hutus deliberately executed ten Belgian peacekeepers, calculating
correctly that the old colonial power would have no taste for such
terror and would order the immediate withdrawal of its
contingent. These were the most highly trained soldiers in General
Dallaire's command and without them he was powerless to stop
the slaughter. He warned in a cable that some of his remaining
UN troops would 'hand over local people for inevitable killing
rather than use their weapons to save local people'.

The leader of the Tutsi army, General Paul Kigame, poured
scorn on the international speculation about whether anyone
could have stopped the slaughter of one million of his people.
He told me that if the UN troops had simply been given orders to
put a few rockets into the Akazu's radio station broadcasting the
detailed orders for the genocide, hundreds of thousands of lives
would have been saved. If the UN had allowed its original force
of 2500 troops to rapidly disarm the marauding Hutus and
confiscate the massive stockpiles of machetes assembled for the
bloodletting, this too would have greatly reduced the scale of the
slaughter. The French also stand condemned for their weapon
sales to the Hutus and the Belgians will never be able to erase the
shame of withdrawing their trained soldiers. The United States
and Britain have yet to explain why, within the Security Council,
they refused to call this killing 'genocide' until it was too late.

After the peacekeeping debacle in Somalia, President Clinton
understandably was reluctant to send more American troops into
an African war zone. Rwanda made Somalia seem like a picnic.
This was clearly genocide, as confirmed by General Dallaire and

yet the American ambassador to the United Nations, like his British counterpart, was given instructions for weeks not to agree to a debate on 'genocide' because this would require the United Nations to take immediate action. Given that the Americans and the British have the best intelligence in the world, they really did not need General Dallaire's many secret cables, his warnings about 'crimes against humanity' and the Hutu threat to 'exterminate the Tutsis', to know what was going on in Rwanda. Perhaps there is another reason why Clinton appeared so weak and vacillating.

While France had sold the Hutus sufficient arms to kill a million Tutsis, the United States and Britain were supporting General Kigame's Tutsi army. If the Security Council had intervened in the early weeks of the genocide it would have frozen the forces on the battlefield, with the Hutus still in Kigali and the Tutsis encircling them. The result may well have been a compromise, an attempt to share power. But then the French would have maintained their influence. From the perspective of American and British national security types who sit around tables like the Akazu and determine who should live and die 'in the national interest' it would have been far preferable to let the Tutsi army press on to outright victory. The United States for the first time had a possible sphere of influence in Central Africa and the old masters, the French, were in retreat. These are the games great powers play while the pawns are destroyed in one tragic war after another.

The horror we were seeing in Rwanda was beginning to have a disturbing, accumulative effect on all of us. Mike Hourigan felt physically and mentally exhausted but was determined to press on when General Kigame agreed to let us investigate some dangerous parts of Rwanda that had been closed since the genocide. My film team, cameraman Phil Donoghue and sound-recordist Mark Brewer, were the same colleagues who had gone into Rwanda with me during the war. The producer, Julian Cress, was making his first visit and told me that he felt he was in a constant state of shock. The scale of the mass graves was difficult for us all to come to terms with, but we agreed to try to film one final extraordinary scene before we put our camera down.

Driving south, I rode on an RPF truck, sitting between young Tutsi soldiers holding rocket-launchers and watchful for the marauding Hutu squads still roaming the country. This was the heart of the recruiting ground for the Hutu militia, the Interahamwe, the core weapon of the genocide. These were the farming villages where men piled into trucks and drove off to form massive rolling death squads, filling their vehicles with corpses each day. We passed through Ngoma where about 350 000 Tutsis were massacred. The local prosecutor for the Butare region told me that he had stopped arresting Hutus. There were too many killers to prosecute. The stress felt by the survivors having to exist side by side with mass murderers was illustrated in one of the camps where hundreds of Hutus were being subjected to a kind of re-education program before they would be allowed to walk home to their land. These were men and women who had murdered time and again but they expressed no remorse. Tutsi soldiers, weapons slung over shoulders, danced with the Hutus in a strained display of friendship but it seemed a fairly futile attempt to erase the hatred. The tragedy of Rwanda was that the political elite manipulated this fear and loathing into a national hysteria, a country-wide psychosis that turned men and women into beasts. There was so much madness and trauma that only sheer exhaustion brought a pause in the carnage.

Near the southwestern town of Gikongoro we moved down a track to a schoolyard where about 25 000 Tutsis were massacred. There were mass graves down through the valley below us and some had been exhumed to reveal the scale of the killing. I walked across the school grounds with Mike Hourigan, hands across our mouths as the smell of death again filled our nostrils. We counted seventy-two classrooms in this school. Inside was one of the greatest horrors of the most terrible twentieth century. Fifty thousand corpses were piled on wooden racks. Dusted in white lime, the skin was stretched and dried into terrible death masks. I saw whole classrooms full of dead children, tiny, twisted corpses with skulls caved in, small hands up to their faces in a last gesture of fear and helplessness. Many of these people still wore the clothes that they had died in, khaki pants, a floral dress, a child's T-shirt.

I gasped when I saw the dead mother with her arms clutching her dead baby. There were more stakes thrust into the abdomens of the women, more feet severed from young children, more men beheaded. It was staggering, soul-destroying, unforgettable horror.

After sucking in a lungful of fresh air, I stepped back into the classrooms. Phil kept the camera rolling because he knew he must. He was angry like I was because the world had allowed this to happen. Mike said it would happen again because the United Nations and the great powers had not the will to prevent a repetition of this tragedy. By now some of us were on the verge of throwing up, so putrid was the stench. Mark whispered to me that maybe he had seen too much of this because it was disturbing him no more than all the other occasions. Phil and I were shaking. Julian was white-faced, eyes wide, a young man who would never forget this place as long as he lived.

I urged them not to wear emotional armour, not to hold back the tears, not to stay silent about this school full of death. Tell your loved ones about it. Tell everyone you can. It may be the only thing that keeps a man sane. I felt that we should tell the whole world about it, because Rwanda was the world's crime of silence.

CHAPTER NINETEEN

LIKE A SHOOTING STAR

There are pictures to paint everywhere. There are stories being scribbled in the sky. They have no beginning or end as stars are born and moons keep rising. The seas swell, rain falls, living creatures breathe the air but the earth's crust still hides so many secrets at its core. Trees whisper what we no longer see. Animals have knowledge we have forgotten. The poems of nature are worth listening to all around this beautiful world.

(JOURNAL 1989)

Maurice and Katia Kraft were vulcanologists who lived and died for their fiery passion. While most people looked at volcanoes and thought of death, they knew that the earth's core held the real meaning of life. Without volcanoes the earth would be a dead planet, just a rock with no energy at its centre, no oceans, no breathable atmosphere, no life at all. Meeting this remarkable man and woman, sharing an awesome adventure to the top of an active volcano, made me look at our time on earth in a very different way.

Instead of tearing off the pages of the calendar, Maurice and Katia measured time in geological age. About 4.6 billion years ago a cloud of stardust condensed into our planet, Earth. In another four and a half billion years or so, they believed, the earth would explode into stardust again, engulfed by our sun.

They were full of life but not afraid of death as they pursued one of the most dangerous professions in the world. Their glorious obsession was to try to understand what lay at the centre of the earth and to try to predict its violent outbursts.

As we loaded our backpacks for a 3000-metre climb to the top of Mount Etna, Sicily's active volcano, Maurice and Katia explained the dangers. If we were trapped near a lava flow the temperature would be around 1000°C and we would need asbestos suits covered in aluminium to reflect the infra-red heat waves. My film crew did not have such suits. If Mount Etna continued to blast out huge boulders, which could be the size of a car, then a helmet really would not do us much good. I wore a ski cap. Poisonous gases sometimes were thick in the air around Mount Etna's main crater. We had two gas masks between four people. I was so keen to try to get to the top of the mountain that I resorted to my usual measure of risk when working with a master.

'How many times have you and Katia managed to get close to an active volcano?' I asked as we walked to our cars.

'Oh, about one hundred and fifty,' Maurice said.

'Do you think we can do it?'

'Sure.' But then he added, 'There is also a chance we could be killed.'

Maurice had been fascinated with volcanic eruptions since the age of seven when his parents took him to see Mount Stromboli, a volcano that has been erupting north of Sicily for around two thousand years. Katia was eighteen years old when she saw the same volcano. The pair met during their university days and formed a lifelong bond that grew from an uncommon interest. She became an expert geochemist and he was a geologist, but it was not rocks and dead mountains they would spend their lives studying.

Soon after our earth was born it turned molten due to radioactive decay and the impact of meteorites. As the planet cooled, the heavier materials sank, forming layers from the rocky crust to the mysterious inner core, thought to be a solid sphere of hexagonal iron crystals. Most scientists agreed that the elements at the centre were giving off so much heat that the rock melted into magma which rose under the pressure of gases to become lava as it burst through fissures in the earth's surface. But no one was certain what caused the mightiest volcanic eruptions, superplumes that could fill the sky with ash, alter the global climate and even influence the evolution of life itself.

Maurice told me that if he could he would journey to the centre of the earth like Jules Verne's adventurers. He dreamed of inventing an asbestos canoe to take him on a lava flow for one hell of a last ride. Katia joked that she would be there to take the pictures. Maurice said that he got the idea after realising that when wearing special asbestos gloves he could make balls of lava and juggle them. It was an amazing life they shared, travelling, filming and studying many of the world's 500 active volcanoes on land and still more under the sea.

In Central Africa, near Rwanda's border with Zaire, they climbed 4000 metres up the side of Mount Nyiragongo, the forbidden volcano, then down inside to camp on a platform of rock inside the crater. It was so hot that their boots melted and their clothing and tents were eaten away by the acid in the air. But for Maurice and Katia it was a once in a lifetime opportunity to closely study Nyiragongo's lava lake, hot enough to instantly fry them if they put a foot wrong. Fortunately they were not in the crater when the volcano exploded in 1977. The lava racing across the plain at about seventy kilometres an hour overtook 150 people and a small herd of elephants. Maurice later cut open the hardened mounds of lava and found hollow sculptures of the elephants. The flesh had frizzled away but the moulds captured a likeness of the creatures, in a similar fashion to the human moulds found at Pompeii in Italy.

Katia believed that many people developed their fear of volcanoes after hearing the story of Pompeii, buried under lava in 79 AD. She pointed out that only 2000 people had died in that eruption. If Mount Vesuvius exploded today hundreds of thousands would be killed, she said. In a still more crowded country, like Indonesia, with the world's largest and most dangerous volcanic field, the death toll would be even larger unless people had reliable warnings of extreme geothermal activity. It was this factor that drove the Krafts and other vulcanologists to take tremendous risks. A dozen colleagues of Maurice and Katia (there are only about 350 vulcanologists in the world) had been blasted into invisible pieces. Even this was not going to keep them from another attempt on Mount Etna, a volcano they loved for its beauty and power. They hoped to learn enough about Mount Etna to not merely forecast its volcanic activity, but to accurately gauge the violence of its outbursts.

With the windchill factor it was about seven degrees below freezing as we trudged up the sides of Mount Etna, or la Vibre (the Viper) as the Italians call it. We could see where the snake-like lava flow had devoured stone cottages just a few years ago as Maurice and Katia were filming close by. John Little and I found the climb so stirring it almost rid us of our fear. Mark Brewer's concern was his feet were turning blue. Phil Donoghue found the strange brew of sulphurous gases very hard on the lungs and grabbed for a gas mask. There were all sorts of evil belching sounds and at times a low roar from the devil's pit, the main magma chamber at least thirty kilometres below. Maurice said there was another magma chamber much closer to the surface, maybe five kilometres below our feet. When Mount Etna blew I understood why he said this mountain was 'alive'.

(JOURNAL 1989)

At the top of Mount Etna we were standing on the spot where nine tourists had been killed and another twenty-three injured when they took their eyes off the sky during a sudden violent eruption. As I rubbed the falling ash from my eyes, Maurice panted out another warning. When you hear the loud explosions from down inside the volcano, a 'bomb' is on its way. No matter how large these awesome blocks of rock, your only chance is to watch the sky and sprint before they crush you. Just as Katia was telling us with a chuckle that it was like dancing with the volcano, Mount Etna shook violently, as if the whole peak was about to collapse. From inside the vast darkness of the crater, there was a rumbling that became a roar and then a great blast of stone and ash came flying into the sky. We all leaped back from the crater's edge but with eyes straining we could see that the ejected rocks were very small. Fortunately they fell away from us. Then we noticed that here and there the rim of the crater had crumbled away, with huge chunks falling into the hell down below.

'Don't worry about it,' chuckled Maurice, 'ninety-two per cent of people die in bed. Most journalists and most vulcanologists die in bed. This would be an amazing way to go.'

The crew crept closer towards the cloudy abyss, making wisecracks as you do at such times, waiting for a break in the gaseous cloud so that we could begin filming. Again Mount Etna roared without warning. Eyes were on the sky but we could not see a thing. The vapour was so thick we could barely see one another. So there we were trying to film a thought-provoking conversation on the edge of the biggest hole in the ground I had ever seen and all I could think about was something as big as a Fiat crashing down on top of us.

'The big boulders fly out at around five hundred metres a second,' Maurice said, 'and the most deadly volcanic blast will come at more than one thousand kilometres an hour. Those are the ones that vulcanologists fear because there is nothing left of you or your pictures. You just disappear. Let's face it my friends, there's simply no point worrying about it.'

When the cloud had slowly cleared and I peered down into the crater, thinking of the magma's path from that mysterious core, of the life force of our planet there before our eyes, I suddenly understood what Maurice and Katia had been telling us. As the ground trembled beneath our feet I lost my fear and stood in awe of the volcano's power and beauty. I realised why some societies had worshipped this natural wonder. The geological calendar Maurice and Katia followed began to make sense. Why live in fear of anything, especially mortal men, when four and a half billion years from now we will all be stardust anyway? We laughed together and threw arms around shoulders as we sauntered around the crater's edge.

It was an exhilarating dance with Mount Etna, and pure joy to share with the world the wit and wisdom of this fearless man and woman. Coming down we paused to film another brilliant display as the sky grew darker. Mount Etna glowed as molten lava burst into the night sky as it had done for the last 500 000 years. The first day's filming was complete, the core of a story that would be shown around the world, and three or four times on Australia's *60 Minutes*, thanks to Maurice and Katia's breathtaking images on the volcanic front line. Our camera was packed away. We began to thaw out as we settled down with a Sicilian family to eat rabbit sausage and drink red wine in a stone cottage on the rich volcanic slopes.

'I really hope I see many more volcanoes as beautiful as Etna, but after one hundred and fifty-one days like this I have seen so much I have no right to expect more,' Maurice said.

'You are not afraid now, but have you ever known fear?' I asked.

'When I was young I worried more. If I was really frightened I just pressed my eye to the camera viewfinder and the volcano would look much smaller.'

Phil Donoghue nodded, understanding perfectly.

'I am so small,' Katia said, 'I have a much better chance than Maurice. Look how much sausage he eats.'

'Sometimes I have seen "bombs" bigger than I am fly out of a crater,' laughed Maurice, 'and I found myself not filming at all, just standing there watching this rock go a thousand metres into the air. The volcano for me is the most beautiful thing in the world. For me, and for Katia, this is a dangerous life but we truly do not care. I do not want to die asleep in my bed. I would like to die on a volcano.'

We clinked glasses and saluted Mount Etna.

Less than two years later, Maurice and Katia Kraft were filming a volcano in Japan when a catastrophic blast reduced them to stardust. On their cosmic calendar they are part of the continuum. Our time on earth is so short. How glad I am to have known these shooting stars.

> There is an Aboriginal dreamtime story about a bright star that fell from the sky a long, long time ago and landed in the desert at a place called Kundimulul. We flew there, north from Alice Springs, turning west at Rabbit Flat, across the Great Sandy Desert until somewhere out the back of the Billiluna Aboriginal Station we could see this amazing sight rising out of nowhere. The Wolf Creek Crater was created by a meteor that plummeted from the heavens about 300 000 years ago. It's almost a kilometre in diameter, the second largest meteorite crater on earth, and like the others out here in the desert, it is perfectly preserved.
>
> (JOURNAL 1993)

Stargazing is quite possibly man's second-oldest pastime and it certainly is a favourite of mine because in Australia we not only have clear skies, we have the best preserved collection of meteorite craters. One-third of the world's stellar crash sites are right here in our backyard. While many others on earth have crumbled away over millions of years, the unique stability of our central desert has saved for us the kind of scenery you would see on the moon.

The Wolf Creek Crater, or Kundimulul, in Western Australia is a scientific sacred site as well as a place of beauty and power in the Aboriginal dreamtime. To the local Aborigines the falling star has a mysterious connection with water. To Eugene and Carolyn Shoemaker, American comet-watchers who had been drawn to these remote parts of Australia for more than ten years, comets were great cosmic snowballs of ice, dust and gas that might explain where earth's water came from.

Gene, a veteran geologist and adviser to the American space program and Carolyn, an amateur astronomer, were two-thirds of a remarkably successful comet-hunting group from Arizona. With astronomer David Levy they discovered at least forty comets including the gigantic 'Shoemaker-Levy 9', a string of icy pearls up to five kilometres in diameter. As this necklace wrapped itself around Jupiter, one of the pearls bigger than a football field slammed into the far side of that mighty planet. It left a crater larger than the Earth. Shoemaker-Levy 9, first spotted by Carolyn, is still up there, orbiting Jupiter like a moon. But sometimes, maybe once in a thousand years or so, one of these space giants — like our recent visitor Hale-Bopp — will get a gravity boost from Jupiter and come streaking back our way.

Gene Shoemaker was the granddaddy of the meteor catastrophe theorists. Soon after he began to study these heavenly bodies he also started calculating the odds of them crashing to earth. If we are talking big boulders there are millions crossing the earth's orbit. Far more dangerous are the meteors and asteroids about the size of a football field — and there are at least one hundred thousand of them. But the giants of space get even bigger. There are at least two thousand asteroids the size of a mountain, from one to seven kilometres in diameter, crossing the earth's orbit. In fact there may be a lot more because Gene believed that he and his colleagues had only identified about 5 per cent of what may be up there. If the 'space mountains' fall from the sky, the Big Crunch may come a lot earlier for many of us.

Gene and Carolyn showed me in Central Australia the most spectacular evidence of what a giant space invader might do to the earth. Gosses Bluff is an awesome crater twenty-two kilometres across. Some of the original walls have been worn away by erosion, but you can see the extraordinary uplift where the crater collapsed and rose again in the middle. Gene believed that the asteroid or comet that created this natural wonder was about two kilometres in diameter — today that would mean a major human catastrophe. It would not extinguish life on earth but would throw up so much dust into the atmosphere, blocking out sunlight and cooling the earth rapidly, that our world could lose an entire year of crop production. The loss of human life would be devastating. As Gosses Bluff was created by an impact 140 million years ago, Gene calculated that there was only a fairly small chance of another one like it in the next century. Roughly a one in a thousand chance.

Gene remembered how a woman in the United States reclining on her living-room couch watched a small meteorite crash through her roof, ricochet off her radio and thump her on the thigh. That is the risk of being a couch potato when you could be wandering around Central Australia looking at some of our nineteen impact craters, four of them relatively new like the Henbury cluster near Alice Springs. These craters were formed when a meteor about twenty metres in diameter came down just six thousand years ago. It was going fifteen times faster than a rifle bullet and as it hit the shockwaves of the earth's atmosphere it broke into a dozen big pieces which created the craters. It's a wonderful place to spend a day walking. You can pick up chunks of melted shale that were turned to glass by the heat. Under a microscope you can see the precious elements of the meteorite, like gold and platinum, far richer than in earthly rocks.

Despite the panic Hollywood movies try to whip up to avoid disaster at the box office, we are here on earth for such a short blip in time that meteors — like volcanoes — should be a subject of wonder, not fear. Like Maurice and Katia Kraft, Gene and Carolyn Shoemaker had an intriguing way of looking at these powerful natural forces.

In Gene's view, we are the progeny of comets. They contain carbon, hydrogen, nitrogen and oxygen in about the same proportions found in the human body. To these astronomers, we really are made of stardust.

Gene's favourite T-shirt depicted two dinosaurs looking up as a huge meteor streaked across the sky towards them. One dinosaur looks at the other and says, 'Oh shit!' A meteor, or a series of meteor strikes, indeed was believed to have been a major factor in the extinction of the dinosaurs 65 million years ago. But that meteor's 300-kilometre-wide crater is buried under marine limestone at the northern tip of Mexico's Yucatan Peninsula.

This kind of catastrophe, causing the extinction of a species, happens about once every hundred million years. Do you see what I mean about the odds? If human civilisation taps into its real potential and we last, say, one million years, the odds of us being wiped out by a meteor are one in one hundred. On a year to year basis the risk is incredibly small.

If we lose this real-life game of 'Space Invaders' and a giant asteroid crashes into our world, cities would be destroyed by the largest ever nuclear explosion, tsunamis would flood the land and our species could end. It seems to me there is a far greater chance that we will poison our earth or its atmosphere, or wipe ourselves out through war, than go the way of the dinosaurs.

We exist today, Gene and Carolyn helped me see, only because that huge meteor hit the earth 65 million years ago and destroyed the dominant life form. Mammals were given a miraculous chance to evolve. A so-called 'catastrophe' created ecological space for a new species to develop. Now it is our turn to show what we are truly made of and to create a civilisation that might reach for the stars.

My six-year-old son, Will, recently asked me, 'Daddy, what will come after the people on earth?' With a child's sense of wonder and illuminating honesty he had observed the passing of the dinosaurs and concluded that humans too had a finite time on the cosmic calendar.

'We have the chance to build a great civilisation,' I answered, 'if we look after the earth and one another. Maybe with spacecraft like your grandfather helped design we will fly to another world some day before the sun engulfs the earth.'

Gene Shoemaker, who had a vital advisory role in the American space program, certainly believed that we could stretch our wings and fly beyond the maps of Magellan, Columbus and Cook. He was not much interested in the debate about knocking down meteors with nuclear weapons in space. He wanted their water so that it could be broken down into fuel and used by our rockets and space stations already up there. This made the meteors a precious commodity capable of extending our exploratory reach and sustaining the human journey somewhere up there in the stars.

It was not a meteor that ended Gene Shoemaker's life on earth. On a lonely road in the outback, a mundane collision of motor vehicles turned his sky to black. He was a great loss to astronomy. Whenever my family assembles our telescope to look at the beautiful moons of Jupiter or our own golden moon with its vast craters, I remember Gene, laughing about the odds.

> *The physicist Stephen Hawking called it the 'discovery of the century, if not of all time'. The Cosmic Background Explorer satellite, COBE, has sent back pictures of the afterglow of the Big Bang. It proves that our universe was created in a massive primordial explosion. This is as close as we may get to an image of creation itself. It is mind-blowing that humanity has reached so high into the heavens. What a triumph for Bill, to have been part of this extraordinary quest.*
>
> (JOURNAL 1992)

My wife's father, William D. Hoggard II, was one of many fine minds and steady pairs of hands that spent about fifteen years focused on one great mission. The astrophysicists called it the search for the Holy Grail. Gene Shoemaker likened it to looking for the largest and oldest fossils that ever existed in our universe. My father-in-law, Bill, saw it as a space ride back to the beginning of time. Bill's role, after NASA's tragic accident with the Space Shuttle *Challenger* in 1986, was to help figure out how a complex satellite designed for launching from the shuttle could be reconfigured for a ride into space on top of a rocket. The mind that once had focused on teaching mathematics at the US Naval Academy in Annapolis turned to intense number-crunching, the sort that reduces my brain to mush. But what we shared in this family was great conversation about the profound meaning of COBE's very human quest.

One of Bill's friends, John Mather, was in charge of this NASA project. In his backyard in Maryland on America's eastern shore, Mather showed me his tomato plants. A tomato was like our early universe, he said. But we could not say whether our universe was connected to ten, one thousand or a billion other universes. We lived within one little tomato but it was possible we were connected to others by a cosmic tomato vine. I really loved this stuff. Mather reminded me of that wonderful Peter Sellers character in the film *Being There,* but out of these simple observations grew the most challenging ideas. COBE was looking for the things that made our tomato-universe grow: the seeds, the vine, the cosmic climate.

Bill's rocket successfully boosted COBE far enough to start sending back postcards from the edge of our universe. The spacecraft found for the first time minute differences in the temperature of the cosmic background radiation. A computer turned this information into an image of cool blue and hot pink. At this point you need a bit of imagination, but what the scientific team was cheering was an image of creation.

The project's astrophysicist, George Smoot, explained that right now we are living about fifteen billion years after the 'Beginning'. COBE was taking snapshots of roughly 300 000 years after the Big Bang. If you put this in human terms, our universe today is middle-aged, but thanks to COBE we could look back to see a baby photo taken when it was just five hours old.

As Stephen Hawking may be the greatest mind since Einstein, I will take his word on the scientific importance of COBE's confirmation of the Big Bang theory. In my family the discovery became a hot topic of discussion. What did it mean to us? If the universe has a middle-aged spread will it get in shape and settle down or keep growing like a fat man who finally explodes? If we are looking at the baby photo, who or what made the baby?

The COBE team had to admit that we were at the outer limits of human knowledge. The astrophysicist Smoot felt that looking at these images was like looking at God. It was a deeply moving experience. John Mather was not inclined to religious metaphor but was simply thrilled that humankind had come so far. Now it was time, I suggested, for the imagination to take over where the laws of science could not venture. We simply do not know if our 'laws' apply before the Big Bang. Can you imagine a neverending series of Big Bangs with no beginning or end to time, where space spirals inwards and outwards forever? You might see the creator orchestrating each event, like the birth of our universe or our own birth. Or perhaps you see no room for a creator in this place of no beginning and no end? Are we looking at creation or the continuum?

For me there is a fathomless beauty and peace in contemplating these things. To understand the nature of happiness you have to find your own idea of our human purpose. To exist for a time in timelessness is an immensely pleasing thought. To continue in the continuum is our destiny. Am I imagining this? Maybe, as Einstein said, the most incomprehensible thing about the universe is that it is comprehensible.

CHAPTER TWENTY

BEAUTIFUL EXTREMES

I know of no man or woman who has seen Antarctica
and not been changed forever. It is the closest experience
I have had to making a journey to another star. For in this
world of ice, all of the shapes are beautifully disorienting
— a magnificent iceberg, an awesome crevasse, cliffs of
blue ice that refract the light and seem to flow like a
frozen waterfall, great pyramid mountains perfectly
sculpted, vast fields of ice gleaming in the midnight sun,
and always the whiteness of the snows, the swirling
blizzards of blinding white.

(JOURNAL 1989)

The quest to be first to reach the North and South Poles was a twentieth-century phenomenon, just like the race to be first on the moon. The United States naval officer Robert E. Peary claimed to be the first to reach the North Pole in 1909 and he probably made it to within ten kilometres of his mark. Just two years later Roald Amundsen reached the South Pole ahead of Captain Robert Scott. As we know from his journal the British adventurer was devastated to find a Norwegian flag flying and messages from Amundsen. To Scott this meant someone else had 'discovered' the South Pole. When we reflect now on the drama and the tragedy of that race, did it really matter who was first? Scott and his team chose to travel without huskies and perhaps for that reason perished, seventeen kilometres from supplies that may have saved them. While there is great romance and tragedy in these polar journeys, the explorers' journals convey a different kind of experience, suffused with the uniqueness and seemingly unearthly beauty and awesome natural forces of the great white wilderness. This was the allure for me of Antarctica.

In the polar spring of October 1989, I flew to Chile with hopes of intercepting the longest trek ever made across Antarctica. A team of six men from six different countries was attempting to be the first to travel by foot and husky-drawn sled 6450 kilometres across the entire continent. Learning much from Scott and the other brave men who had trudged the ice before them, the Trans-Antarctica Expedition had organised food caches to be dropped from Twin Otter aircraft. Most were found but some were lost in the constantly shifting snow. In the fearsome southern winter they had been battling winds of 160 kilometres an hour and temperatures as low as –43°C. A blizzard in the Antarctic Peninsula had kept them tent-bound for thirteen days. But these adventurers had a purpose to sustain them in their most desperate hours. By combining the strengths and talents of men from the United States, Britain, France, China, Japan and the Soviet Union they wanted to show that international co-operation was the best way of preserving the uniqueness of the increasingly endangered polar wilderness.

Scott was right about Punta Arenas, Chile. What an awful place. This rusty tin town, constantly buffeted by gales, was our gathering point as a small band of journalists tried to hitch a ride on an aircraft that was to carry food and fresh huskies down to the Trans-Antarctica Expedition. The trouble was the ancient DC-6 hired for our 3000-kilometre flight across Drake Passage could not get off the ground. This ex-Canadian fire-fighting plane, nicknamed the 'Albatross', was supposed to fly us across the stormy sea, over the ice and down the Antarctic Peninsula to a rendezvous point at Patriot Hills, near the Ellsworth

Mountains. This is one of the most spectacular areas of Antarctica and I was certainly prepared to give up most of my annual holidays and travel solo without a *60 Minutes* film crew to make the trip of a lifetime. When I walked up from the port, pushed and shoved by the wind, and knocked on the doors of the charter company appropriately named Adventure Network International, the risks and challenges began to mount. I learned that the DC-6, a four-engined workhorse, was not equipped with skis but was going to attempt a rare landing on a patch of blue ice. It would carry 44-gallon drums of fuel that would be quickly rolled out onto the ice for refuelling and a hasty take-off. Any delay ran the risk of the engines freezing up and the Albatross would be stranded.

I went to the hangar to have a look at the old plane hoping it would be as sturdy as the reliable DC-4s that had carried me on adventures twenty years earlier around the far-flung islands of the South Pacific. The DC-6's engines were leaking oil as they often do. The inside of the plane had been stripped with just a few seats remaining to provide room for supplies and for the huskies to sleep on the floor. The only insulation to protect us from the extreme temperatures was sheets of taped-up cardboard painted grey. This would mean wearing our polar gear for the trip south. Of more concern to me were the engine problems that the mechanics were struggling to repair. I had a friendly conversation with the Canadian chief engineer who told me that the plane was not really the one for the job, but, he believed, it would get there.

The difficulty of travelling to Antarctica in the 1980s came not only from the distance and the isolation, but from the competing claims to control of the wilderness. Governments, scientists, mineral exploration companies, tour operators and adventurers had priorities that sometimes conflicted. Commercial sightseeing flights had stopped after an Air New Zealand DC-10 crashed into Mount Erebus in 1979, killing all 257 people aboard. As a result, sea travel was the most reliable passage to Antarctica, but not an option that would get me remotely close to the husky-driven expedition. As I walked away from the hangar I knew that only the greasy old Albatross could get me there.

Four times the DC-6 attempted its mission and four times it failed to make it all the way. One engine faltered, one engine caught fire, there was a small electrical fire in the cockpit, a generator problem, faulty spark plug and on it went. Three times the weather closed in over the designated landing spot at Patriot Hills, a dangerous white-out that could have spelled the end for the Albatross. After our third attempt to cross the windswept Southern Ocean, many of the journalists packed up and went home to the United States, France and Germany. I could see the risk and the degree of superstition that builds up when you strike out three times. But the truth was that the veteran pilot, a seventy-year-old Canadian, had made the correct decision each time and everyone was still alive. You have to know when to go on and when to turn back. The Canadian engineer assured me that he had fixed all of the mechanical problems and so I fastened my seatbelt for the fifth time and set off on the most exciting and nerve-racking ride of my life.

Some of the huskies were so nervous that they did not lie down at any time during the flight. These spirited animals had been specially bred from Siberian husky, malamute and timber wolf stock to give them the strength for a brutal trek never before completed by man or beast. I stroked the dogs to calm them as we flew through darkness, the engines throbbing but not missing a beat. After nine very slow hours we crossed the point of no return, when we simply had to land somewhere soon to refuel. Our merry band of brothers knew that now it was all up to the Albatross and our veteran pilot.

The DC-6 made radio contact with the expedition somewhere down below but with the thick cloud and the total whiteness we were lost for some time. They could not see us and we could not see a thing as we flew between the peaks of the tallest mountains in Antarctica. The Omega navigation system was not working and we were getting very low on fuel. After one hour of circling, the pilot glimpsed the coloured markers planted by the expedition and we dropped through a break in the clouds, thundering down towards a huge icefield. In the near white-out conditions it was extremely hard to see anything from our side windows except the black rock of the mountains. The pilot was having difficulty too. As we landed, the wheels of the DC-6 clipped a ledge of ice and we bounced about four storeys into the air. As the plane came down again the right wing tipped the loose snow but the pilot kept control. In a savage wind, on a patch of blue ice, the Albatross had landed.

As we unbolted the rear door the six members of the Trans-Antarctica Expedition cheered heartily. Their co-leader, the forty-five-year-old American Will Steger, told me that he had covered his eyes after seeing the DC-6 bounce. He was convinced that the Albatross was going to crash, and that would have been a disaster for the expedition as well as us. The French co-leader, Jean-Louis Etienne, a forty-three-year-old doctor of sports medicine, gave me a bearhug and introduced me to the others. The Russian scientist Victor Boyarsky was waving a bottle of vodka that we had brought him from Punta Arenas. I met the Chinese glaciologist Qin Dahe, a man the cynical media had suggested would not be tough enough for this marathon on ice. The Japanese adventurer Keizo Funatsu, who was an economist back home, and the British master of dog-sledding, Geoff Somers, already had begun to unload the highly excited huskies, so relieved to be on solid ice that they immediately left their mark.

Four months of Antarctic winter showed on the faces of the expeditioners, with patches of frostbite on noses and cheeks. But there was great camaraderie and a cheerfulness that opened its arms to the strangers who had come with the huskies they needed to reach the South Pole by Christmas. From there they still had to cover another 1210 kilometres never before crossed on foot, through the zone known as the Area of Inaccessibility to the Soviet scientific base at Vostok.

Working with the crew of the DC-6 we had the plane unloaded and refuelled in less than an hour. With a thumbs up from the pilot and a great roar of the engines, the Albatross took off. Aboard was a correspondent from the American ABC network with his cameraman who had taped a quick interview with Will Steger and the inevitable piece to camera to show that they had been to Antarctica. The correspondent's highly experienced producer had been one of those who had abandoned the trip in Punta Arenas. As we shook hands to say goodbye, the American correspondent warned me that if I stayed behind with Pierre Le Petit, a French sports-cameraman I had teamed up with to co-produce a documentary, then there was a very good chance we would be stranded in Antarctica. The beauty of the mountains surrounding the Patriot Hills camp and the spirit of these six brave trekkers made me decide to try to stick with the expedition as long as we could until the Albatross came back with more supplies in a week and took us home.

Heading north towards Drake Passage the DC-6 ran into a gale and, low on fuel, had to make an emergency landing. The Albatross ended up in a snowdrift on King George Island, a rocky outcrop at least a three-day sea voyage from Chile. Drums of fuel had been dumped on this island for just such an emergency, but massive snows now buried them. The American film team offered cash to the aircrew for the first man to find a fuel drum but not one was uncovered. The Albatross spent the next two weeks stuck on King George Island while I had the time of my life in Antarctica.

Geoff Somers, the British adventurer, and I soon struck up an easy companionship, for I understood his great affection for the sled dogs. To him, the huskies were the real heroes and they did it a lot tougher than the men. They had tried protective boots on the dogs to cushion the punishment of the ice but abandoned them when the snow trapped inside the boots started to give the huskies frostbite. After a day running across the ice and snow, these hardy animals ate a solid brick of space-age, high-protein dog food. When we crawled into our tents, still freezing, they curled up and slept half-buried under the snow. On the rare nights when the wind dropped, a few of the fiercest males would sit like wolves and howl mournfully in the great emptiness of the frozen continent. Maybe they were calling Geoff Somers's lead dog, Thiulie, who was tied up outside his tent, away from the others. The only female in the pack of thirty-six huskies, Thiulie was on heat. Somers chuckled and said that it would only make the pack run faster.

Minnesotan schoolteacher Steger had a similar affection for his huskies. Three years earlier he had led the first unsupported dog-sled expedition to reach the North Pole and it was on that trek that he met the Frenchman Jean-Louis Etienne, notching up a record of his own as the first to ski solo to the Pole. It was up there at the other end of the earth that the pair decided to attempt their most difficult journey of all. Remembering that Amundsen had needed dogs to get to the South Pole first, Will and Jean-Louis recognised that the huskies were their only chance of traversing the entire continent.

It was far tougher than anyone expected and they came close to tragedy several times as they crossed the ice and snow concealing massive crevasses that could swallow a sled-team whole. When one of the dogs plunged in his harness into a deep crevasse, Will and Jean-Louis lay on the ice, slashing at ropes and hauling on the harness to free the choking husky. Learning from other famous expeditions that had seen men, sleds and supplies disappear into these seemingly bottomless chasms, the Trans-Antarctica team divided their supplies between three sleds, knowing that at any time they could lose one. But Steger never thought of abandoning the husky. They worked hard to set the dog free and then everyone cheered, such was the bond between the men and the animals. They were mutually dependent for survival and otherwise alone.

As the weeks wore on, the vastness, the almost overwhelming feeling of aloneness, had a powerful effect on all of us. The isolation was an extraordinary experience on this odyssey, building up with each new footstep on the virgin snow. Although the coastal parts of Antarctica supported thirty-five species of penguins, six types of seals and a dozen kinds of whales, I saw no other living creature in the inner region of this white wilderness, just the bright reds, oranges and blues of our team of men and a yapping pack of huskies.

It made me appreciate the extraordinary courage of the men on Douglas Mawson's first expedition with Sir Ernest Shackleton in 1907, who walked 2027 kilometres in 120 days to get close to the South Magnetic Pole. This is the point where the compass needle dips vertically and points to the extremity of the earth's axis of rotation, as distinct from the true South Pole, reached a few years later by Roald Amundsen, and then by Robert Scott.

When I saw the scale of the ice sheet I was full of admiration for the mental and physical strength of all of the polar explorers who have pressed on to the edge of human limitation and beyond. I had a new measure of respect for what the men on Douglas Mawson's Australian expedition (1911–12) had gone through. Lieutenant Belvedere Ninnis fell to his death in a crevasse. As his sled was carrying most of the food supplies it left Mawson and Dr Xavier Mertz facing a slow death from starvation. Mertz eventually became so weak that he too died. As I surveyed the emptiness of the ice around me, I thought of Mawson, alone, 160 kilometres from his base. He must have been in agony, feeling responsible as the expedition leader for the death of his men. Exhausted, suffering from severe frostbite and near blinded by the snow, he could have surrendered to the cold and lain down to die like the Iceman. But somehow he found the strength and spirit to go on for three more weeks, until he reached a supply cache and survived.

After a century of exploration in Antarctica, we have satellite navigational equipment, improved clothing and space-age food packs, but the environment is still as harsh as in Mawson's day. We slept in small tents, the only warmth inside double-layered sleeping bags. The temperature even in the spring was still way below freezing point and on some days with the wind chill it plunged to −79°C. It was like a sharp knife in the back as we went 'wind-walking', hunched over and straining in the face of the cyclonic killers. Sometimes the wind blew so fiercely that it was not safe to walk outside. I used to rig a sheet of canvas inside my tent door as a heat trap for the little warmth that came from our bodies. It was so cold one day that the metal thread on my frozen camera lens peeled off in my gloves. Bowel movements in the big freeze were a risky business. We built a snow wall to break the wind, so to speak, and then had to perch above a bucket without getting stuck to the freezing metal. After days in our heavy Arctic gear when the armpits really started to smell like a husky, I took

Victor Boyarsky's advice and discovered the early morning shock of a Russian snowbath. This involved stripping off and slapping on powdery snow, while yelling like a madman.

Every day the expeditioners faced the same menu: cereal, butter and cheese, pasta and peanut butter, dried meat and fat. Everyone lost weight but the whole team pushed forward. Even Qin Dahe, the Chinese scientist, proved all of the doubters wrong and showed tremendous grit when the going was toughest.

I hate the cold and my usual idea of paradise is a dive in a turquoise sea or catching a summer wave to a white sandy beach. But here each day was full of such wonders, like the thrill of seeing spectacular mountains that had never been named or watching the wind funnel the snow across vast sheets of blue ice, that I forgot the cold and became absorbed in the beauty around me.

The news of the DC-6, relayed to us through broken radio contact with South America, was an endless stream of bad weather, bad luck and bad planning. Will Steger was embarrassed by the delays and we discussed emergency alternatives like trying to travel by dog-sled to the coast to be picked up by a steel-hulled sailing vessel. The ships that had been trying to cross the massive seas to carry fuel to the DC-6 had been driven back to port. My view was that as we were well supplied and in good hands we should be patient. With Pierre Le Petit, I used the time to film the scientific work of the expedition.

Victor Boyarsky's instruments set up outside his tent confirmed that there was an alarming depletion of protective ozone right above our heads. It was the discovery of this hole in the ozone layer in Antarctica a few years earlier that alerted scientists and environmentalists to the dangers of weakening the earth's protective shield. For years most of us living in industrial countries had been releasing chlorofluorocarbons (CFCs) into the atmosphere without realising that we were destroying our only real protection from ultraviolet radiation. Victor was concerned about the added risk of skin cancers and cataracts, not to mention the damage to plants, animals and marine life, unless we phased out CFCs and gave nature a chance to heal itself.

A little-discussed consequence of the ozone hole is that ultraviolet rays appear to be slowing the growth of marine plants by as much as 30 per cent and this could alter the fragile ecosystem of Antarctica. Boyarsky speculated that unless we took the ozone hole seriously our generation might inflict as much damage as those responsible for the harpooning of more than one million whales in Antarctic waters. We could look back and see the folly of the hunters who drove some whales and fur seals to the edge of extinction, but it was more difficult to accept the consequences of our own actions.

As Qin Dahe dug coffin-like trenches in the ice and snow he found further evidence of our carelessness. Traces of pollution reached down through the layers of ice, the legacy of industrial pollutants blown to the ends of the earth. This disturbed Qin Dahe because like all scientists he had hoped we could preserve the purity of the 'cleanest place on earth'. No one yet understood Antarctica's major impact on our global climate, but it was clear that half a century of scientific settlement had also contaminated the continent. Some of the oil spills had been disastrous. Fortunately Greenpeace had begun annual inspections of the national bases in Antarctica and already this had made a great difference. If we are going to preserve the most pristine place on earth we have to do better. Conscious of this, Pierre and I collected our garbage and frozen human waste and hauled it out of there. I trust that all we left were our footprints.

Jean-Louis Etienne, resting on his dog-sled one day and surveying the breathtaking surroundings, espoused passionate support for the proposal to declare Antarctica a permanent wilderness park. The biggest obstacle he saw would be to lift the ban on mining and oil drilling. On the surface geologists had found low-grade gold, iron, coal, copper and zinc. Despite the difficult conditions, nations without natural resources (or with technology to burn) would be under great pressure to explore the option of mining in Antarctica. Some believed there was oil on the bottom of the Ross Sea. Jean-Louis shrugged. How could anyone jeopardise the only chance left for humankind to live in perfect harmony with nature somewhere on this earth?

After filming memorable days and sunlit nights with the expedition we had to let them travel on to meet their deadline. If too much time were lost they would run into the teeth of the next winter and no one believed they could survive that hardship twice. Men hugged and shook hands. I took a letter from Geoff Somers to give to his brother Chris in Australia, but Will Steger joked that it had no chance of getting there. Will was still worrying aloud that the DC-6 might never make it back to pick us up. The team left us their spare sleds, a few very tired huskies and enough food to get us to Christmas. I waved goodbye to the most united bunch of human beings I have ever met, truly unforgettable strangers. Each man had said that he would like to be buried on the ice if he died there. All six agreed they would finish together or no one would finish. Pierre's camera was rolling as the men and the sleds slowly faded to white.

We spent seventeen days stranded in the base camp waiting for the return of the Albatross. On a short-wave radio, Pierre and I listened to broadcasts about the Germans tearing down the Berlin Wall. The whole map of Europe was changing and yet down here men who spoke very little of one another's languages were getting on like brothers. It was strange to be in a place devoid of life and yet to feel so much a part of the human race. This is how isolation clears the mind. When you cannot see the trees and smell the flowers your senses are sharpened. The appreciation of life itself deepens. When you are separated from all those you love those feelings intensify. It had been many weeks since I had spoken to my wife, Kim, but I got a radio connection to Chile and then a telephone hook-up to her desk at the State Department in Washington.

I have never felt so far away from you and yet so close.
Yesterday when our voices met across the radio wave
I felt the pulse quicken, an electric touch of hearts and

minds. Out of this whole world of nature, in our garden
perfumed by flower and sea, how did your atom find its
way to me? In this land of ice it seems so clear. These
weeks have been lived between mountain and sky,
footprints in pure snow, blizzard days when our frozen
tents are lost in great white-outs, and the wind is howling,
moaning, or is it the husky's cry that leads me out under
the midnight sun, a mirage of warmth in this cold place,
so vast all of civilisation has disappeared from the
horizon. Here at the end of the earth, as far as I have ever
gone, I feel so deeply connected to you, in love with you.
Tonight the wind is a sigh for home.

(JOURNAL 1989)

I spent many days wandering the frozen hills with Pierre and
our camera. We had the gear so we did a bit of mountain
climbing on some minor ridges. The Ellsworth range was
magnificent in any direction we chose to trek. Usually after four
or five hours we returned to our tents, dug out the snow that
had blown in and then closed our eyes on days that had no real
beginning or end.

The value of such time is that it gives perspective to all the other
crowded hours of life. Perhaps it was only the pure adventure and
sense of accomplishment, but coming from Australia, a chunk of
land once connected to Antarctica, I felt a peculiar sense of
completeness. During the Jurassic period, 200 million years ago,
Antarctica was the centre of Gondwanaland, a supercontinent
with a warm climate, covered in forests and teeming with reptiles
and some of the earliest mammals. This is not speculation.
Geological evidence of the supercontinent was first detected in
Gondwana, India. When the gigantic Gondwanaland began to
break up 160 million years ago, bits like Australia, Papua New
Guinea, Africa, India and South America stayed in the warm
zone. But Antarctica drifted off on its own to where it now lies
at the South Pole. As I wandered around one of the most

inhospitable frozen deserts, I realised that the earth's journey had been every bit as interesting as our own.

When we finally received a radio message that fuel had been flown to King George Island and the Albatross was airborne again, I began to look longingly at a mountain I had been staring at for several weeks. It was a perfect pyramid of blue ice, unnamed and almost lost in the clouds on the horizon. I studied the map, packed some food and gear, and went for a walk.

As I crossed the ice sheet and the tents began to recede I was enjoying the silence. I stopped to listen. Nothing. I walked on until I had gone so far that when I spun on my heels I could see only snow and ice. It was like standing in a vast crater on another star. The weather was clear and I hoped that the clouds would not close in, lowering a veil between this mysterious mountain and me. Under my feet were clear pools of ice with tiny rocks arranged in myriad patterns. I had learned to warm and cool down my body to stop the sweat. Remove a glove. Open a zip. Turn down the furnace.

I slipped crampons onto my boots and began a steep climb up a long sloping ridge that I hoped would give me a clear view of my mountain. I whispered its name now, secretly to myself. My heart beat faster as I climbed ridge after ridge. 'Oh God!' I said aloud. My brain was drenched with the beauty before me. To the south there was a majestic range of mountains so much grander than I had seen, black rock blotched with white snow, running down into smaller and smaller peaks until they faded into an opalescent blue sky that went on forever. To the north was another mesmerising sight, a huge plateau of blue ice that fell away like a frozen waterfall, catching the rays of the sun. It was a masterpiece. This was nature unspoiled, original and awesome.

Above the ridge where I was standing I could see one last rocky ledge, considerably higher. Could it be more glorious from there? I started up again carefully, watching my footholds as the wind grew stronger. I slipped just once and paused to look carefully at the snow, the rock and the ice, measuring the difficulty and the danger. I could hear the great climber Reinhold Messner whispering, *You have to know when to go on and you have to know when to turn back.* Foot by foot I climbed, bent to the wind, watching the icy drop to my right and the splendour of the valley to my left. I climbed for another hour and then I raised my hands high and laughed. There was my mountain, a temple waiting for worship. I whispered her name, told her how I had searched for her, how she was perfect and how I would always treasure her memory. Just then, like a will-o'-the-wisp, the snow at my feet was swirling, not a warning, but a whisper, *Go home now.*

The return of the Albatross was as dramatic as its very first landing on the blue ice. The plane disappeared into a hollow then emerged suddenly with snow and ice streaming behind it, all four engines roaring. For the next hour we worked in a frenzy to load and refuel as the wind was gusting to fifty knots. There were screams and shouts as the wind spun the DC-6 forty-five degrees with a grinding noise on the ice. The alloy ladder propped up to the rear door buckled and bent like a piece of wire.
I ducked under the plane as a sheet of metal hurtled past my head. As the pilot replaced the wheel chocks,
I grabbed the strongest wooden sled to use as a makeshift ladder for us to reach the high door. There was some apprehension on the faces of the crew as we buckled up and the engines thud-thud-thudded into life. The crosswind was so dangerous that the pilot was pointing the Albatross straight at the Patriot Hills which seemed oh so close in front of us. This would be a near thing. We were roaring across the ice sheet, lifting frantically. Come on baby, go, go. Almost on top of the hills the Albatross swung right, sweeping into a magnificent curve. It was superb, swashbuckling flying and we applauded loudly before slumping back in our seats. On the way up the Antarctic Peninsula in daylight we saw the towering Vinson Massif, icebergs as long as a city block, channels of sparkling water cutting through the ice, strange uplifts

resembling frozen volcanoes and crevasses arranged in
enormous parallel lines like a trap for anyone brave
enough to try to cross this continent.

(JOURNAL 1989)

The Trans-Antarctica Expedition made it to the South Pole before Christmas, the first dog-sled expedition to do so since Roald Amundsen's. Will Steger lost one of his favourite huskies, Tim, and a pup lost a leg to frostbite. A dog named Yeager set some sort of record by being the first to sled to both the North and South Poles. Thiulie became the first female to cross Antarctica. All six men and their three sleds completed the 6450-kilometre journey, crossing the Area of Inaccessibility and reaching the Soviet base at Vostok in March 1990. Will Steger summed up the feelings of us all when he said that Antarctica was beyond anything he ever thought existed.

CHAPTER TWENTY-ONE

A WORLD TO SHARE

I dived from the boat with lungs full of air and out of the blue sea it swam towards me. It was moving slowly like a gliding submarine, about ten metres long and ten tonnes in bulk. I was face to face with a whale shark, the biggest fish in the sea. The enormous head moved from side to side. The mouth, big enough to swallow me whole, was wide open. In less than a minute it powered past me, one huge eye watching, but unconcerned by my presence.

I burst to the surface and climbed back onto our boat to borrow a lightweight scuba tank from my diving companions, Ron and Valerie Taylor, the underwater adventurers. We were on Ningaloo Reef, the world's longest stretch of fringing coral, so close to the shore that you could swim out to the dugongs and turtles along the white sandy beaches near Exmouth in Western Australia. The whale sharks liked the outer edge of the reef and a spotter plane had just radioed that another was heading our way. The skipper cautiously slowed our boat to a crawl. It was another colossus, at least twelve metres long.

This time I was determined to stay with the whale shark longer, and swimming hard I could just keep pace with it. Val had warned me not to touch the whale shark's powerful tail as this could send it to the murky depths. I kicked down closer to its huge blue-grey body, mottled with white circles like an Aboriginal dot painting. The whale shark had half a dozen passengers, tiny sucker fish called remoras. A yellow and black pilot fish was leading the way and we were being escorted by two sleek black kingfish down below. I had swum with dolphins, sea lions, turtles, stingrays and sharks, but this gentle giant of the sea was putting on the most exhilarating performance I had ever seen as it powered through the water to feast on one of the huge clouds of plankton that drew the whale sharks to Ningaloo Reef.

As the whale shark slowed, Ron had his camera rolling. He was only metres in front of the gaping jaws as they strained water for the plankton, in through the mouth and out through the ten large gills that showed that it was indeed a fish, not a mammal. The skin was not smooth like a dolphin's but looked sandpaper rough, like a shark's, because that is what we were staring at wide-eyed, a shark as big as a whale. As I kicked down and slowly passed one of its great eyes, it appeared to survey me momentarily and then turned back to its feeding. I moved around towards its cavernous mouth. It looked big enough to park a Volkswagen.

The jaws were working steadily, its wide-open lips, or 'velum', hiding thousands of small teeth. We were entranced as the giant paused, its tail drooping slightly, and its head sweeping from side to side like the biggest vacuum cleaner we had ever seen. I was wondering how many of us would fit inside that huge mouth when with one flick of its tail the whale shark surged forward. Ron, Val and I darted aside and felt the bow wave as the leviathan accelerated quickly to a good ten knots and then glided off into the blue. I floated, suspended in another world, savouring the majesty of the biggest fish in the sea.

As we clambered back onto our boat, Ron and Val were as excited as I was, for in forty years of diving around the world they only had managed four previous encounters with whale sharks. Some marine biologists spent their whole careers cruising the coast of California, the Seychelles or the waters of the Philippines to achieve a single dive with these giant fish. Yet here at Ningaloo Reef we were to see twenty whale sharks over a couple of days. One of the rarest and most mysterious of the

25 000 kinds of fish in the sea had chosen to come regularly and in great numbers to our shores.

A physician in Exmouth, Dr Geoff Taylor, who had been studying the whale sharks for a decade, said that he and his family had been lucky enough to spot them at most times of the year along the 260 kilometres of the Ningaloo Marine Park. We had come at the best time. Every March after the full moon the Coral Coast spawns new life. Ningaloo's spectacular corals explode with millions of tiny pink and white balloons, eggs and sperm for the next living community of coral. The surface waters turn oily with a light pink film of coral eggs and within days the big plankton feeders like the whale sharks and manta rays are feasting on their favourite plankton soup, a banquet that usually lasts until late April.

On our next dive, Val and I had a rare delight, catching up with a female baby whale shark, about three metres long. Val said that no one was sure where the females gave birth, or whether a baby like this had hatched from an egg outside the mother or stayed in utero until she was ready to swim. There was so much we still did not know about the whale sharks. They had been known to grow to eighteen metres and almost forty tonnes but only the so-called juveniles — and they were mainly males — appeared to like Ningaloo Reef. It was definitely a boys' club. That baby was the only female whale shark in the twenty we sighted. It made us wonder where the females were hiding and whether somewhere in the marine world there was a secret nursery like the extraordinary places where whales breed. There have been rare sightings in the temperate zones around the globe but whale sharks' migratory patterns are highly mysterious. I felt all the more fortunate to be watching this spectacular ballet in the deep at the only place in the world where they were so friendly and accessible.

The largest whale sharks we saw all had bulging bellies. It was hard to believe that these giant powerhouses were running on plankton and would rather eat the tiddlers of the sea like anchovies and pilchards than swallow us whole. Ron and Val said there was no reason to fear the whale sharks, there had never been an attack at Ningaloo Reef, and they laughed at old yarns about these giants trying to gulp down modern-day Jonahs or even whole fishing boats in the Seychelles.

'Another diver saw a whale shark out here on Ningaloo Reef feeding on a baitball of tiny fish and the whale shark accidentally swallowed a whole turtle,' said Val. 'But it spat out the turtle immediately. It didn't swallow it. So I think if you get sucked into that mouth it'll just spit you out too . . . and,' she added laughing, 'we'll just film it all. It would be a great sequence.'

I came to share the Taylors' view that while the smaller whale sharks were shy and best observed at a considerable distance of about ten metres, the big ones showed not the slightest irritation at our company unless a diver's air bubbles were right in its face and disturbing its feeding. I don't like divers who blow bubbles in my face either. There is such peace gliding through a tranquil world that belongs to other creatures that it seems best to move as calmly as the whale sharks.

The prime feeding time for the whale sharks is at night in the moonlight and so they have a lot of time completely undisturbed. The ten-tonne giants we saw in daylight often seemed to be attracted to our boat and some surfaced close by us. It is this kind of behaviour that leads divers to speculate that some whale sharks, like some playful whales and frisky dolphins, may enjoy seeing us as much as we enjoy seeing them. We have no hard evidence of that and it is just as likely that the whale sharks are more intent on grazing plankton and want to make sure that we do not get in the way. It is still an awesome and inspiring experience to be so close to such a gigantic creature that appears to be carefully avoiding any injury to us. If divers and tour boats recklessly interfere with these giants they may start avoiding us altogether in daylight and feeding only at night when it is a slightly scarier proposition swimming on the outer reef.

The constant threat to whale sharks is commercial hunting, especially when we have no reliable estimate of how many whale sharks exist in the world. Although harpooning whales and whale sharks, turtles and dugongs has long been banned in Australian waters, other countries do not protect the giant fish. Taiwanese fishing fleets routinely kill whale sharks. With due respect to cultural differences, this is as senseless as killing a tiger to use its bones and penis as an aphrodisiac. If you don't have to eat it and it is not going to harm you, why kill it? The flesh of whale sharks is described as soft and tasteless and brings a lousy price in the poorest fishmarkets. They are harpooned still in the Maldives where some argue that this is a traditional food source and essential for human survival.

Japanese fishermen, whom I have confronted over the years because of their senseless slaughter of whales, surprisingly have an admirable reverence for the whale shark and consider it an omen of good fortune. If you think about it, when the waters are rich enough to lure the giant of the sea, there should be a plentiful catch of more edible fish to keep the fishermen happy. At Ningaloo Reef, the local fishermen share this view and have been among the strongest supporters of a decade-old environmental campaign to banish yet another threat to the whale sharks, oil drilling along the Coral Coast.

The Australian Geological Survey estimates that there may be as much as three billion barrels of oil to be found around our coast. The North West Shelf one day could overtake Bass Strait as the country's main source of oil. But if one of the cyclones that are commonplace between November and April strikes an oil rig or an oil tanker anywhere near Ningaloo Reef, the marine reserve could be facing a disaster like the *Exxon Valdez* spill in Alaska. In 1979 an exploratory well in the Gulf of Mexico spilled 475 000 tonnes of oil. The Australian industry, however, is rightly proud of its record. After drilling thousands of wells and producing billions of barrels of oil it has spilled only a few hundred barrels in Australia. However, the lobbyists of the Australian Petroleum Exploration Association betray their motives when they float proposals for direct drilling right inside the Great Barrier Reef or along the spectacular coral fringe of Ningaloo Reef.

Oil is a valuable resource, but the Great Barrier Reef and its equally precious western counterpart are a priceless part of our national heritage. Australia's oil ends up being owned by oil companies, not Australia. A national resource is sold anywhere in the world where the oil companies can make the most profit. These are issues of fairness that the government and public need to debate. But it is dishonest of the oil industry to pretend it is a clean industry when oil tankers, the prime movers of the product, have had numerous accidents with ugly consequences. The cyclonic weather in the west combined with the appalling condition of many ships has left our shores littered with rusty wrecks. An old Greek tanker, the *Kirki,* spilled 17 000 tonnes of oil off the coast of Western Australia in 1992 when part of its bow broke off and the prospect of that kind of accident at Ningaloo Reef horrifies Ron and Val Taylor.

'The test drilling close to Ningaloo Reef must stop,' said Val. 'With the whole North West Shelf to explore for oil, can't they leave this place untouched for all of Australia to enjoy?'

'This is one of the wonders of the world,' added Ron, 'and it should be shared with everyone.'

'You will not see whale sharks like this anywhere else,' Val said, casting her eyes over the pink plankton sheen of the sea. 'Believe me we have searched for them. These past few days have been among the best we have had anywhere in the ocean. I think if the whale sharks chose this place, people deserve to be able to see them forever.'

I wanted our final dive to never end. We put our camera away and everyone in the crew swam with the whale sharks. If you are young enough at heart to pull on fins, mask and snorkel, head west to Ningaloo Reef. It is the thrill of a lifetime. Before the sun goes down take your boat across the shallow turquoise lagoon and along the tranquil waters of Yardie Creek Gorge. Little black-faced wallabies stare down from the red rock walls. Wedge-tailed eagles soar above the Cape Range. Along this shoreline all of the vital nutrients from the land run down to feed the brilliant living coral reef, a place unspoiled for countless thousands of years.

Striking the balance between developing our natural resources and re-establishing a harmony with nature long lost in this age of technology is one of the greatest challenges facing human civilisation. The sharpest scientific minds believe we are in the earth's sixth great period of extinction. In Australia most people realise that we perhaps have killed off more species in the last two hundred years than anyone else on earth. We have clear-felled most of our ancient forests, taken too much water from river systems like the mighty Murray–Darling and we continue to be one of the biggest and most irresponsible producers of greenhouse gases. Yet many Australians, including our most brilliant scientists, are part of a worldwide enlightenment, a positive, rational, scientific movement which believes that we have the knowledge to live with nature rather than make war on it.

I remember the ugly mess when a tourist and supply ship, the *Bahía Paraíso,* ran aground in Antarctica in 1989, spilling 170 000 gallons of fuel, killing newly hatched penguin chicks and the krill that fed other fish, whales and birds. Humans have accidents frequently. It is an unavoidable consequence of our most important industries. The vital decisions to be made, and we all should be part of them, are where to exploit natural resources, how to regulate this process responsibly and how to measure their real value. I believe that wherever we live there is at least one important environmental challenge that we can influence personally.

Lake Cowal is the largest wetland in New South Wales and one of the biggest in Australia. So many of the wetlands in my home state have been drained for irrigation that Lake Cowal is among the last few unspoiled habitats for many of our unique native birds as well as exotic birds from Russia, Japan and China that each year make extraordinary pilgrimages to this place. There are swans, pelicans, cormorants, ibis and a variety of ducks in bountiful numbers. As you move quietly along canals between the tall grasses you will see rookeries with up to one million birds. I went there on the first day of spring because nature's nursery was under threat.

(JOURNAL 1995)

Scott Cardamatis, an intelligent and principled environmentalist, guided me in a small boat around the spectacular sights of Lake Cowal. Outside of Kakadu, I had not seen such an abundance of birdlife. Scott knew the lake well but on every visit found the rookeries a source of new wonder. Now, however, he was angry because there was a gold rush under way, right here on the shores of Lake Cowal. One of Australia's mining giants, North Limited, had filed plans for a gold mine and we could see test drilling preparations being made. Land councils, local politicians, cattlemen and unemployed workers were divided on the merits of the gold mine. It was estimated that the mine could run ten years, employ hundreds of people, and earn around one billion dollars. Most of that, of course, would go to shareholders in North Limited. The public would benefit indirectly through government revenue from the mine. That seemed fair enough — unless the real price of extracting the gold at Lake Cowal meant damaging the wetlands and jeopardising the almost inestimable value of one of nature's richest nurseries.

Rather brazenly, because it enjoyed the best environmental reputation of any of the Australian mining companies, North Limited declared that it could safely gouge a huge open-cut mine in the lake itself, the same lake where at least a million birds were breeding. Next they would bulldoze four big dams for the tailings, the cyanide-contaminated brew left over from the mining process. These dams would sprawl for 240 hectares. Think of about 450 football fields full of poison. North Limited rejected the argument that cyanide extraction of gold was poisonous. The company told the state government that birds were not attracted to tailings dams and that only a dozen birds had been found dead in their existing gold mine, Northparkes, at Parkes in western New South Wales. My *60 Minutes* team began a long investigation and found quite the opposite.

After an inside tip, Scott made an unannounced visit to the Northparkes gold mine with our camera and was shocked to find a dam of death. Thousands of swans, cormorants, gulls and ducks had been poisoned by the cyanide-laced tailings. The shores of the dam were covered with dead birds in various stages of decomposition. Scott wandered around trying to count the bodies. When he waded in to retrieve what looked like a freshly killed swan, he was spotted by two men in a hovercraft, pulling dead birds out of the dam. He immediately was taken to the mine manager, Dick Swann, who asked whether Scott had picked up that distinctive, bitter-almond smell of cyanide. After being put under a shower and dressed in a pair of overalls, Scott found himself listening to the lament of the mining men who suddenly realised that their secret was out. Their environmental reputation was about to be challenged publicly.

I wanted more scientific evidence before I confronted the mining giant and a night visit to the tailings dam produced a very dead example of Dick Swann's namesake. For an independent analysis we began with the chief veterinarian at Sydney's Taronga Park Zoo, Larry Vogelnest. He was adamant that the swan had died, painfully, after ingesting a massive dose of poison, heavily damaging its gastrointestinal tract.

We also found a local bird expert, Neville Schader, who had spotted endangered birds, including the Superb Parrot, in and over the tailings dam. Neville's sighting of piles of dead birds months before confirmed that this was not an isolated incident but a problem with the management of the cyanide levels used in the extraction of the gold.

If we were to believe the mining company, its normal cyanide levels at the proposed gold mine and tailings dams around Lake Cowal would be below 50 parts per million. Our sources at other mining companies told us that it was inefficient, expensive and hazardous to allow higher levels of cyanide to build up in the tailings. When we turned on our camera, an exasperated Dick Swann admitted that at the Northparkes tailings dam the levels had blown out to 300 parts per million. I challenged him with the analysis of our secret samples taken on the night visit to the tailings dam. These registered a cyanide level of 520 parts per million. I told Dick Swann that now we knew why Scott Cardamatis had been rushed into the showers.

An embarrassed Northparkes already had begun a public relations campaign to hose down the damage. Its first press release said that several hundred birds had been killed at the Northparkes tailings dam. A revised environmental impact statement lodged with the government increased the kill to over one thousand. After I toured the tailings dam with Dick Swann his final estimate shot up to two thousand dead birds. He pointed out that helicopters had been brought in to frighten away the birds. Northparkes had ordered a propane gas gun to deter birds and was looking at ideas like covering the dam with net, streamers or floating coloured balls. What had happened was an unfortunate accident and the amount of cyanide used would be cut in half at Northparkes. But Mr Swann could not give me any form of guarantee that it would not happen again. He said he was not in the business of giving guarantees.

The headquarters of the mining giant in Melbourne understood that it had a serious problem and called in a public relations specialist to advise it in its response to the *60 Minutes* story. Other Australian mining companies polluting the rivers of Europe, Papua New Guinea and right here at home were spending a small fortune trying to put their spin on the truth. To conceal a rapacious hunger for profit they suggested that common sense complaints, even questions about their behaviour, were the objections of ratbag greenies or fanatical, one-eyed conservationists.

While both sides of my family came from the land, I had uncles who worked as miners. My grandfather gave miners beef on credit during the Great Depression and, as I have mentioned, helped build them a hospital in the Hunter Valley. I have been three kilometres underground with coalminers and to the snow-covered reaches of the world's richest gold mine, Freeport's giant open-cut mine in West Papua. I mention this to emphasise that I have no grudge against mining companies and have treated them with the same fairness and honesty as I have conservationists. It was revealing to see the bitter and personal tone of the industry's counter-attack.

The *Australian Mining Monthly* reported in its October 1995 edition that I had 'levered open the front door' of the Northparkes gold-mining operation (I think they meant metaphorically speaking) and that our 'raid' and my 'aggressive cross-examining' amounted to a 'masterpiece of eco-terrorism'. 'The mercenary precision of the *60 Minutes* crew in its penetration and unhalting derision of the Northparkes camp — until then one of our environmental flagships — was awesome.' Up near Lake Cowal some people who supported North's gold-mining ventures went further and organised a mock lynching of me.

On the other hand, the great Australian conservationist Milo Dunphy wrote to me saying that Northparkes had circulated the full transcript of my interview which was so damaging to the company that he could scarcely believe it had published it. This man had fought long and hard to convince our government that between irrigation and drought our wetlands were in dire straits. He was still furious that the Northparkes mining operation had been allowed at all, as it was over the headwaters of the Bogan River which ran underground there in gravel beds.

The truth always has powerful consequences. Despite the huge campaign mounted by the mining giant and the millions of dollars it forked out for environmental impact studies in which the company selected and paid the 'experts', the *60 Minutes* report, the result of many months of work by my old team of Cress–Donoghue–Brewer Inc., brought a swift response in federal parliament. The Senate passed a motion calling for urgent action to reduce the environmental damage from tailings dams around the country. Evidence was cited of similar accidents by other miners, including the death of 60 000 birds at Kalgoorlie and glaring mismanagement at Katherine, Cobar and Telfer. The Senate also heard evidence about tailings dams around the world. These studies indicated that mining engineers had not yet mastered the technique of stopping leakage, even when the tailings dams adjoined cattle properties and vital water catchment areas.

In the end there was just one man who had the power and the ultimate responsibility to make a decision about the company's failure to control its cyanide levels at the Northparkes gold mine and how this should affect the proposed mine at Lake Cowal. The Premier of New South Wales, Bob Carr, without doubt one of the most informed and environmentally sensitive political leaders in Australian history, ordered an Independent Commission of Inquiry.

The Australian Heritage Commission and the Environmental Protection Authority noted the potential for ecological impact but did not object to the mine if strict conditions were honestly adhered to. The National Parks and Wildlife Service had much stronger concerns and other conservation groups unanimously opposed the development. Environmentalists were not convinced that the mining company had solved the problem of seepage from the tailings dams and of course produced their 'experts' who cited the dismal international record. The inquiry's final recommendation was that the gold mine and tailings dams would not jeopardise the agreed importance of the wetlands and that North Limited should be given approval to develop the mine, subject to it meeting strict environmental conditions. This meant keeping the cyanide process under 50 parts per million and keeping those one million birds out of the tailings dams.

The weight of the final decision now fell on Bob Carr's shoulders. The premier understood the political reality that allowing the gold mine to go ahead would be quick revenue for the government. There were taunts from the Opposition that no state premier would turn his back on a gold mine. Maybe the company would be luckier this time with the bird kill? Perhaps as their experts said they could keep the cyanide levels down. After weighing up all of the evidence available to Cabinet, the premier admitted that this was one of the most difficult but important decisions of his political life.

'We have agonised over the details,' Carr announced in 1996. 'We have decided to reject the development. The risk is simply too great. We're not prepared to endanger a wetland and all the wildlife that depend on it and run the risk that fifty years, one hundred years from now, there would be kids in Australia who would say, "How could they have taken that away from us, how could they have done that, back in that generation?". We want to pass on something precious to the generations that come after us.'

Like Scott Cardamatis, the premier recognised that the price of gold at Lake Cowal was too high. Each man felt a responsibility, a burden of conscience, and each had to take action for what he believed was the public good, no matter how much derision he faced from some quarters. Around the world I have met other equally courageous men and women, inspirational people who have become the true custodians of our land and water.

> *John Cronin is the only man in America who lists his job as*
> *'riverkeeper'. In medieval times a riverkeeper used to guard*
> *England's leafy streams against poachers but John is more*
> *interested in polluters. On behalf of a Fishermen's Co-*
> *operative he is leading a campaign to clean up the Hudson*
> *River which runs through New York State, past Manhattan*
> *and into the Atlantic Ocean. This fishery that for hundreds of*
> *years has supported Native Americans, British and Dutch*
> *settlers and modern-day New Yorkers has been contaminated*
> *by toxic waste, chemicals, sewage and other human garbage.*
>   (JOURNAL 1992)

It may have looked like one man in a little boat moving up and down the mighty Hudson but John Cronin was armed with a great legal power open to every American citizen. As a result of that nation's forty or so environmental laws, if the government was not prosecuting an offending polluter, every individual citizen had the right to do so. Cronin also had a powerful ally, Bobby Kennedy Jnr, the son of the late Robert Kennedy.

When I asked Kennedy why he had turned his back on politics to become one of America's most successful environmental lawyers, he spoke passionately about his belief that the only way most of us can make a positive difference to this world is to think globally but act locally. He contributed to the Clean Up the Hudson campaign the brilliant idea of using students at Pace University in New York, where he taught law, to bring environmental cases against the industrial polluters.

'I could handle maybe three or four cases at a time but these students are the cream of the crop at a school specialising in environmental law and so with their help we can act against fifteen polluters at a time. If they don't win they don't pass the course,' he laughed, 'and we haven't lost a case yet.'

The Hudson campaign has been a brilliant success, with scores of big wins against companies like Exxon, one of the world's largest corporations, the chemical giant DuPont, the Remington Arms Corporation and the Indian Point Nuclear Power Plant. Most paid compensation to the New York State government. Exxon chose to settle out of court, contributing US$1.5 million to the government's clean-up of the river, as well as a 'donation' of several hundred thousand dollars to the fishermen's clean water campaign.

'The fish and crabs are healthy,' Cronin told me as we coasted on the Hudson's strong current. 'Heavy industry has done a lot to clean up its act. The cities and municipalities are the main polluters now. It's just people and their utilities in our cities and towns. That's why I say we all make a difference. Whether it is the Hudson or your Hawkesbury every river needs a riverkeeper.'

If there is any river in the world that needs a miracle it is the Ganges. From the headwaters high up in the Himalaya all the way to the sea it is a cesspool carrying the waste of some 600 million Indians. Here in Varanasi, one of the world's oldest cities, a magnificent centre of art, music and literature long before the rise of Athens and Rome, people go down each morning to bathe in a poisoned river. They have been coming here for 3000 years believing that the Ganges is sacred, their 'mother', Ganga-Mai. The Hindus say that Shiva created the universe here. The Buddhists believe that Buddha preached his first sermon here. All I know is children are dying of cholera in the villages. The waterborne plagues are killers. And for four days now, the crew and I have been sick as dogs with amoebic dysentery.

(JOURNAL 1997)

In the scientific world, Dr V. B. Mishra is known as a brilliant Indian hydrologist who has led an international campaign to save the historic city of Varanasi and the lives of millions who drink, wash and bathe in the river Ganges. To Hindus, he is 'Mahantji', the high priest of one of Varanasi's largest temples, one that steps down onto the ancient bathing *ghats* alongside the Ganges.

Watching this ageing man take his morning 'holy' dip it was hard to see how he reconciled his head and his heart. The modern mind that understood that he was bathing in the midst of 1350 million litres of daily sewage surely would overrule the heart that said this was his ancient religious duty. Not so, Mahantji said. It was the wish of millions of Hindus to come here at least once in their lifetime to bathe in the Ganges — even if it killed them.

I was introduced to Mahantji by a pair of Sydney schoolteachers, Sue and Colin Lennox, who almost every year travelled to Varanasi to work for his research foundation monitoring the bad health of the river. Back home, the Lennoxes started the Oz Green campaign that successfully cleaned up Manly Lagoon in the northern suburbs of Sydney. Here the scale of the challenge was far more daunting. They showed me raw sewage pouring into the Ganges right alongside Mother Teresa's local hospice. We walked past canals where men performed all their ablutions, including cleaning their teeth, in a flow of raw sewage. In the villages surrounding the city, the water wells were too polluted to be used and people had resorted to drinking the contaminated river. This was happening up and down the Ganges.

Mahantji's scheme for the salvation of his city and its people was not mystical, but practical, achievable science, supported by some of the best experts in the west. For about thirty million dollars he could build a series of oxidation ponds on a sandy island in the middle of the river. This, he said, could process Varanasi's effluent and become a successful model for other Indian cities. This inspiring man has travelled the world tirelessly, trying to find the seed money for a project that could mark the beginning of a planetary clean-up of our degraded rivers. Mahantji's work has even been captured cleverly in a children's animated television series shown in both developed and underdeveloped countries.

Perhaps the next generation will be better informed and wiser than this one.

After spending only a few days around the suffering village children we soon were coming down with their illnesses. This is how it works in the brotherhood of man. For most of our time in Varanasi my crew and I had the chills, headaches, blurred vision and vomiting that are just part of life for the locals. Mahantji had been gravely ill many times himself but he continued in his dual role of holyman and health worker, saying that this was his duty to *Ganga-Mai*.

When I visited the famous Cousteau Institute in Paris I found a similar conviction that the fate of the Ganges, the Hudson and our own mighty Murray–Darling should be of great concern to us all. The late Jacques Cousteau and his team had assessed the best studies in the world, from UNESCO's to the World Bank's, and come to the conclusion that if current trends continue the demand for fresh water would exceed supply by the year 2030.

The greatest undersea explorer of all time was a hero of mine, not only because of his obvious courage, but because he discovered how to illuminate the beauty of nature and the fragility of its many interdependent parts. Even at eighty-seven, Cousteau was still diving into the mystery of the sea, trying to learn something from every minute of his life and sharing it with those who would listen to his wisdom. Cousteau lived through the greatest explosion of human population and the most rapid industrial expansion the earth has experienced. There are few people who have seen more of the world. For these reasons we would be wise to remember his words in the last year of his life. Cousteau said that the world's most pressing environmental crisis, the one that we all must address with urgency, is the rapid dwindling of our most precious resource: fresh, drinkable water.

'We are drawing blank cheques on future generations,' Cousteau said. 'If we don't pay . . . they are going to have to pay.'

CHAPTER TWENTY-TWO

EVOLUTIONARY THOUGHTS IN THE GALAPAGOS

ON THE GIANT TORTOISE

Slowly, slowly
Down through the years,
I have survived
Despite my fears,
My world is changing
I can't stay the same,
I guess it's just
Mother Nature's game.

(JOURNAL 1995)

If you want to see how life began on earth and is still evolving there is no better place than the Galapagos Islands. While cruising the sixteen main islands, several dozen small islets and reefs, I watched one night as a volcano erupted on Fernandina. I left the wooden charter yacht, *Rachel III*, at a safe distance and paddled a rubber dinghy to within twenty-five metres of the glowing red lava, growling and hissing as it poured into the sea. I plunged an arm into the water and found that the lava flow as big and grand as Niagara Falls had warmed the usually cold current to the temperature of a hot bath. It was this volcano and others arising from a crack in the sea floor about three million years ago that created the archipelago where Charles Darwin cracked the code of evolution on earth.

The gnarled black rock I saw in daylight was barren and lifeless for centuries until seeds blown on the wind found their way there. Birds that could fly the 900 kilometres from South America came to nest when plants appeared. I saw albatrosses, pelicans, gulls, gannets, yellow warblers and blue-footed boobies. I watched that sleek fisher of the seas, the black frigatebird, puff up its distinctive red bulb under its beak. When I spotted the numerous tiny finches, with different shaped beaks and colours depending on which of the islands they lived on, I thought of Darwin. The great British scientist spent five weeks here in 1835 on the voyage of the SS *Beagle*, staring at creatures like the tiny finches until slowly in his mind he formulated his brilliant theory of natural selection.

When Darwin sailed through these islands they had been settled or visited by humans for at least three centuries, but he was struck by the tameness of all the creatures here. It is still the case. The most famous resident of the Galapagos, one estimated to be 150 years old, so heavy it would take six men to carry him, walked straight up to meet me, probably because he was thinking of lunch.

The giant Galapagos tortoise is an evolutionary marvel. On some islands where there is plenty of foliage to eat the tortoises have short necks and the common dome-shaped shell. Where there is only prickly scrub and tall cacti to graze, the shells have evolved into a saddle shape, with a distinctive peak that allows much longer necks to reach the available foliage. Dr Chantal Blanton, an American biologist in charge of the Charles Darwin Research Station when I visited the Galapagos, told me that there were anecdotes suggesting some of these giant land tortoises had survived to be 200 years old. The international scientific team was supervising the birth of hatchlings in order to study the length of time these creatures could live. It is an interesting thought that this wrinkled old reptile, with its waddling, elephantine legs and its portable home in that hard shell, has learned how to live at least twice as long as we do.

Year after year Chantal and her colleagues were coming up with brilliant new elements of evolutionary theory. Darwin's general idea of survival of the fittest meant that creatures that lived through the hard times handed on their genetic characteristics to their young. Finches needed a certain shaped beak to survive on certain Galapagos islands. But Chantal believed that in nature there was a degree of 'benign neglect'. Sometimes creatures managed to arise and keep going just because there was nothing to take them out.

As I discovered what had been happening to the giant tortoises of late, Chantal's observation was disturbingly relevant. Modern-day pirates on floating fish factories had invaded the protected waters of the Galapagos, and when challenged by the scientific team had taken out their anger by slaughtering over a hundred of the tortoises. The international fishing fleets also had been spotted poaching shark fins, a delicacy in many countries, and *bêche-de-mer* (sea-cucumbers), which some people claim (without any scientific basis) are an aphrodisiac. With about four hundred fishermen now illegally camped on the isolated islands, clearly the human threat to some species was a deadly new ingredient in the evolutionary game.

Does that dark cavern of the human brain still conceal a primitive violence, driven by what Carl Sagan called the reptilian complex? Whether it was slaughtering in cold blood the tame tortoises of the Galapagos or one million Tutsis in Rwanda, these killers were clearly not using the neocortex, the 85 per cent of the brain that would tell them such behaviour was madness.

I sat on the rocks throwing a stick to a barking sea lion pup that retrieved it for me as playfully as my dog at home, Ned Kelly. Perhaps the men who hunted such creatures to the edge of extinction believed they were superior. To hell with the giant tortoises, the hammerheads, the white-tipped reef sharks and sea-cucumbers, man came first. Blanton said she knew people in government institutions and lofty world organisations who genuinely believed that nature was there for the taking. But that was not her belief or the mandate of the Charles Darwin Foundation and the Galapagos National Park Service which were determined to protect and conserve Darwin's favourite laboratory. In Darwin's age the impact of humans on this world already was painfully clear. In our own time the war against nature and against ourselves has become more violent and threatening to the earth than the greatest primordial struggles.

On the *Rachel III* I sailed through timeless days, swimming with the sea lions from a little island near Santa Cruz, past the fur seals clinging to Redondo Rock and on to the land of dragons. On the blistered, black shore of Fernandina, thousands of fierce spiked heads were turned towards me. The magnificent marine iguanas, the only sea-going lizards in the world, are a spectacle unique to the Galapagos. I had a permit from the National Park Service to go ashore on the landing site. It was like walking with the dinosaurs. The dark-skinned bodies were basking on the hot rocks, poking out their red tongues and snorting salt through their nostrils. There were countless thousands of them covering the hardened volcanic lava and a constant procession swimming ashore through little channels.

Another remarkable evolutionary tale, the original iguanas probably were carried on great clumps of driftwood swept out from Ecuador's rivers in flood and pushed on the powerful current all the way to the Galapagos. Most other creatures would not have been fit to survive such a voyage but the hardy reptiles, the tortoises and iguanas, made it through the sea without much food or fresh water. The common green iguanas from South America changed over time, developing the dark skin they needed to survive without shade. As most of the Galapagos Islands are arid they would have struggled to find the green leaves their ancestors fed on and so they grazed on seaweed along the shore. Their claws grew longer to allow them to cling to the rocks as waves came rolling in and they developed an amazing ability to swim in the sea.

Pulling on fins, mask and snorkel, I joined the iguanas underwater, watching their sinuous, snake-like action propel them through the shore break and out to the seaweed on the bottom of the cove. I was no match for them on a dive to the bottom. Darwin had experimented by tying stones to the reptiles to keep them underwater and found that they could hold their breath for almost an hour. Most of the agile little divers I was watching spent at least ten minutes down below, buffeted by the tide, and then came ashore to rest.

It is fascinating to think about how these Galapagos dragons learned to swim so well. Many lizards can swim a bit when they have to, but the marine iguanas are the only habitual swimmers among them. As I watched them grazing on the algal beds I remembered Blanton speculating that perhaps the early iguanas had found their way out there at a very low tide. They may have survived the harsh dry years in the Galapagos by discovering this food even before they knew how to swim and dive so efficiently. I thought of other possibilities. An adventurous iguana may have plunged off the rocks and gone surfing. Or was it a few brave lizards, the ones who instinctively knew that they would perish from hunger unless they had the strength to reach that green new world?

I hauled myself up on the warm rocks, basking in the sun with the dragons. I watched one swim ashore with head held high like the prow of a tiny Viking ship. As a land-living, air-breathing creature like the iguana, the only way I could compete with him for manoeuvrability and endurance under the sea was with my scuba gear. Technology put me on level, but not superior, terms. After about one hour we both would have to come to the surface when his air and my air tank ran out. The iguana in his world seemed beautifully adapted to nature. In my world I was dependent on technology for survival.

The natural advantage we now have over most creatures is our extraordinary intellect. Dolphins, whales, chimpanzees and gorillas have demonstrated clearly that we are not the only ones with great mental powers, yet no other species even approaches the technological skill of my six-year-old son or the linguistic virtuosity of my seven-year-old daughter. As adults we can repair a human heart, control machine intelligence, fly a starship and even search for other possible intelligence in our universe. Our negative traits — the impulse to violence, habitual warmongering, reckless elimination of other species and disregard for the earth — are held in check only by the capacity of some human minds to act thoughtfully. The dragon in our brain may roar and belch fire but with one clear positive thought the beast is banished.

> *He looks his best*
> *his head held high,*
> *especially when*
> *she walks by,*
> *the rules for lizards*
> *are just the same,*
> *a guy's a guy,*
> *a dame's a dame.*

(Journal 1995)

When the dragons of the sea are ready to mate the males try very hard to woo the sleek wet females lying on the rocks and glistening in the sun. The spikes on the male's neck stand fully erect and many display a lime green band across their body, a throwback to their ancestors on the South American continent. Each season leaves the older males looking battleworn after fighting to defend their breeding territory. The female chooses a soft place to nest, dropping as many as five hen-sized eggs, covering them with soil and then staying on top for days. Without the protection of their vigilant mothers the next generation of dragons is not guaranteed a safe passage into life. Herons and other hunters watch for the hatchlings, speckled when they are young to help camouflage them inside the warm craters of ancient dormant volcanoes. On some of the Galapagos islands the young iguanas are being devoured by new predators introduced by the men who came in ships. Feral cats rule the scrub even within sight of the research station on Santa Cruz. Dogs, goats and horses also have done their share of damage, but without doubt the gravest threat to the Galapagos is humankind.

Because of their isolation from humans for all but the most recent pages of the geological calendar, the Galapagos Islands are still as precious as they were in Darwin's day. Here it is possible to contemplate where life has been and where it is headed next. Wherever I looked there was fascination in this natural world. On some islands, plants that once had male and female parts on the same stem had evolved, through natural selection, into plants that had separated the males and the females. It made me wonder where humans were headed.

Will men continue to use their power to suppress women or will we become true partners? Will women need men to reproduce? As we unlock the secrets of our genetic code, will humanity clone itself? I once met the Italian scientist Dr Severino Antinori and his sixty-two-year-old patient, Rosanna Della Corte, who became then the world's oldest mother almost a decade ago through a controversial mix of technology and nature. Now Antinori and his colleagues are convinced that their hour of creation is near. Man wants to try his hand at the masterpiece without really understanding what he is painting.

My own journey through the natural world, my meetings with remarkable men and women, my experiences at the edge of the abyss and at the pinnacle of human endeavour convince me that our destiny is calling us to one higher evolutionary plane. For humanity to be truly civilised we need a New Man and New Woman, but with an evolution of mind more than body. Their minds will not surrender to violence, ignorance or superstition. Their world will be sane and balanced. Their children will live in harmony with nature and one another. They will be the ones to reach the stars.

Some of the most unforgettable days of my life were spent in good company aboard the *Rachel III*, listening to the stories of people who had spent their lives trying to understand the complexity and interdependence of all living things.

On the longer passages between the islands, I sat on deck under the sails and wrote poems to Kim and stories for Claire and Will, hoping to keep their eyes wide open with wonder, to inspire their own search and to nurture their love of this beautiful world.

As the wind drove us towards Fernandina, we came across a marvellous sight. A pod of sperm whales appeared, then another and another. I counted thirty-five whales sailing like a great armada spread out on both sides of our yacht. Our crew and scientific guides had spent years sailing these waters and said that they had never seen such a spectacle. The whales were breaching, diving and crashing enormous tails on the foam. Like huge black buttresses the massive bodies heaved high into the air and then powered down into the sea they ruled. Standing in the bow, drenched in spray, I lost all track of time. If we are just a human speck in this endless journey, at such times we become one with nature.

When the whales left us, the *Rachel III* glided into darkness. There was silence except for the canvas flapping and the sound of the boat on the sea. The moon lit our passage and all the glorious possibilities of a sky full of stars unfolded before us. Ahead I could see the glow of the volcano. The whole mountain was molten red lava, falling down to the sea, with huge red tongues licking the shoreline. One day like this is poetry. It brings a hush to words of anger or fear. We end our alienation when we discover that we are all part of the same story. Find harmony with nature and we find ourselves, and then our hearts are full. Listen to the wind and the rain. Feel the land beneath your feet. Stand naked in the rays of our sun. We are all stardust.

SELECT BIBLIOGRAPHY

For fifty years I have drawn on the knowledge in so many books that here I can only point to influences in the development of my ideas, books mentioned in this memoir, some manifestos that I thought worth questioning and reference texts for the history that has left an indelible imprint on my mind.

Abzug, Bella & Mim Kelber, *Gender Gap,* Houghton Mifflin Company, Boston, 1984.

Ancona, George, *Riverkeeper,* Macmillan, New York, 1990.

Baker III, James A., *The Politics of Diplomacy,* G. P. Putnam's Sons, New York, 1995.

Bernstein, Carl & Bob Woodward, *All the President's Men,* Simon & Schuster, New York, 1974.

Beschloss, Michael R. & Strobe Talbott, *At the Highest Levels: The Inside Story of the End of the Cold War,* Little, Brown, Boston, 1993.

Bowden, Tim, *One Crowded Hour: Neil Davis Combat Cameraman,* William Collins, Sydney, 1987.

Breslin, Jimmy, *How The Good Guys Finally Won,* Viking Press, New York, 1975.

Bronowski, Jacob, *The Ascent of Man,* Little, Brown, Boston, 1973.

Bugliosi, Vincent & Curt Gentry, *Helter Skelter,* Norton, New York, 1974.

Butterfield, Fox, *China: Alive in the Bitter Sea*, Times Books, New York, 1982.

Carter, Jimmy, *Keeping Faith: Memoirs of a President,* Bantam Books, New York, 1982.

Chasov, Yevgeni, *Nuclear War: The Medical and Biological Consequences*, Novosti Press, Moscow, 1984.

Darwin, Charles, *The Origin of the Species*, W. M. Benton, Kent, UK, 1952.

Eisenman, Robert & Michael Wise, *The Dead Sea Scrolls Uncovered*, Element Books, Dorset, 1992.

Faludi, Susan, *Backlash: The Undeclared War Against Women*, Chatto & Windus, London, 1991.

Faust, Beatrice, *Apprenticeship in Liberty*, Angus & Robertson, Sydney, 1991.

Foote, Shelby, *The Civil War: A Narrative*, three vols, Random House, New York, 1958, 1963, 1974.

Greer, Germaine, *Sex and Destiny,* Harper & Row, New York, 1984.

Halberstam, David, *The Powers That Be*, Alfred A. Knopf, New York, 1979.

Hawking, Stephen W., *A Brief History of Time*, Bantam Press, London, 1988.

Jaworski, Leon, *The Right and the Power*, Gulf Publishing Company, New York, 1976.

Jefferson, Thomas, *The Writings of Thomas Jefferson*, Library of America edition, Washington, 1854.

Leakey, Richard & Roger Lewin, *The Sixth Extinction*, Doubleday, New York, 1995.

Lenin, Vladimir Illyich, *On Just and Unjust Wars,* Progress Publishing, Moscow 1984.

—— *State and Revolution*, New York International Publishers, New York, 1932.

Manchester, William, *The Glory and the Dream*, Little, Brown, New York, 1974.

Marx, Karl, *Das Kapital*, English edition, New York International Publishers, New York, 1887.

Morris, Desmond, *The Human Zoo*, Jonathan Cape, London, 1969.

Ratliff, William E., *Castroism and Communism in Latin America, 1959–1976*, AEI Hoover Institution, Washington, 1976.

Reagan, Ronald, *An American Life*, Simon & Schuster, New York, 1990.

Romer, Elizabeth, *The Tuscan Year: Life and Food in an Italian Valley*, Atheneum, New York, 1985.

Romer, John, *Testament*, Henry Holt, New York, 1988.

Sagan, Carl, *The Dragons of Eden: Speculations on the Evolution of Human Intelligence*, Random House, New York, 1977.

Schmidt, Dana Adams, *Armageddon in the Middle East*, John Day Company, New York, 1974.

Shevchenko, Arkady N., *Breaking Moscow*, Alfred A. Knopf, New York, 1985.

Shostak, Seth, *Sharing the Universe*, Berkeley Hills Books, Berkeley, 1998.

Smoot, George & Keay Davidson, *Wrinkles in Time*, Little, Brown, London, 1993.

Steinem, Gloria, *Outrageous Acts and Everyday Rebellions*, Holt, Rinehart & Winston, New York, 1983.

Strauss, Leo & Joseph Cropsey, eds, *History of Political Philosophy*, University of Chicago Press, Chicago, 1963.

Thiering, Barbara, *Jesus the Man,* Doubleday, Sydney, 1992.

Thoreau, Henry David, *Walden: Or, Life in the Woods*, Princeton University Press, Concord, 1854.

Williams, Robyn, *Scary Monsters and Bright Ideas*, University of New South Wales Press, Sydney, 2000.

Wu, Hongda Harry, *Laogai: The Chinese Gulag*, Westview Press, Oxford, 1992.

ACKNOWLEDGMENTS

The Australian author Thea Astley, teaching at Macquarie University in the 1960s, urged one of her most restless students to 'use it all', referring to the journal entries about my travels. The New York novelist Dan Jenkins and veteran correspondent Richard Growald expressed enough interest in the 1970s to encourage more elaborate philosophical musings. The former US Secretary of State James Baker III and the New South Wales Police Commissioner, Peter Ryan, showed appreciation of my access to moments of important history, especially the horrors of war. The film director Peter Weir discussed the beauty of quiet observation in faraway places. The archeologist John Romer opened up the world of ancient history and introduced a method of critical analysis new to me. The astronomers Eugene and Carolyn Shoemaker, vulcanologists Maurice and Katia Kraft and NASA scientist John Mather indulged my insatiable curiosity about the journey ahead. Robyn Williams's writing, ABC broadcasting and personal encouragement were inspirational in maintaining a belief that the public is interested in scientific knowledge. My thanks to the Australian cricket captain, Steve Waugh, for introducing me to the publisher and expressing his own interest in my stories. Kim Hoggard, my partner, whom I have shared so much with for so many years, read the manuscript and gave honest and thoughtful criticism, in particular supporting the most personal revelations. My editor, Amanda O'Connell, brought an enthusiasm and fresh interest in the historical events and a sensitivity towards the strangers who have become the unforgettable characters in my life. The entire HarperCollins team — management, editorial staff, designers, typesetters and publicists — were delightful and a pleasure to work with. And finally, there are not words to thank Julian Cress, who travelled with me to so many extremes, from Cambodia to Rwanda, and to all the other cameramen, editors, photographers and fellow journalists who shared the adventure of my life, you will never be forgotten.

INDEX